ASSAULT ON THE
LIBERTY

JAMES M. ENNES, JR.

ASSAULT ON THE *LIBERTY*

The True Story of the Israeli Attack on an American Intelligence Ship

Random House New York

Opinions or assertions expressed here are those of the author and do not necessarily reflect the official view of the Department of the Navy or any agency of the United States government.

Grateful acknowledgment is made to the following for permission to reprint previously published material:

Newsweek: Excerpt from "Periscope," June 19, 1967. Copyright 1967, by Newsweek, Inc. All rights reserved. Reprinted by permission.

The New York Times: Excerpts from *The New York Times,* June 18, 1967, and July 7, 1967. Copyright © 1967 by The New York Times Company. Reprinted by permission.

The Shreveport Times: Excerpts from *The Shreveport Times,* June 18, 1967. Reprinted from *The Shreveport Times,* Copyright 1967.

United Press International: Story about Israel's attack on U.S. ship *Liberty,* June 10, 1967. Reprinted by permission of United Press International.

Library of Congress Cataloging in Publication Data
Ennes, James M.
Assault on the Liberty.
Includes index.
1. Israel-Arab War, 1967—Naval operations.
2. Liberty (Ship)   I. Title.
DS127.6.N3E56   956'.046   79-4793
ISBN 0-394-50512-3
E 59   a

Manufactured in the United States of America
468975

FOR

WILLIAM ALLENBAUGH

PHILIP ARMSTRONG

GARY BLANCHARD

ALLEN BLUE

FRANCIS BROWN

RONNIE CAMPBELL

JERRY CONVERSE

ROBERT EISENBERG

JERRY GOSS

CURTIS GRAVES

LAWRENCE HAYDEN

WARREN HERSEY

ALAN HIGGINS

CARL HOAR

RICHARD KEENE

JAMES LENAU

RAYMOND LINN

JAMES LUPTON

DUANE MARGGRAF

DAVID MARLBOROUGH

ANTHONY MENDLE

CARL NYGREN

JAMES PIERCE

JACK RAPER

EDWARD REHMEYER

DAVID SKOLAK

JOHN SMITH, JR.

MELVIN SMITH

JOHN SPICHER

ALEXANDER THOMPSON

THOMAS THORNTON

PHILLIPE TIEDTKE

STEPHEN TOTH

FREDERICK WALTON

Of the events of the war, I have not ventured to speak from any chance information, nor according to any notion of my own; I have described nothing but what I either saw myself, or learned from others of whom I made the most careful and particular inquiry. The task was a laborious one . . .

Thucydides,
History of the Peloponnesian War, i.c. (404 B.C.)

Acknowledgments

This book could not have been written without the advice, assistance and active support of many people. I am indebted to numerous persons still on active duty in the Navy whose detailed recollections were invaluable, and to others, in and out of government, who assisted but who must go nameless here. I am grateful to Jay Whitehair, whose reaction to a very early draft was inspirational, and to Sylvester Jordan, who repeatedly urged me to write the book; to Philip Scott and Martin Elzy of the Lyndon Baines Johnson Library for their patient attention to my many requests; to the Navy Judge Advocate General and the Navy Historian, who are conspicuous in government as prompt and willing sources of information about the attack; to the United States Department of State for showing, through their interminable foot-dragging, that a cover-up still exists; to Weetie Armstrong, George Golden, David and Paula Lucas, Lloyd Painter, John Scott, George Wilson and others close to the attack for their active support and cooperation; to James and Julie Carroll, Joan Cassidy, Jose Chiriboga, George Clarren, Robert and Jo Ann Devaney, Peter Hutchinson, Robert and Fran Kephart, William McCollum, Jr., Roy Noorda, David Normandin and Richard O'Neal for their support and encouragement; to Pierre Mion, who provided helpful advice while the book was being written and who graciously consented, under trying conditions, to paint the dust-cover battle scene; to Neil Sheehan for introducing the book to Random House and to Tom Williams for helping to introduce the author to Neil Sheehan; to Robert and Peggy Marshall for repeated errand running, messenger service, manuscript criticism, research assistance and encouragement; to my daughter Julie for her many hours in the Library of Congress and elsewhere tracking down vital scraps of information; to my son, Mark, and my neighbors Diane Campbell and Stanley Price for help with proofreading and criticism; to my mother, Margaret Ennes, who (along with the publisher) suggested the title; to my wife, Terry, for her patience, repeated readings, criticism, encouragement and support; to Linda Schmid, and to my daughter Carolyn, for help with the index; to copy editor Carolyn Lumsden for her sharp eye for detail; and most of all to my editor, Robert Loomis, whose relentless pursuit of clarity and conciseness contributed immeasurably to the final product.

James M. Ennes, Jr.
July 1979

Contents

ASSAULT ON THE
LIBERTY

Prologue

The history of a battle is not unlike the history of a ball. Some individuals may recollect all the little events of which the great result is the battle won or lost; but no individual can recollect the order in which, or the exact moment at which, they occurred, which makes all the difference . . . But if a true history is written, what will become of the reputation of half of those who have acquired reputations, and who deserve it for their gallantry, but who, if their mistakes and casual misconduct were made public, would not be so well thought of?

Wellington,
Letter to a historian, August 8, 1815

United States Technical Research Ship *Liberty* sailed from Norfolk May 2, 1967, on a routine patrol of the African coast. Five weeks later she was suddenly and overwhelmingly attacked in international waters by the air and naval forces of Israel. Her decks were strafed with machine-gun fire and scorched by napalm; she was crippled by rocket and torpedo damage; her life rafts, readied for survivors, were machine-gunned in the water. Thirty-four of her crew died; scores were seriously wounded.

Even before the wounded were evacuated, a news lid went down over the entire episode. This story was not to be told. The Navy's own failures were never exposed or acknowledged, and Israel's fragile alibi was nurtured and protected. Israel claimed that the ship was at fault for being near the coast, for "trying to escape" after being fired upon by jets, and for not informing the Israeli government of her location; and our government tolerantly kept those assertions from public knowledge. Israel claimed that the attack resulted from mistaken identity, and our government quietly accepted that excuse.

Three weeks after the attack, the Pentagon released the lengthy *Summary of Proceedings of the Navy Court of Inquiry,* but the report added little to the public knowledge and it failed to fix blame.

Complaints came from everywhere.

"The published [report] leaves a good many questions unanswered," said the New York *Times.* [1]

"This naval inquiry is not good enough," said the Washington *Post.* [2]

"They must have known . . . that *Liberty* was an American ship," said the Washington *Star.* [3]

". . . the action was planned in advance," said Drew Pearson and Jack Anderson.[4]

"Only the blind—or the trigger happy—could have made such a mistake," said *The National Observer.* [5]

". . . the attack . . . was deliberate," said California Congressman Craig Hosmer. "Those responsible should be court-martialed on charges of murder . . ."[6]

"How can this be treated so lightly? What complaint have we registered?" demanded Mississippi's Thomas G. Abernethy.[7]

"The story has been hushed up," said Louisiana's John R. Rarick.[8]

Despite the outcry, the public affairs apparatus of the Defense Department succeeded in keeping most *Liberty* crewmen away from the press. Without witnesses to interview, the press had no story to tell.

"These errors do occur," said Secretary of Defense McNamara in a report that neatly summed up the position of the Department of Defense. Senator Bourke B. Hickenlooper of Iowa pressed McNamara for a better explanation during a Senate Foreign Relations Committee hearing, but got nowhere. The attack was an "inexcusable error of judgment and professional tactics," the Secretary

1. The New York *Times,* July 1, 1967.
2. The Washington *Post,* June 30, 1967.
3. The Washington *Star,* June 30, 1967.
4. The Washington *Post,* June 16, 1967.
5. *The National Observer,* July 3, 1967.
6. *Congressional Record—House,* June 29, 1967, p. 17893.
7. Ibid., pp. 17894–5.
8. Ibid., September 19, 1967, pp. 12170–6.

conceded, but he insisted that it was an understandable wartime error.[9]

Little more was printed anywhere about the *Liberty* affair. The crew soon dispersed and the ship was deactivated. I began taking notes, interviewing and corresponding with other survivors of the attack, and piecing together this story of what *really* happened on and around June 8, 1967.

9. Senate Foreign Relations Committee hearing, July 14, 1967.

Chapter 1

AFRICA, SUDDEN ORDERS AND A PROPHECY

The fear of spies seems to be endemic in every crisis in every military campaign.

Alan Moorhead,
Gallipoli, 1956

Liberty was a different sort of ship. A "Technical Research Ship," she operated alone, far from the rest of the fleet. The Navy said her task was to conduct research into electromagnetic phenomena, radio wave propagation and the like. Newsmen called her a "spy ship."

Hastily built for World War Two freighter duty, *Liberty*'s keel was laid on February 23, 1945, by Oregon Shipbuilding Corporation, Portland, Oregon. Launched just forty-two days later, the ship was delivered to the Maritime Commission on May 4, 1945. As SS *Simmons Victory,* she was chartered under general agency agreement by Coastwise (Pacific Far East) Line, San Francisco, for service during the closing months of the war; after the war she performed routine supply duty for States Marine Lines, serving in both the Atlantic and Pacific oceans.

During the Korean War, *Simmons Victory* crossed the Pacific Ocean eighteen times to supply and support American forces fighting in Korea, and during the same period made countless shorter trips throughout the Far East, usually unloading her cargo at Suyong Bay, Pusan, Korea. Finally, in 1958, weary and streaked with rust, she was placed in the national reserve fleet in Puget Sound at Olympia, Washington.

The Navy, though, had special plans for SS *Simmons Victory.* Technical Research Ships were being developed as part of an ambitious program of seaborne intelligence-collection platforms. First chosen for this duty were three old Liberty hull freighters, which in 1963 became Technical Research Ships USS *Oxford,* USS *Georgetown* and USS *Jamestown.*

Next selected were two Victory hulls, eventually to become USS *Belmont* and USS *Liberty.* Acquired by the Navy from the Maritime Commission in February 1963, *Simmons Victory* was delivered to Willamette Iron and Steel Corporation, Portland, Oregon, for conversion to a Technical Research Ship. And it was no small task: the work required twenty-two months and cost twenty million dollars even before the installation of specialized equipment for the new role.

The government has never revealed the mission of Technical Research Ships beyond an official statement that reads: "The mission of this ship is to conduct technical research operations in support of U.S. Navy electronic research projects which include electromagnetic propagation studies and advanced communications systems."

Jane's Fighting Ships (the standard reference for such things) called the ships mobile bases "for research in communications and electromagnetic radiation," and added that they were "considered electronic intelligence ships." Indeed, despite the official double talk, *Liberty* and her sister ships were widely and openly known for what they really were. Merchants, bar girls and other ships' sailors called *Liberty* a "spook ship." *Liberty* sailors were called "spooks." And the compartment aboard ship where the "spooks" worked became known by nonspooks as "the spook shop."

"Spooks," however, seldom acknowledged that there was anything special or different about their work, claiming instead to have quite ordinary, humdrum jobs. Even today, *Liberty* sailors are bound by stringent oaths of secrecy that severely restrict their freedom to discuss the ship's "technical research" mission.

Technical Research Ships were named after American cities and towns. In 1963 America had sixteen cities and towns named Liberty, plus a number of burgs, villages, hamlets, corners and similar places; *Liberty* was named after *all* of them—and was the fourth ship of the line to carry that name.

On April 1, 1964, *Liberty* was classified AGTR-5 (an *auxiliary* or noncombatant vessel of *general* or miscellaneous type assigned to *technical research* duty—the *fifth* U.S. naval vessel so classified); and on December 30, 1964, she was commissioned at Bremerton, Washington, Commander Daniel T. Wieland, Jr., in command.[1]

After sea trials and acceptance by the Navy, she was eventually assigned to Africa, where she would crawl endlessly along the coastline from Dakar to Cape Town and back to Dakar. Every few weeks she would stop for fuel and supplies, and on these occasions her crew would be permitted two or three days ashore at Monrovia or Luanda or Abidjan or occasionally further north at Las Palmas; but for the most part duty aboard *Liberty* was unexciting.

Technical Research Ship duty was, however, considered "career enhancing," an appraisal that ensured ample volunteers from among those careerists willing to endure the isolation and family separation; and so, early in 1967, I called upon two friends, Lieutenant James G. "Jim" O'Connor and Lieutenant Commander David E. "Dave" Lewis, to see if there was a job for me in the ship's research ("spook") department. Family separation was not attractive to me, but career enhancement was appealing after a year of staff duty.

I was impressed with the ship from the beginning. The quarterdeck watch was sharp-looking, alert, courteous and helpful. The ship was spotlessly clean in spite of being in a repair yard at the time. The crew was busy, friendly and good-natured. This was a happy ship, and I had the impression it was a good ship for duty.

After an hour or so, O'Connor and I prepared to go ashore. "Oh, Mr. O'Connor," called the petty officer of the watch as we crossed the quarterdeck, "the executive officer would like you and your guest to stop by his stateroom before you leave."

Lieutenant Commander Philip McCutcheon Armstrong met us at the door to his stateroom with his hand outstretched. "Hi, Jim," he said. "Call me Phil. What are you drinking?"

Drinking? Drinking aboard ship was a serious offense. The ancient Navy prohibition of liquor aboard ship was violated by an occasional alcoholic or a particularly brave sailor, but casual drinking aboard ship was something new to me. Drinking by the executive officer was unheard of.

1. Commander Wieland took the ship through her conversion, outfitting, commissioning, shakedown, specialized training and two African deployments. On April 25, 1966, he relinquished command to Commander William L. McGonagle and went on to assume command of Mine Division 44.

"Lock the door," he warned. "Scotch?"

No quick, warm shot from a contraband bottle for Philip. He drank only Johnny Walker Red Label scotch. Like a good host, he also offered bourbon, gin, a variety of mixes and fresh ice from an insulated bucket. And to assure that the ice didn't melt quickly in warm shipboard water, a personal water spigot dispensed ice-cold water piped in from a water cooler in the passageway outside.

"Is the captain as loose and easygoing as the XO?" I asked Jim later.

"No, not at all. Captain McGonagle is stiff and proper, and seems not to know that the XO drinks. The XO does about what he wants. He's the one that really holds the ship together."

"Does he *often* drink in his stateroom?" I asked, although I thought I knew the answer.

"Most of the time," Jim said. "During the day, while the ship is underway, he'll usually have a cold drink hidden in a drawer or under his hat on the desk. He says he always had a taste for booze, especially scotch, and claims he made a fortune at the Naval Academy selling booze by the drink to his classmates."

"The Old Man is straight?"

"Like an arrow."

It was with some misgivings that I asked the Bureau of Naval Personnel to terminate my plush staff assignment in the Second Fleet flagship, heavy cruiser USS *Newport News,* and to transfer me to USS *Liberty.* At the same time, a *Liberty* officer asked for an early transfer, and my friends in *Liberty* asked the Bureau to approve my request. Weeks later I received orders to report for duty in time for the ship's summer deployment to Africa. And on May 1, just one day before her scheduled sailing from Norfolk, I relieved Lieutenant John Gidusko, *Liberty*'s electronic material officer, to find myself in charge of the ship's division of electronic maintenance technicians.

———

Our Norfolk departure was delayed by a defective hydraulic line, which caused purple hydraulic fluid to leak down an antenna mast and all over a large section of deck. Shipyard technicians, known as "yardbirds" to my men, had been working for weeks to install new high-pressure piping. During the night the yardbirds had pronounced the work completed and walked off the job—all without the concurrence of anyone in authority and without testing the system under pressure. Now, when tested, the system leaked.

The commanding officer, forty-two-year-old Commander William L. McGonagle,[2] was already on the bridge preparing to get underway when I brought him the news. Mooring lines were singled up and we were only moments away from sailing when I asked him to remain in port for another few hours so that I could recall the workmen and seal the leaks. He was not pleased, but he agreed to stay.

While the men worked, McGonagle summoned me to his cabin. "Now, this time," he told me, "I don't want any elaborate testing. I don't want any testing at all. If the leaks are not repaired this time, they are not going to be repaired until September, when we come back to Norfolk."

McGonagle, it turned out, was what sailors call a "steamer"—a sailor who wanted always to be underway, "to steam." He longed for the sea and was noticeably restless in port. He simply would not tolerate being delayed by machinery that was not vital to the operation of the ship. No matter that the use and evaluation of the antenna system was an important part of our mission.

The workmen left shortly before 1500, and *Liberty* was underway fifteen minutes later. As directed, I did not test the system until we were well away from Norfolk, and when I did check I was not surprised to find that it still leaked. These leaks seemed minor, though, and we were hopeful that we could control them ourselves.

After several days of being tossed about in the stormy Atlantic, we reached the African coast and turned toward the ship's first scheduled port call at Abidjan, capital of the Ivory Coast. *Liberty* slowed to four knots, the lowest speed at which she could easily answer her rudder, and crawled south.

Arriving at Abidjan, all of the officers and most of the men soon gravitated to the expensive but comfortable Ivorian Hotel, which we found to be a haven of hospitality in a grim and inhospitable city. Elsewhere in Abidjan we were either snubbed by arrogant Frenchmen or stared at by destitute native Ivorians, but here we felt at home. Besides, the hotel boasted the only American-style hamburgers in Africa, and we took special pride in these, even at $3.50 each, since the hotel chefs had learned the art of American hamburger-making from our own ship's cooks. In return for cooking lessons, the hotel offered modest discounts to *Liberty* sailors.

On our second day in Abidjan, I returned alone about midnight

---

2. See Appendix J, page 250, for an official biography of Commander McGonagle.

from a dinner party held for *Liberty* officers by the American air attaché. Leaving the taxi at the end of the dark pier, I walked toward the distant island of light that held the ship. From far down the pier I could see perhaps a dozen people clustered under a streetlight near the gangway. The air was still and heavy with moisture as the temperature hovered in the nineties. As I came closer I could see that most of the visitors were young Ivorian women in Western dress, who stood about cajoling our sailors in fractured English. One very pregnant girl with a huge black escort stood apart from the rest and carefully surveyed each returning sailor.

"What's going on?" I asked the petty officer of the watch as I came on board. A husky boatswain's mate, he wore a .45 caliber pistol in a holster at his belt.

"Not much, sir," he said, pausing to chuckle at the scene ashore. "The pregnant one over there," he said as he pointed toward the quiet couple, "says one of our sailors knocked her up when we were here last trip. She's waiting for him so she can announce the good news. Says he'll marry her and make her an American."

"Uh-huh." I nodded. "And where is the proud father?"

"He's hiding in the compartment. We told her he went ashore; he's not about to go out there."

"And the others are local business girls?"

"Yes, sir. They do it standing up behind the packing crates for five packs of cigarettes when they can get customers. Our men just talk to them and tease them a little, but no one will go with them."

———

In Washington, meanwhile, Lieutenant Commander Birchard "Bud" Fossett wrestled with the scheduling of Technical Research Ships. The political situation in the Middle East was getting dangerous, and Fossett's seniors in the Department of Defense wanted to move a Technical Research Ship into the eastern Mediterranean Sea, near the area of tension. Fossett sought out Lieutenant John "Terry" McTighe, who was a staff liaison officer recently moved to Washington after a tour of duty in *Liberty*'s sister ship, USS *Oxford*.

"I think it would be easy to do," said McTighe. "*Liberty* is in port in Abidjan." After some quick calculations, he added: "She could be in the eastern Med in about two weeks, if we could get the move approved quickly."

Fossett and McTighe discussed the shift with McTighe's civilian boss, Francis A. "Frank" Raven. Then they gathered some other staff members and met with Raven's boss, the deputy section head. After long discussion, the group—except for Raven—agreed that *Liberty* should be moved. Raven insisted that the plan was unwise.

"The ship will be defenseless out there," Raven argued. "If war breaks out, she'll be alone and vulnerable. Either side might start shooting at her. The only way she would be safe would be to set up a special defense and intelligence system just to protect *Liberty,* and that wouldn't be practical. I say the ship should be left where it is."[3]

Raven might have prevailed, but he was interrupted by a summons to a meeting elsewhere. The system churned on without him, and with no further objection the group agreed to recommend that the ship be moved. Final approval was sought from the section head, John E. Morrison, Jr., an Air Force brigadier general. Morrison asked many questions before consenting, but finally he agreed that the move was necessary and proper. Because the matter was urgent, he agreed to ask the Joint Chiefs of Staff to assume direct control of the ship.

McTighe drafted the message. He assigned it "Flash" precedence —a speed-of-handling indicator usually reserved for enemy contact reports—and delivered it to supervisor Jane Brewer, who released it for transmission.

———

I poured a cup of coffee and stood talking with the men on watch. Time passed slowly as the ship's officers and most of the men straggled aboard. First came Captain McGonagle, who arrived alone and ramrod straight at about 1230, followed over the next half-hour by the remaining *Liberty* officers who piled out of mini-taxis in groups of three and four to negotiate the one hundred yards or so of pier, each in his own way.

All the officers were aboard now, but I resolved to remain awake until most of the men had returned and the assembly on the pier had broken up.

3. Frank Raven is no ordinary bureaucrat. In 1941 (according to David Kahn, *The Code Breakers* [New York: Macmillan, 1967]) twenty-seven-year-old Navy Lieutenant (jg) Francis A. Raven recovered the key pattern of the Japanese "purple" code. Building upon earlier work by noted cryptologist William F. Friedman, who had recovered the *basic* purple key, Raven discovered how the key was formed—the key to the key. With this knowledge, cryptanalysts could rapidly decrypt most of the Japanese "purple" messages, even those encrypted in daily keys that had not previously been solved.

"There's been a lot of heavy drinking lately," said the boatswain's mate. "Before our last trip there was an article in the paper by that woman prophet up in Washington—what's her name?"

"Dixon? Jeane Dixon?"

"Yeah, that's her, Jeane Dixon. Well, it was in the paper in Norfolk that Jeane Dixon said the USS *Liberty* was going to sink. That was before our last trip, and nothing happened, but a lot of guys were scared all trip. The night before we got to Monrovia last February it was really bad. A lot of guys slept on the main deck 'cause they were too scared to sleep below."[4]

"They thought that was the night the ship would sink?"

"Yeah, and they didn't feel any better when we didn't. A lot of guys think the ship is doomed. One guy in the deck force—they call him 'Greek'—is taking notes for a book he's gonna write, called *The Last Trip of the USS Liberty* or something like that."

"And all this just because of one newspaper article?"

"Well, after the article, everything that happens reminds people of the prediction. Like today, a steam pipe burst in the generator room and a lot of steam came out and there was a lot of noise. It was a while before the valve could be shut off because it was so hot and you couldn't see through the steam, but finally LeMay got it turned off —Bill LeMay, the second-class electrician. He was in sick bay, just had an appendix operation and wasn't supposed to be out of bed yet, but he went down there and got it shut off. Well, after it was all over I heard two guys talking. One guy says, 'We were lucky. I thought for a while that was the one that would sink us,' and the other guy says, 'Yeah!' So you can see a lot of guys are nervous."

Traffic on the pier thinned out as we talked. Occasionally a lone sailor would come aboard, but mostly the area was quiet as the several Ivorian women and the one man stood silently watching the ship. A prostitute attempted to open shop in the shadow of the ship's truck parked near the gangway, but she was put out of business when the truck was moved under a streetlight. Finally, by four o'clock in the morning, most of our three hundred sailors were aboard and the girls were gone. The mid watch had been relieved by the morning

4. The reported prophecy was widely discussed among *Liberty* sailors, some of whom report reading it in *The National Enquirer*. The newspaper, however, was unable to identify the article for me. Jeane Dixon, in a letter to me dated October 30, 1974, denies that she has ever made any prediction about USS *Liberty*. Nevertheless, the belief was widely held among the crew that a prophecy was made, and the belief contributed to a feeling of unrest in the ship.

watch. The pregnant girl was still standing her silent and rather sad vigil with her husky friend when I decided to turn in.

I climbed the short ladder to the 01 level, one deck above the main deck, to the room I now shared with Jim O'Connor. Jim was the duty officer and had been the only officer aboard for most of the day. He was asleep now, and on call. My self-imposed long watch on the quarterdeck was quite unnecessary, I told myself as I lay in bed waiting to fall asleep.

Suddenly the room filled with light from the connecting passageway as a sailor entered with a message for the command duty officer. Jim woke quickly, held the message in the red glow of a Navy flashlight, and then swore softly as he climbed out of his upper bunk and pulled on his trousers. The duty officer was often called for high-precedence messages or for other matters of ship's business, but it was relatively unusual for him to dash around in the middle of the night.

"What's going on?" I asked.

"You might as well get up," Jim said, ignoring my question. Snapping the bright room light on, he added, "We're going to sea," as he left the room to show the message to the executive officer.

Still hoping that whatever the message said was less momentous than Jim seemed to think, I lay on my back with my eyes closed, trying to ignore the lights that Jim had left on and hating him for leaving them on.

In a few minutes I heard the executive officer giving some sort of hurried instruction to someone. I couldn't hear the conversation, but the tone was urgent. As doors opened and closed and plumbing made gurgling noises where there had been only nighttime ship's machinery sounds, it became clear that something unusual was happening.

As I groped sleepily for my shoes, Jim returned. "I thought you'd be up," he said.

"I thought you'd tell me what's wrong. What's all the excitement about?"

"It was a message from the Joint Chiefs of Staff. Whoever heard of JCS taking direct control of a ship? We're to get underway as soon as possible and make our best speed for Rota, Spain."

"What for?"

"God only knows. They didn't say. They just said that we'd get further orders at Rota."

"When are we leaving?"

"The captain expects to sail at 0700, less than three hours from now, and he expects to do it with all the crew aboard and fresh groceries too. It will be a busy three hours, but Captain Magoo usually gets his way."

Reveille sounded over the ship's general announcing system as I finished dressing. It was not yet 0430.

Lieutenant George Golden, the ship's engineer officer, stood half-dressed in the passageway outside his stateroom, lecturing the other officers. "Okay, you college pukes!" he cried as sleepy young officers passed by carrying towels and shaving kits. "I told you smart-ass college pukes we were going to war. This uneducated Smoky Mountain Jew is the only one here who knows what the hell is goin' on."

Golden would not soon let anyone forget that he had been the first to foresee a Mediterranean cruise for *Liberty*. He knew from news reports that the Middle East was about to boil over, and he knew from having been aboard for three years that *Liberty* tended to go where the action was. "We're going to see the Pyramids," he had announced at breakfast.

Forty-two years old, George Golden saw the world from a Navy destroyer before most *Liberty* sailors were born. He served in a dozen ships, saw more than two dozen major battles of World War Two, and was eventually commissioned directly from the enlisted ranks in 1960. Golden was not the oldest man aboard, but he had spent the most time at sea and was considered the "saltiest." Whenever *Liberty* crossed the equator, it was Golden who presided as King Neptune over the traditional crossing ceremony. Now he indulged in a favorite pastime, called "Harass the College Pukes."

Soon the ship was alive with weary men who had expected to be allowed to sleep late and so were even less prepared than usual for middle-of-the-night reveille. But awaken they did. Most of them. Golden had gone back to bed. He and several enlisted men could not be roused, and they were allowed to sleep; but fully 95 percent of the crew were awake, dressed and ready for work ten minutes after reveille sounded.

A few early risers were startled to see McGonagle on the quarterdeck, barefoot and in his underwear, orchestrating the many details of getting the ship underway. He paced about, barking orders, making telephone calls, and summoning officers and chiefs as though unaware of his appearance. There was much to be done.

Our late-returning sailors had to be found. Philip Armstrong obtained the cooperation of the Ivorian police, then personally headed into town with the ship's truck and some sailors who knew the late-night haunts. Even in a city of 180,000 people, American sailors remain conspicuous. The last man was aboard within an hour.

Fresh groceries had been scheduled for delivery late in the day through an arrangement with the American embassy. McGonagle called the embassy, and the groceries arrived before 0600, accompanied by an embassy representative to help with any other problems that might arise. Within a few minutes working parties were organized, groceries were carried below and stowed, the ship's vehicles were hoisted aboard and secured for sea, and all the lines were singled up, ready to be cast off.

Meanwhile, the ship's engines were lighted off and pressure was built up in the boilers to prepare the engineering plant for getting underway. At 0650, when the civilian pilot came aboard to guide us out of the tricky Abidjan harbor, the crew was at special sea detail and ready for sea. It was still dark as we cast off. The pier was empty. The pregnant Ivorian girl was not in sight.

===

Few of the officers saw the message until we were at sea and gathered around the wardroom table for a late breakfast. Although relayed by and ostensibly "from" Commander Service Squadron Eight (COM-SERVRON EIGHT), our "operational commander" in Norfolk, it was clear from the text and from other messages that this order came from the Joint Chiefs of Staff:

MAKE IMMEDIATE PREPARATIONS TO GET UNDERWAY. WHEN READY FOR SEA ASAP DEPART PORT ABIDJAN AND PROCEED BEST POSSIBLE SPEED TO ROTA SPAIN TO LOAD TECHNICAL SUPPORT MATERIAL AND SUPPLIES. WHEN READY FOR SEA PROCEED TO OPERATING AREA OFF PORT SAID. SPECIFIC AREAS WILL FOLLOW.[5]

Rota, 3,000 miles to the north, would require eight days of hard, full-speed-ahead steaming.

Golden's lucky guess looked like a good one. Egypt and Israel had been scrapping for years; border clashes were routine; both sides were becoming increasingly belligerent as chances for peaceful settlement faded. Our station off Port Said would put us about a hundred miles from the Israeli/Egyptian border.

Soon, however, we received further orders placing us even closer

5. COMSERVRON EIGHT message 240020Z May 1967.

to the developing conflict. After leaving Rota, we were to proceed, again at "best speed," to the eastern shore of the Mediterranean, where we were to patrol a prescribed dogleg pattern just thirteen miles off the hotly contested Gaza Strip. From the beginning there was great fear among the crew that these orders were unwise, that tempers were too hot to permit a lightly armed, neutral intelligence vessel to patrol casually within sight of what could very soon develop into full-scale war. Officers tried to reassure the chiefs, chiefs tried to reassure the men, and we all tried to reassure each other, but everyone was uneasy about this assignment.

Typical was Chief Petty Officer Raymond Linn. Chief Linn, due to retire that month after thirty years of service, loved the Navy and enjoyed the ship and didn't want to leave. In Norfolk he had begged for "just one more trip, one more liberty port," and somehow it was decided that he could return to the United States on one of the embassy flights in time to make his scheduled retirement date. So Chief Linn was still with us, and now even this old salt was concerned.

We drank strong Navy coffee from oversized mugs in the communication center as he told me the story. The Navy was this man's life. He had been a sailor before Pearl Harbor and he had survived World War Two, but this mission was different.

"I've never seen anything like this," he told me as he sat at his desk, checking messages for errors. "It's crazy to send an unprotected ship on an intelligence mission in a war zone. Spies just don't prance around like that in broad daylight near the front lines."

"I'll bet the Joint Chiefs will pull us back if a war starts," I said. "If shooting breaks out, we should get a change of orders within two hours."

"I hope so," he said, "but I wouldn't bet on it. I keep thinking that we will be a sitting duck, just begging to get our ass shot off, and I wouldn't even be here if I hadn't cried about how I wanted one more trip. I'd be home taking rocking-chair lessons. Wouldn't it be ironic if I got killed out here?"

Chapter 2

SPAIN

Nothing is so unmanageable as a sailor, except by his own officers.

Letter by unknown British Army officer,
Walcheren expedition, 1809

On June 1 we arrived at the U.S. Naval Station at Rota, intending to remain only long enough to take on fuel and stores. *Liberty* tied up quickly near the permanently stationed submarine repair ship, USS *Canopus,* and settled down to business.

Waiting on the pier to meet us were three enlisted Marines and three civilian technicians, all sent to *Liberty* on temporary duty for her new assignment. Civilian Allen Blue from Rockville, Maryland, was quite unhappy about being here. "I got back from my last trip," he explained, "just in time to take my wife to the hospital to have a baby. She's still there. As soon as the baby was born I got called away on *this* trip. Hardly had time to say goodbye. Jesus! If I'd known working for the government would be like this, I'd have gone to work for General Motors."

Soon fuel lines were connected to the pier. Trucks arrived, were unloaded and were replaced by more trucks. Long lines of perspiring sailors carried food and supplies below.

Captain McGonagle was anxious, as usual, to get our business taken care of and get underway, so it was only reluctantly that he agreed to stay a few hours longer while the submarine repair crews helped stop another hydraulic leak in our new antenna system. This was the same apparatus that delayed our departure from Norfolk, and it had kept several of my men busy ever since. The temperamental contraption had been aboard for nearly a year and had never worked for more than a few hours at a time, so it was understandable that McGonagle had no patience with it.

Purple fluid dripped from several hydraulic piping connectors. Any repair would be temporary, the submarine repair crews told us, because the shipyard had used low-pressure fittings that were never intended for our high-pressure system. Eventually, all the fittings would have to be replaced. Meanwhile, the men thought they could make some repairs that would get the system back in operation, if only for the time being.

The antenna served an experimental communication system known by the acronym TRSSCOMM, for Technical Research Ship Special Communication System. Elaborate sensors, complex computers, sensitive hydraulic systems and a television camera with a powerful zoom lens all worked together to keep a sixteen-foot antenna dish aimed in the right direction on a moving platform that pitched and rolled unpredictably. Pronounced "triss-comm," the system beamed a 10,000-watt microwave signal to the earth's natural moon and bounced it back from the moon to a receiving station on earth. The highly directional signal would not give away the ship's position and would not interfere with incoming radio signals, as conventional radio transmitters would. But it was not dependable. We could communicate beautifully with Cheltenham, Maryland, whenever the system was in operation and *both* stations could see the moon; unfortunately, these conditions were seldom satisfied all at the same time.[1]

---

1. TRSSCOMM was the brainchild of Navy Commander William C. White, the deputy director for logistics on a Washington-based Navy headquarters staff. Commander White conceived the idea of adapting for shipboard use a discarded Air Force moon-relay microwave system; the system itself had been in operation for years, but using land-based terminals. White arranged to take custody of the surplus transceivers, appeared personally before a congressional committee to appeal for installation and redesign money, and then coaxed the first shipboard system into operation on USS *Oxford* (AGTR-1) in February 1964, after two years of work. Commander White was eventually rewarded for his effort with a Navy Commendation Medal and an accompanying citation that concluded: "The magnitude of this unique and most significant accomplishment places it in the front rank of historic happenings in the annals

When it became clear that repair would be an all-night job, men were allowed ashore until midnight—a privilege known in the Navy as "Cinderella liberty." Over two hundred sailors streamed off the ship, most of them crowding into the small enlisted men's club operated by the Naval Station.

As command duty officer this day, I soon became the only officer on board a quiet ship. The few men on board were mostly either on watch or catching up on sleep lost during previous watches. Even the men who had been working with TRSSCOMM were able to rest while replacement parts were machined on the submarine tender.

===

Philip Armstrong, anticipating a long, dry summer, organized a "booze run" to one of the larger local liquor stores. Four officers squeezed into a tiny Spanish taxi for the short trip to town, and quickly bought four cases of whiskey. Lieutenant Lloyd C. Painter and the ship's doctor, Lieutenant Richard F. "Dick" Kiepfer, arrived in separate taxis in time to chuckle at the spectacle of Philip stuffing a final case of Johnny Walker Red Label scotch into an already overburdened cab, and watched the cab vanish in traffic as it headed back toward the Naval Station.

Lloyd Painter and the doctor, reflecting a peculiar Hunger, ordered two cases of Spanish Terry brandy, several cases of scotch and bourbon, and an assortment of wines, brandies and liqueurs, and waited while the proprietor brought the huge order in from the back of the store. While they waited, a man entered from the street and stood quietly by the cash register. He was a tall, lean man, conservatively dressed. Painter took him for an American.

The proprietor returned with a loaded dolly and quoted a price in Spanish pesetas. Painter asked if he would accept dollars and the man said that he would.

"He can't take dollars!" announced the heretofore silent stranger as the proprietor disappeared into the back of the store with the dollars that Painter gave him. "He can't take any American money," the man insisted.

---

of Naval Communications." Nevertheless, the system never worked well on any of the ships. Although the design and concept were sound, no hydraulic system seemed capable of handling the heavy antenna for more than a few hours without leaking. In 1969, when Technical Research Ships were taken out of service, TRSSCOMM was allowed to die. A Navy communicator who had access to the final cost and traffic volume figures calculated that the few messages passed by TRSSCOMM cost taxpayers about five dollars per word.

Painter, shorter than the intruder but broader and stronger, was in no mood to trifle with busybodies or pranksters, and chose to ignore him.

The stranger became louder when the proprietor returned with the change, in pesetas, and began counting it into Painter's palm. It was obvious now that the man had been drinking. He must be drunker than he looks, or else he's crazy, they decided as they helped the liquor dealer push the loaded dolly toward the street.

"No!" the man cried. "You can't take that! Look!" he said, flashing an official-looking ID card and badge. "I'm a U.S. government agent. You can't spend American money in this country. I'll have to place you under arrest!"

Certain now that the man was a lunatic, and a half-drunk lunatic at that, the two officers ignored him as they continued to load the waiting cabs. There was scarcely room left for passengers as they climbed in. Painter was cramped and uncomfortable. Kiepfer's six-and-a-half-foot frame didn't fit the tiny Spanish taxi under the best of conditions, and it took care and some pain for him to squeeze in among the cargo.

They were astonished to see their antagonist standing in front of the store, waving his arms and yelling in a loud and nearly hysterical voice: "Help! Help! Call the police! Arrest these men! Help! Police!"

"This guy is nuts," Painter called to the doctor.

"He's drawing a crowd," said Kiepfer.

"Back to the ship," said Painter to his driver.

"Follow that cab," said Kiepfer in Spanish to his driver.

As the cars started to move, the man stepped into the street in front of Painter's car, forcing the driver to stop. Then he threw himself across the hood of the tiny car and resumed his frantic call for police. Painter's driver, reserved up to this point, began waving his arms and yelling in Spanish.

Dick Kiepfer remained in his cramped position overlooking the scene as Painter extricated himself from the besieged lead taxi. The stranger unfolded himself from the hood of the car as Painter approached with a shrug and a disarming look of apology.

"Look, mister, we don't want to cause any trouble," he said as his knee came up hard into the man's groin. The stranger's eyes rolled back in his head as he fell unconscious on the sidewalk.

"Let's go!" Painter yelled, ignoring the crowd that was rapidly gathering.

"Wait!" insisted Kiepfer. "He could be hurt." Kiepfer was out of the cab now, fumbling with the man's belt with one hand while checking his pulse with the other.

"He's okay. Now help me get his pants down," Kiepfer ordered as the astonished crowd murmured. Down came the stranger's trousers, revealing an enormously swollen scrotum that somehow assured the doctor that the man was not seriously injured.

"He'll live," said the doctor. "Let's go!"

Most of the populace of Rota seemed to be standing on that sidewalk as the men reboarded the taxis and again ordered the drivers to drive.

=====

I finished a quiet dinner alone in the wardroom and was preparing to watch an ancient movie with the duty steward when a messenger came to announce in a ceremonial tone that "the officer of the deck requests your presence on the quarterdeck."

A chief petty officer from the Naval Station stood on the quarterdeck talking with Chief Joseph A. Benkert, our officer of the deck. "Sir, I must ask you to recall your men," he said. "They're all crowded into the one little club. They're getting out of control. It's hot. There have been fights, and now they're throwing beer bottles. I'm afraid there will be real trouble if you don't pack them all back aboard."

After talking with the chief for a few minutes, I told him that I couldn't recall the crew just because some of the men were difficult to handle. I explained that the men were restless after a long period at sea, and were apprehensive about the uncertainty ahead. Arbitrary recall now would be explosive, I told him. When he remained unconvinced, I offered to send men from the ship's duty section to supplement the already-beefed-up shore patrol, and assured him that I would certainly abide by any orders from higher authority requiring the recall of our men. He finally agreed to return only individual offenders, and accepted my offer of four husky sailors to further supplement the shore patrol contingent.

While we talked, Painter and Kiepfer drove onto the pier in their two overloaded cabs, where the presence of the shore patrol car alerted them to the gathering on the quarterdeck. Certain that the incident in town had preceded them to the ship, Painter walked back to Kiepfer's cab where the two officers discussed their predicament.

In a few minutes they saw me leave the quarterdeck.

"He'll not return. He's going back to see the rest of the movie," Kiepfer guessed correctly.

A few minutes later they saw the shore patrol chief leave the ship with the four additional shore patrolmen that I had provided. Never one to miss an opportunity, Kiepfer approached the shore patrol chief.

"Trouble with the liberty party, chief?"

"Yes, sir, a little trouble at the club. Nothing we can't handle."

"Well," said Kiepfer, assured now that the shore patrol was not looking for him, "before you leave I'd like to borrow your men for a few minutes. We just got back with some of the ship's welfare and recreation liquor and need some help stowing it below."

So Kiepfer turned apparent adversity to advantage. The shore patrol party carried two carloads of contraband liquor aboard ship and stowed it while the command duty officer watched a movie.[2]

For the next few hours, weary, bloodied and beer-soaked sailors stumbled back aboard, many in the custody of the shore patrol, loudly profane and insistent that they were being abused. Our usually well-behaved crew seemed to be going crazy.

Soon there were more signs of discontent. At about ten o'clock the messenger brought another urgent call for me to come to the quarter-deck. Chief Benkert was still on duty.

"Big trouble, Mr. Ennes," Benkert announced. "Some nut is loose in the deck-force sleeping compartment with a loaded gun. He says he'll shoot anyone who comes near."

Benkert and I inched our way into the darkened compartment to find a young black sailor cowering in a corner, frightened and unarmed. After some coaxing, he told us of being tormented by a group of bullies, and he surrendered the .22 caliber snub-nosed revolver he had hidden under some bedding, far from his reach.

I promised to investigate the bullying charge, and offered to ask the captain for leniency if the man had been bullied as he claimed.

2. Welfare and recreation liquor is liquor purchased by the ship's welfare and recreation officer for official ship's parties, which are always held ashore. What the shore patrol helped carry was *not* welfare and recreation liquor.

Benkert arranged for a place for him to sleep, well away from his tormentors.[3]

An hour later I was called to the quarterdeck again as the shore patrol chief returned another batch of unruly sailors. He complained to me that sailors were now systematically throwing their beer glasses and bottles at the walls of the club as they finished each drink. Again I advised him to collar any troublemakers, but refused to order a wholesale recall of the crew.

Men were coming aboard in groups of ten and twenty now. Many of the younger sailors were ill, arrogant and itching to fight. They were barely restrained by the more experienced men. The officer of the deck, with the help of his assistants, was keeping fairly good order under the circumstances as I watched from a distance. Suddenly someone cursed; pandemonium broke loose. Like a waterfront riot scene, nearly fifty men launched wild attacks upon whoever happened to be standing nearest.

The ship's officers, led by the executive officer, arrived at this moment in two taxis. Lieutenant Commander Armstrong—yelling, "Wade into them! Hit 'em! Slug the sons of bitches!"—launched an attack through the center of the struggling mass. This counteroffensive by nearly a dozen relatively sober officers so shocked the men that they abruptly stopped fighting. Men stood in silence for a moment, confused and frustrated, and then sullenly made their way off the quarterdeck and down toward their sleeping compartments on the second deck.

The XO and I stood alone a few feet from the quarterdeck. He leaned on a railing and stared out across the pier as though in deep thought. Finally he said, "You have to hit 'em. You have to wade in and just pound the crap out of 'em. It doesn't do any good to tell people to stop fighting. You have to knock them senseless."

Although I did not agree, this was not an argument that I could win. Our conversation shifted to the morale of the men, the fighting ashore and the fear that seemed to be behind these things. Here was

3. Years later I learned that this incident was not the isolated case of racial unrest that it seemed at the time. *Liberty* men told me that three disparate factions existed among the junior enlisted ranks: Chicanos, who for the most part had several years' service and consequently held relatively senior positions; Blacks, who were mostly younger than the Chicanos and junior to them; and Whites, who were spread throughout the structure and were a majority in numbers but not necessarily in power or influence. The incident I observed was simply one outward manifestation of a struggle that was usually of lower key, and was usually kept from the knowledge of officers and chiefs.

a crew that until recently had been happy and hard-working. Almost overnight they had become insolent, angry and antagonistic.

"They're scared," said the XO. "Once we leave Rota, we don't know when we'll get mail, liberty, groceries or anything else. And with orders to Israel on top of that crazy Dixon prophecy, half the crew is convinced we're going to sink."

Suddenly we were interrupted by a sharp cry from a chief petty officer. "Hey! There's a riot below!"

Quickly rounding up most of the officers and several chiefs, Philip Armstrong led an angry half-dressed "police force" into the Research Operations Department sleeping compartment. There we found nearly a hundred men surging toward their imagined enemy, the deck-force sailors who slept in a forward compartment.

Sharply barked orders were ignored or lost in the din as the mob thundered through an empty mess hall. Somehow Philip got ahead of the men, blocked a door, and collared the ringleaders. Many were larger and stronger than Philip, but none was willing to defy the executive officer.

Sullenly, the men retreated to their sleeping compartment, where they were rudely ordered to bed. As a few half-drunk officers and chiefs bounded about the compartment to keep a hundred mostly very drunk sailors at bay in their bunks, the scene made me think of a lion cage at a circus.

Some of the officers, clearly surprised and impressed with their own authority under the circumstances, raged about, badgering the men. One officer moved through the compartment, hounding men who were slow to get undressed. "You," he would say, "snap it up there."

"Sir," a man replied, "why don't you leave us alone so we can get some sleep?"

"Shut up and get in your bunk!" said the officer. "You're on report!"

Was this the ship that had impressed me so recently with its high morale?

The excesses of some of the "policemen" led men to hurl brazen wisecracks about the room, and these served to increase the abuse. Hoping that silence and darkness would restore order where "discipline" had failed, I quietly turned out the lights and crossed my fingers. In a few minutes all was quiet and most of the men were sleeping.

The deck force, meanwhile, slept peacefully, unaware of the aborted assault. The battle had been a one-sided affair.

======

Late the next morning I reported to Captain McGonagle that the men of the submarine tender had completed their task. Working all night, they had machined some new high-pressure fittings to repair our worst leaks. Although we still had several minor leaks, the system now held adequate pressure and operated satisfactorily. Until the remaining leaks got worse—which was inevitable—they could probably be controlled with drip cans and rags.

Chapter 3

THE MEDITERRANEAN

Lloyd Painter, who had relieved me earlier as command duty officer, now made preparations for getting the ship underway. As he stood on the quarterdeck with Captain McGonagle, waiting for the harbor pilot to come aboard, an official-looking black limousine nosed onto the pier.

"What's this?" asked McGonagle.

"I don't know, Captain. It doesn't look like the pilot," Painter remarked as the car stopped by the gangway. A dignified-looking American got out of the back seat and climbed the gangway to the quarterdeck.

"Take me to the captain," the man demanded.

"I'm the captain," said McGonagle, offering his hand. "What can I do for you?"

"I'm the senior agent here for the United States," announced the unsmiling visitor. If he identified himself or his agency any further,

Painter didn't hear. "You're going to have to stay here, Captain. Two of your men beat up one of my agents last night, and I have ordered a full investigation. We know it was either officers or chiefs from this ship."

Painter struggled to appear preoccupied with the details of getting the ship ready for sea.

"I'll be happy to cooperate in any way I can," said the unflappable McGonagle, "but I'm afraid we can't hold an investigation today. I have orders to go to sea."

The man seemed to lose some of his confidence as he looked around and saw that the pilot had arrived. Men stood ready to cast off the mooring lines and a crane was in position, ready to remove the gangway.

"We are getting underway immediately," McGonagle continued. "I suggest you leave the ship at once unless you intend to hold your investigation at sea."

"This is very serious, Captain. It must be taken care of. When will you be returning to Spain?"

"I am not at liberty to discuss ship movements, sir," replied McGonagle. "If you have a charge to file against a member of my crew, you should send a written complaint through official channels. Meanwhile, please excuse me, as I intend to get this ship underway."

McGonagle escorted the visitor to the gangway, saluted smartly, and turned to address Painter.

"Raise the gangway, Mr. Painter. I'll show the pilot to the bridge."

Painter felt the blood returning to his brain as the chief boatswain's mate signaled the crane operator to remove the gangway. The black limousine drove to the end of the pier and stopped. Painter watched the car until the ship was well past the sea wall that enclosed the harbor. He did not see the car move.

=====

The ship passed through the Strait of Gibraltar during the late afternoon, en route to a point thirteen miles off the Gaza Strip, 2,300 miles away on the eastern shore of the Mediterranean Sea. Captain McGonagle ordered a speed of seventeen knots, which was about the top speed we could maintain, and *Liberty* plunged through the water with a bone in her teeth, thirty-five-knot winds over the decks much of the time. In the distance we could see three Soviet destroyers, which matched each course and speed change to maintain a constant distance of about 6,000 yards off our starboard quarter.

Apprehension toward our mission increased as men in my division reminded me of their fears that we would get involved in a Middle East war. Nasser was clearly itching for a conflict with Israel. He had expelled the 3,400-man United Nations peacekeeping force. Next, he ordered a blockade of the Gulf of Aqaba to cut off Israel's oil from Iran, and he assembled an invasion force along the Israeli border. It seemed that war would explode at any moment, while USS *Liberty* —not built or trained for combat and armed only with four quite ineffective .50 caliber Browning machine guns—prepared to enter the scene.

My yeoman, an experienced senior petty officer, developed blood-shot eyes, clammy skin and a hunted look. Reminding me of the now frequently discussed Dixon prophecy, he told me that he had not slept well for several days and had recurring nightmares of being trapped in a compartment of our sinking ship after a torpedo attack. I sent him to Dr. Kiepfer, who prescribed tranquilizers in the day-time and sleeping pills at night. He slept with this chemical help, but remained paralyzed by fear that he would drown in a water-filled compartment.

═══

As time passed, I became better acquainted with our executive of-ficer, thirty-eight-year-old Lieutenant Commander Philip McCutch-eon Armstrong, and I began to appreciate his remarkable personality and the considerable influence he had upon the ship. I soon found Philip to be one of the most intelligent, articulate, iconoclastic and thoroughly likable individuals I have ever known. He was also troubled.

Philip, as we have seen, was an exceptionally heavy drinker who imbibed almost constantly—about a quart of whiskey every day. Yet I never saw him drunk. Like everything else in his life, he paced his drinking carefully and kept his ethanol intake within carefully estab-lished limits. He maintained tight control and strict discipline wher-ever he considered it important, and simply ignored regulations— such as the Navy's prohibition of shipboard alcohol—with which he disagreed.

The XO's philosophy—his single-minded devotion to the job at hand coupled with contempt for convention and disregard for awk-ward regulations—quietly spread among the officers and crew, and seemed almost to become the philosophy of the ship. In port, for example, Philip virtually abolished regular working hours although he demanded peak performance; men were free to come and go as they chose, provided that their responsibilities had been met. The result was that *Liberty* sailors never felt compelled to remain aboard in port just because it was a workday, yet they seldom hesitated to work late when the job called for it, often working all night or all weekend on their own initiative when that seemed necessary. Also, like Philip, the men rarely hesitated to violate a regulation when they thought they could get away with it.

The freewheeling habits of Philip Armstrong and the *Liberty* crew were more than just a shipboard secret. A few days before I reported to the ship for duty I was cornered by a staff officer in the cruiser *Newport News.* "Be careful, Jim," he warned. "There's a lot of drinking in that ship, and if you're not careful you'll get burned."

"Come on," I coaxed. "Tell me what's going on."

The story came out slowly. "I know an officer who did *Liberty*'s IG inspection," he said, "and he just couldn't ignore all the drinking he saw. Not excessive so much as open and widespread. Would you believe the XO offered a drink to the inspecting officer? My God!"

I was already well aware of Philip's shipboard drinking. I had shared a drink with him on my first visit to the ship. "Did the IG put it in his report?" I asked.

"No, he wrote a good report—then he reported privately to Admiral Renken.[1] *Liberty* has such a good record and Armstrong is such a crackerjack XO that no one wants to move quickly. Admiral Renken plans to put a spy aboard and get a firsthand report before he decides what to do."

When I told my friends Jim O'Connor and Dave Lewis about the likelihood of a spy being placed aboard, they were not surprised. Illicit shipboard drinking is so common, they admitted, that the chiefs use a crushed-ice machine to keep their beer cold. A drunken sailor once offered a drink to the conning officer on the bridge. And on a recent trip dozens of sailors were caught smoking marijuana in their sleeping quarters. Finally there was a crackdown. Drugs had been eliminated, my friends believed, and shipboard drinking was at least discreet and under control.

"What was the captain's part in all this?" I asked.

"McGonagle was never told," Jim said. "The XO decided not to tell him. And if he found out on his own, he kept it to himself."

---

1. Rear Admiral Henry Algernon Renken: born 1908; U.S. Naval Academy, class of 1931. As Commander, Service Forces, U.S. Atlantic Fleet (COMSERVLANT), Rear Admiral Renken was COMSERVRON EIGHT's operational commander and thus one step removed from *Liberty* in the command hierarchy.

Lewis explained that it would be almost impossible for the captain *not* to know that the XO, at least, was drinking. While others might succeed in hiding an occasional drink from the captain, the XO drank too much and saw him too often to keep such a secret. However, if the captain knew, he carefully avoided a confrontation. McGonagle's habit of whistling when he walked through officers' territory—and always the same tune—helped assure that drinking would be kept out of his sight. My friends suspected that McGonagle was just feigning ignorance until he had enough evidence to justify a court-martial or an unsatisfactory fitness report.

In addition to the large amount of liquor he drank, Philip was a chain smoker who admitted to smoking five packs of nonfiltered Philip Morris cigarettes daily, or about one cigarette every ten minutes while awake. Once I watched him consume forty cigarettes during an evening of conversation. He sucked cigarettes with such enthusiasm that they barely had time to form an ash before he crushed them out—the last cigarette still a long red cinder as he reached for the next one.

And although his vices implied a certain tension, the overall impression he made was one of relaxed self-control. Only his hands seemed to reveal the inner tension: they trembled, and they displayed fingernails that had been restlessly chewed to tiny crescents set well back from the end of knobby fingers.

Someone asked Philip once if he didn't worry about his health. Wasn't he afraid the heavy drinking, insatiable appetite for nicotine, insufficient sleep and other bad habits would shorten his life? "Of course," he answered. "I have often told Weetie not to expect me around after forty. I'll burn out before then, but I'll have one helluva time first." And Philip was serious. Back in Norfolk, a carefully drawn *Philip Armstrong Death Book* outlined in precise steps everything his new widow should do.

More than most executive officers, Philip was trusted and welcome everywhere in the ship. Men felt comfortable with him. He had particularly friendly relations with the chiefs—a fact that clearly irritated McGonagle, who did his best to discourage social contact between officers and enlisted men. And Philip openly defied the captain's nonfraternization policy: he lunched regularly in the chiefs' private mess, competed in the chiefs' English darts matches, and included a chief petty officer and a black enlisted steward among his closest friends.

While *Liberty* men were largely aware of Philip's weaknesses, at the same time they felt his warmth, they respected him and they were anxious to please him. Although McGonagle was definitely and firmly in command, it was Armstrong who made things move—who executed McGonagle's orders and made them work. When McGonagle wanted *Liberty* to be the cleanest, sharpest ship in Norfolk, Philip saw that the ship became marvelously clean and sharp. When McGonagle wanted men to train for an exercise, Philip generated enthusiasm for the drills. To a large extent, *Liberty* was what Armstrong wanted her to be. If the *Liberty* crew was tough, impudent, irreverent, well-trained and capable of surviving a sudden assault by vastly superior forces, Armstrong's influence helped make it so.

And *Liberty* was certainly an exceptional ship. During an operational readiness inspection held some weeks before I came aboard, the *Liberty* crew earned the highest marks of any of the ships of her type, an accomplishment for which she eventually would be awarded the coveted Battle Efficiency Award. Philip wanted his ship to have that award, and he saw that his men learned to plug holes and repair damage faster than any ship in the squadron. Philip swore that the case of whiskey he gave an inspecting officer had nothing to do with the high grades the ship won.

=====

When *Liberty* entered the Mediterranean, I had been aboard for more than a month and had seen no drinking by anyone except the XO. I asked my roommate about this.

Jim laughed. "You don't see it," he said, "because the word has gotten around about the spy who may be aboard. Most of the men and some of the officers think you are the spy."

=====

While *Liberty* was in the Atlantic, she was officially under the operational control of the Commander-in-Chief, U.S. Atlantic Fleet. After entering the Mediterranean, her operational control passed to the senior naval officer there, Commander U.S. Sixth Fleet, Vice Admiral William Inman Martin.[2]

Military records do not agree as to just when responsibility shifted

2. Vice Admiral William Inman Martin: naval aviator; born 1910; U.S. Naval Academy, class of 1934; promoted to rear admiral July 1, 1959, vice admiral, April 10, 1967. His is a dual command: Commander Sixth Fleet, and Commander, Naval Striking and Support Forces, Southern Europe.

to COMSIXTHFLT or who was responsible for the ship while she crossed the Mediterranean.[3] However, regardless who was *Liberty*'s designated commander during that period, her movements were really being directed by the Joint Chiefs of Staff in the Pentagon, and any intermediate commander—such as Admiral Martin—served only as a conduit for JCS orders.

Nevertheless, Admiral Martin was curious about this new maverick to enter his domain, and quickly drafted a message welcoming *Liberty* to the Sixth Fleet and announcing his intention to visit. He would come aboard on June 7, his message told us, for a tour of the ship, a briefing on her mission and capabilities, and a conference with the commanding officer.

Liberty was in an uproar for hours. Although the ship routinely entertained senior officers in Norfolk, due to her years of isolated duty she was inexperienced in the dangerous work of transferring live cargo between ships at sea.

Reluctantly, we sent a message explaining that the customary "high line transfer" (hauling the admiral over on lines rigged between the ships) was inadvisable due to our lack of experience, that a helicopter transfer was very dangerous because of the small landing area, and that small-boat transfer presented a severe danger of swamping in the heavy seas. While we all hoped that Admiral Martin would change his mind and stay in the flagship, his next message confirmed the rendezvous times and outlined details of his visit. We set to work preparing a briefing for the admiral and doing some extra work to spruce up the ship.

3. While most military records indicate that *Liberty* "chopped" (changed operational commander) to COMSIXTHFLT on June 7 (a date that has been verified by McGonagle and seems to be borne out by military messages), *Liberty* officers considered that the ship came under COMSIXTHFLT's operational control on June 2, 1967. USS *Liberty* letter AGTR5/03 5750, Serial 145, dated March 11, 1968, and addressed to CNO OP-09B9, informs the Navy Historian that, among other things, USS *Liberty* chopped to COMSIXTHFLT on June 2, 1967—thus confirming the author's own recollections. The date of chop is significant, because the Navy explains COMSIXTHFLT's failure to keep *Liberty* away from the war zone by telling us that the ship was under control of USCINCEUR (United States Commander-in-Chief Europe, an Army officer) until June 7, and that Admiral Martin, therefore, lacked authority to move her before that date.

Chapter 4

APPROACH TO GAZA

Get the message through.

Motto of the U.S. Army Signal Corps

We awoke the morning of June 3 to find continued high winds and cloudy skies. The three Soviet destroyers that had accompanied us through the Strait of Gibraltar were now nowhere to be seen. Senior Chief Stanley W. "Stan" White, a lean young genius of an electronics maintenance technician, greeted me with the sad news that a new and major leak had developed in TRSSCOMM. By now we had nearly exhausted our once ample supply of hydraulic fluid. The new leak had to be corrected quickly and positively or the system would be out of service due to fluid shortage. Together we examined the leaky fitting: a wild Medusa of pipes around a distribution box bled purple goop from several joints. This could not easily be repaired, and if our efforts failed we would be out of business anyway without hydraulic fluid. In desperation we agreed to drastic measures. The shipfitters would weld the baby octopus firmly together at all seams and connections. Later removal would be a problem, but meanwhile the system shouldn't leak.

Liberty stepped up her training. The executive officer scheduled frequent exercises at General Quarters. Fire parties were called away, hoses hauled out and run to imaginary fires, damage control teams drilled and thoroughly refreshed in the techniques of plugging holes and using giant timbers to support bulkheads around supposedly flooded compartments. These men, led by Ensign John Scott, could locate and "repair" imaginary flooding and weakened bulkheads in minutes. The drills helped satisfy the ship's regular training requirements and, more important now, they helped to occupy and reassure the increasingly apprehensive crew.

Sunday, June 4, brought "holiday routine" along with continued wind and rain. In the coordination center on the third deck, someone posted a large chart of the Mediterranean Sea with the *Liberty* track plotted. Ahead of *Liberty* and approaching her was the track of another ship. This was USNS *Private Jose F. Valdez,* [1] a much older and smaller ship on "special project duty" (a euphemism assigned to civilian-manned intelligence-collection ships), and she was on her way home. *Valdez* was identified on the chart as Contact A. To our right was an X drawn lightly on the chart in pencil. The X mark was not otherwise identified, and no one seemed to know what it meant.

Co-ord, as the room was known, was the very heart and soul of the Research Operations Department. This large office just below the waterline housed the analysts and report writers; it was a busy place, with desks and plotting tables along the walls and more desks and filing cabinets in the center. In Norfolk the walls were barren, a requirement of Captain McGonagle in consideration of occasional female visitors. During the first night at sea, however, the men literally covered the walls and cabinets and much of the overhead with hundreds of cutouts from *Playboy* and competing magazines. The previously drab room suddenly took on a splash of color and an aura of eroticism not inappropriate for the gaudiest whorehouse.

1. *Jane's Fighting Ships* lists two "Special Project" or "Special Mission" ships: USNS *Private Jose F. Valdez* (T-AG 169) and USNS *Sergeant Joseph P. Muller* (T-AG 171), and reports that a third such ship, USNS *Lieutenant James E. Robinson* (T-AG 170), was in operation in 1963 and 1964. Each ship was operated by a civilian crew, but carried a military department consisting of about fifteen naval officers and 150 Navy enlisted men. *Valdez* usually operated off the east coast of Africa; *Muller* operated off the coast of Cuba. *Jane's* describes the mission of the ships as the collection of "magnetic radiation information and meteorological observations in support of marine environmental programs." No further description of the ship's mission has ever been released by the Department of Defense.

Yet, despite the frivolous appearance of the room, serious men spent long hours here performing important work.

======

On June 5 we received the inevitable news that war had commenced in earnest. Israel finally reacted to Nasser's provocations with devastating surprise attacks launched simultaneously throughout the Arab countries. Arab airplanes and Russian-built Tupolev bombers burned and exploded everywhere. Superb intelligence allowed the Israeli pilots to leave untouched the many dummy airplanes intended to draw their fire while they destroyed literally hundreds of airplanes on the ground in Egypt, Syria, Jordan and Iraq. Having secured control of the air, Israel attacked the now helpless Arab desert forces. Success seemed assured as Israel pressed her advantage.[2]

In Co-ord an excited sailor used felt marker pens to draw a small Egyptian flag; then he burned the edges with a cigarette lighter to show the ravages of war and displayed the battle-scarred banner at his desk. At another desk an Israeli partisan built a small cannon out of cardboard, painted a Star of David on the gun barrel, and aimed it at the Egyptian flag. This was all in fun, produced from a need to react to the great drama unfolding nearby. Soon national flags of all the combatants were displayed throughout the room, mostly tattered and smoke-damaged as though in fierce battle. War slogans appeared in several languages. PALESTINE LIBERATION read a banner posted as a backdrop to the scene. A few men argued heatedly for the Arabs, posting Arab slogans on their desks and promising to push Israel into the sea, but for the most part the men were strongly pro-Israel and proud of the lesson that "science and technology" was teaching to "ignorance and superstition."

Drills resumed, interfering more than ever with routine work. Stan White's battle station was a fourth-deck repair shop just above the bilges. He was spending several hours daily in this room with one other man, Seaman James Lenau, idly waiting out the completion of drills elsewhere in the ship while his own work fell behind.

Lenau's duty was to report by telephone any fire, flooding, leaking or other damage to the compartments within his area. He wore a telephone headset and, over the headset, a huge battle helmet specially designed to permit the comfortable use of the telephone.

Although White's duty was to supervise the repair shops, the

---

2. See *The Six Day War* by Randolph S. Churchill and Winston S. Churchill (Boston: Houghton Mifflin, 1967) for a detailed account of the war.

shops were not manned, as nothing was being repaired. I changed his battle station to his second-deck office, where he could be in direct telephone contact with *all* repair shops and still do his necessary office work during the drills that did not require his direct participation.

Officers and men continued to worry openly about the safety of our ship and the wisdom of our mission. It was widely expected that the onset of war would cause our seniors to reexamine our assignment. When no change of orders arrived, *Liberty* drafted an appeal to Vice Admiral Martin requesting that a destroyer be sent to remain within five miles of *Liberty* to serve as both an armed escort and an auxiliary communication center. And to make the best use of our own limited ability to protect ourselves, McGonagle established a "Modified Condition of Readiness Three," which he defined in a memorandum to key bridge personnel: "Effective immediately, two men will be stationed on the forecastle as additional lookouts/gun crews . . . Lookouts and forecastle gun mount personnel are to man mounts and defend the ship in the event of surprise air/surface attack while regular General Quarters teams are being assembled . . . Any unidentified surface contact approaching the ship on a collision or near collision course at a speed of 25 knots or more is to be considered acting in a hostile manner and Condition of Readiness One is to be set immediately. . . . Any unidentified air contact approaching the ship on an apparent strafing/bombing/torpedo attack is to be considered hostile . . . It is better to set general quarters in doubtful cases than to be taken by surprise and be unable to fight the ship. Take immediate action as may be required by the situation, then advise me of what steps have been taken."

USNS *Private Jose F. Valdez,* Contact A on the Co-ord chart, had passed us during the night and was proceeding slowly toward Norfolk. The mysterious Contact X, meanwhile, was now on an intercept course with *Liberty.* Still, no one seemed to know who was plotting Contact X, where the plotting information was coming from or just what sort of vessel was being plotted. Now that *Valdez* was on her way out of the area, we were alone in the eastern Mediterranean with Contact X.

On June 6 we received Admiral Martin's reply to our request for an armed escort: LIBERTY IS A CLEARLY MARKED UNITED STATES SHIP IN INTERNATIONAL WATERS, NOT A PARTICIPANT IN THE CON-

FLICT AND NOT A REASONABLE SUBJECT FOR ATTACK BY ANY NATION, Admiral Martin reminded us. In the unlikely event of an inadvertent attack, he promised, jet fighters from the Sixth Fleet carrier force could be overhead in less than ten minutes. Besides, he concluded, every commanding officer has authority to withdraw from danger. Request for escort denied.[3]

But even as COMSIXTHFLT saw no danger, CINCUSNAVEUR in London took a careful look and prepared a sobering message to COMSIXTHFLT and *Liberty*:

TO FACILITATE AREA COMMAND AND CONTROL AND ANY POSSIBLE REQUIREMENT FOR PROTECTION DURING MIDEAST HOSTILITIES, USS LIBERTY WILL BE CHOPPED TO COMSIXTHFLT AT 070001Z JUN 67. OPER-ATE LIBERTY IN ACCORDANCE WITH JCS DIRECTIVES TO DERIVE MAXI-MUM BENEFIT FROM SPECIAL CAPABILITIES. SHIP'S OPERATING AREA MAY BE MODIFIED FOR SAFETY REASONS AS DICTATED BY LOCAL SITUATION.

Then, in an ominous reference to an undependable communication system, CINCUSNAVEUR advised McGonagle that *none* of *Liberty*'s daily position reports had been received for the past four days.[4]

None of this did anything to calm the increasingly agitated *Liberty* crew. On the one hand, COMSIXTHFLT minimized the danger, de-clined our request for an armed escort and made an apparently offhanded promise of help "in the unlikely event" help would be needed; on the other hand, CINCUSNAVEUR warned of the possible need for protection, instructed us cryptically to use the Research Operations Department's "special capabilities" for early warning of possible danger, and advised that we could move to safer water if conditions became hazardous.

COMSIXTHFLT reacted to the CINCUSNAVEUR warning by drafting one of his own:

IN VIEW ARAB/ISRAELI SITUATION AND UNPREDICTABILITY OF UAR ACTIONS, MAINTAIN A HIGH STATE OF VIGILANCE AGAINST ATTACK OR THREAT OF ATTACK. REPORT BY FLASH PRECEDENCE ANY THREATEN-

3. This message exchange comes from the recollections of the author and several ship's officers. Like so many others, the messages cannot be found in message files preserved by the Court of Inquiry or by various Washington agencies.

4. CINCUSNAVEUR message 061357Z June 1967. Interestingly, the phrase "and any possible requirement for protection" was added to the message in ink at the last moment by CINCUS-NAVEUR's deputy chief of staff. This is the very same officer who, two days later, would delay the execution of a JCS order to move the ship to a less dangerous area.

ING OR SUSPICIOUS ACTIONS DIRECTED AGAINST YOU OR ANY DIVER-
SION FROM SCHEDULE NECESSITATED BY EXTERNAL THREAT.[5]

COMSIXTHFLT could have saved himself the trouble. In a command, control and communications environment in which *Liberty*'s
last four position reports had disappeared, no one should have been
surprised that COMSIXTHFLT's message went undelivered. Like so
many other messages addressed to USS *Liberty,* it vanished in the
great quagmire that served as a communication system, never to be
received by the ship.

Vice Admiral Martin, meanwhile, canceled his plan to visit. The
rapidly moving war, he explained, made it impossible for him to be
far from the flagship.

O'Connor took to working around the clock, taking time out only
for brief, fully clothed catnaps. His constant greeting of "Oh, so
much work! So much work!" grew irritating.

And TRSSCOMM was on the fritz again. Although the hydraulic
system had held up since the "big weld" tactic, now the electronics
were causing trouble for the first time. The trouble was in the Klys-
tron, a high-frequency signal generator that weighed several hundred
pounds. With block and tackle the men removed the defective part
and installed the single spare that we carried. I reported to Captain
McGonagle that TRSSCOMM should be back in service after forty-
eight hours of "baking in," or essentially warming up the new part,
and that we should be able to talk with Cheltenham, Maryland, at
about two o'clock Thursday afternoon, June 8.

======

June 7 was sunny and clear, with a calm sea and light following
breezes. We were almost alone in the eastern Mediterranean. The few
ships we saw were all going in the opposite direction, away from the
war, and reminded me somehow of frightened animals fleeing a
forest fire. We passed a huge Texaco tanker, her captain on the
bridge examining us curiously through binoculars. He must have
wondered what business we had in that area.

Probably to provide a break in the routine and to get everyone's
mind off the war, a materiel inspection of the ship was ordered.
Materiel inspections are conducted frequently in the Navy, their
purpose being to uncover and correct rust, leaks, fire hazards, defec-

tive equipment and other deficiencies. The ship is divided into zones for inspection, each zone assigned to an officer who conducts as thorough an inspection as his experience will allow. My zone this day included the ship's forecastle and numerous compartments in and around the bow of the ship. Normally, all spaces are opened for inspection, with the man in charge of the space standing by to answer questions or to receive comments. As I approached each compartment, a man would step forward to introduce himself and to present the space for which he was responsible: "Seaman Jones, forward repair locker ready for inspection, sir." When I reached the second deck I found a heavily padlocked compartment on the port side. No one stepped forward to accept responsibility for this space, and no one admitted knowing who it was assigned to or why it remained locked; yet I sensed that some of these men did know and were unwilling to tell me.

Men hedged and shuffled as they evaded my questions. Finally, a chief quietly told me that here languished Philip Armstrong's personal liquor supply. Nearly everyone on the ship knew what was in that room. How did the captain remain ignorant of it? Inspection assignments were the responsibility of the executive officer. Philip simply arranged for the captain never to be assigned to inspect the area of the ship that housed his liquor cache.

During the afternoon a radio broadcast of news and commentary was directed through the ship's entertainment system. Men gathered around speakers, listening to reports of Israel's stunning successes against the Arab nations and digesting the heated United Nations debates over the issues and the righteousness of the participants. Israeli armor and infantry swept westward across the Sinai as forces encircled the Jordanian section of the divided city of Jerusalem. A unit secured an abandoned airfield at Sharm el-Sheik on the Red Sea overlooking the Strait of Tiran to easily end the Gulf of Aqaba blockade. Arab forces were being killed and captured by the thousands as we steamed toward the battle.

We chuckled as the newscaster quoted an American official assuring newsmen and the world that "no American ship is within three hundred miles of the fighting." Perhaps not at this moment, we thought, but by morning we'll be smelling the smoke.

———

USNS *Private Jose F. Valdez,* according to the Co-ord chart, was still moving away from *Liberty* and toward Norfolk. Many of us wished we were going with her. The only other mark on the chart, the unidentified Contact X, was now erased. The unidentified object had been tracked for days until it merged with *Liberty*'s track, when suddenly the plot was discontinued. I asked Jim O'Connor what X represented, and received the somewhat embarrassed and unconvincing "I don't know" that told me he really did know. Apparently, I lacked the security clearance required to become privy to the activities of Contact X. Clearly, *something* had been charted right across the Mediterranean until it came alongside or under or over *Liberty*. I guessed that we had rendezvoused with a submarine. If we had, perhaps it was still with us; no one was talking about it, at least not in my presence.

———

As evening approached, we knew we would see the Gaza Strip within a few hours. The war was still hot, although now it was largely a mopping-up operation. Egypt had charged the United States with participating in the war on the side of Israel, and had broken diplomatic relations. She was soon followed by Algeria, Syria, Iraq, the Sudan and Yemen. But we relaxed, knowing that the Arab countries, as angry as they pretended to be toward the United States, probably were merely making noise to cover their humiliating defeat. The Arab countries were now barely capable of pressing a serious attack, anyway. They certainly had their hands full with the rampaging Jews.

Late that evening I stepped into Lloyd Painter's stateroom to find Lloyd, Jim Pierce, Philip Armstrong, Joe Benkert, Maury Bennett, Dick Kiepfer and Steward Troy Green, along with some others, quietly gathered around a three-gallon stainless-steel pot. Several looked uncomfortable as they held paper cups behind them or under hats. Someone invited me to sit down. Finally Lloyd broke the heavy silence: "Oh, for Christ's sake, Jim's no spy." Everyone seemed to agree that of course I was not a spy. Someone scooped a paper cup into the pot for me. In the pot floated large blocks of ice and chunks of pineapple in grapefruit juice, rum and some kind of whiskey.

"So we come six thousand miles to watch the war, and we finally arrive just as it's grinding to a close," Lloyd said as conversation resumed.

"You can be glad we're late," said Philip. "Out here all alone, we're an easy target. I hate to think where we would be now if we had been sitting off the Gaza Strip when the war broke out."

"We'd be on the bottom," someone volunteered.

"Yeah," the group agreed.

"Well, you can bet those Sixth Fleet jets wouldn't be much help anyway," said the XO. "Victory ships were made to carry freight, not to survive a serious attack. When these ships went down in World War Two, usually all it took was one well-placed bomb or a single torpedo. We probably wouldn't even last long enough for our jets to make the trip."

"And then woe is the attacker!" a voice added.

"No chance," replied the XO, his fingers dark olive from the cigarettes as he poured part of his drink into an ashtray to extinguish a great smoking residue. "We would be damned lucky to get a written apology. Meanwhile, the government would carefully paint the entire affair with subdued colors so that the great American public would not become too upset. This would be called 'keeping everything in perspective.' Public relations is the big thing, baby, and don't ever forget it."

Abruptly changing the subject, Philip said softly, "I think I finally got Shep figured out. I've always wondered what he thinks of me, and today I solved the puzzle." From his tone, it seemed that the long-expected confrontation had occurred. We waited for him to continue, but Philip was not yet ready to tell us more. "It will all come out in time," he said after a long silence.

Shep was the nickname for Captain McGonagle. Most commanding officers have nicknames. Command, particularly Navy command at sea, places stresses and peculiar conditions upon men, and the commanding officer becomes aloof, powerful, godlike, a father figure, the supreme visible being, the granter of pain and privilege. Captain McGonagle was all of these things, though less visible than some, more aloof than others, absolutely proper and courteous, independent, proud. I asked Philip how the captain became "Shep."

He brightened at the question. The alcoholic concoction had no effect on him; his speech and eyes were clear. The dozens of cigarettes he had smoked clouded the room, but the ship's air conditioning kept the air breathable.

" 'When I was a lad and Old Shep was a pup,
Over hills and the valleys we roamed.
Just a boy and his dog, we were O! full of fun,
And we grew up together that way.'

"You know that? You must know it. Probably learned it in school.

> " 'I remember one time at the old swimming hole
> When I would have drowned beyond doubt,
> But Old Shep was right there, to the rescue he came.
> He jumped in and helped pull me out.'

"I'm sure you know that. Well, months ago all the *Liberty* officers attended an embassy reception at Luanda, Angola. It was a full-dress affair: whites; stiff, high collars in all that African heat; large medals clanking; swords at our sides like John Paul Jones. We all had our gentlemanly limit of drinks, behaved like little ambassadors, and left on time. No car. Long walk. All of us feeling ridiculous in public in ceremonial dress. Damp and uncomfortable in all that humidity. And then someone composed a limerick. Well, not to be outdone, Shep dredged up the old poem and recited it from memory as we walked along. All of it—there are several verses. And he did it with such flair and dramatic effect that none of us has ever forgotten. We were impressed. We really were. We just didn't know until then that deep down in his fitting and proper old hide is the very reincarnation of Old Shep. To us, he will *always* be Old Shep."

And the name stuck. Behind his back, when he wasn't "Magoo," he was "Shep" to the officers. The name was never used around the crew, and it was never used in disrespect. Captain McGonagle was deeply respected. He was not feared, as some commanding officers are, but he was held in awe. The nickname helped to narrow the distance, permitting him to be dealt with reasonably.

I retreated to my stateroom to rest. I was scheduled for the forenoon officer of the deck watch on our first transit of the Gaza Strip.

═══════

While we were talking, Captain McGonagle summoned Lieutenant Commander Dave Lewis to his cabin. McGonagle, too, was uncomfortable with the order to operate within sight of the war. He was prepared to exercise his prerogative to move away from possible danger, but before doing so he consulted with Lewis.

"How would it affect our mission if we stayed farther out at sea, say, fifty miles from Gaza?" he asked.

Lewis was concerned about our proximity to the war, but he was *more* concerned about our mission. "It would hurt us, Captain," he said. "We want to work in the UHF [ultra-high-frequency] range.

That's mostly line-of-sight stuff. If we're over the horizon we might as well be back in Abidjan. It would degrade our mission by about eighty percent."

McGonagle sat quietly for a few minutes as though deep in thought. "Okay," he said. "We'll go all the way in."

After dismissing Lewis, he carefully reread his night orders to the officer of the deck. Captain's night orders are usually quite routine; they advise the conning officer of course and speed changes, landmarks expected and so forth. Tonight, McGonagle added this note: "Keep gun crews/lookouts alert. Call me for all challenges received, or in the event air or surface contacts approach in a suspicious manner."

======

In Washington, meanwhile, staff officers concluded that *Liberty*'s position near Gaza was no longer necessary nor wise. That decision, I have been told, grew from a routine staff study of risks and rewards —not from any clear sense of danger. Perhaps Frank Raven played a part; he had objected to the mission from the start. In any case, the final decision was made at a senior staff level within the Department of Defense, and resulted in a high-precedence late-afternoon message to the Joint Chiefs of Staff requesting that *Liberty* be moved farther out to sea. Like the original order to leave Abidjan, this message was drafted by Lieutenant McTighe; like the earlier message, it was assigned "Flash" precedence.

Shortly before midnight by *Liberty*'s clocks (around the commuting hour in Washington), officers of the Joint Chiefs of Staff reacted to the Defense Department request by preparing a message that directed the ship to remain at least twenty miles from the United Arab Republic (for us, Gaza). At forty-one minutes past midnight, ship's time, that message was delivered to the Army communication center that serves the Joint Chiefs in the Pentagon.[6] It was addressed to the ship through three echelons of command, and was given a conservative "Priority" precedence.

For the order to be executed, it would be necessary for the United States Commander-in-Chief Europe (USCINCEUR) to direct the Commander-in-Chief, United States Naval Forces, Europe (CINCUS-NAVEUR), to direct Commander Sixth Fleet (COMSIXTHFLT) to di-

6. JCS message 072230Z June 1967. See Appendix A, page 226.

rect *Liberty* to remain twenty miles from the U.A.R. coast. Copies were sent to all concerned commanders, and a copy was addressed to USS *Liberty* for information.

The message would not leave the JCS communication center for more than fourteen hours. When it *was* finally transmitted, it was sent in error to the Naval Communication Station in the Philippines. It was never received by any commander until much too late to take action, and it was not received by *Liberty* at all.[7]

The Joint Chiefs of Staff remained concerned about *Liberty*. Shortly before 0200 ship's time, a JCS duty officer placed an overseas telephone call to the office of Admiral John S. McCain, Jr., at his headquarters in London.[8] There he reached Lieutenant Edward Galavotti, a duty officer on the CINCUSNAVEUR staff, and directed Galavotti to recall the ship. Twenty miles was no longer sufficient: *Liberty* was to be moved at least one hundred miles from the coast.

Unfortunately, McCain's staff suffered from an incurable bureaucrat's disease: messagitis.

"Show me a message," McCain's deputy chief of staff demanded. "We can't revise a ship's operating orders without a confirming message." The deputy was perfectly willing to relay the order, he explained later, but first he wanted assurance that the JCS order had been properly "staffed" at JCS and did not, in fact, originate with the relatively junior officer who had relayed it—one Major Breelove in the JCS Joint Reconnaissance Center at the Pentagon. Thus, Galavotti took no action to have the ship moved; instead, as directed by the deputy, he waited nearly four hours for the JCS message that would confirm Breelove's telephone call—a delay that proved to be crucial.

It took JCS a little more than an hour to draft a message telling USCINCEUR to tell CINCUSNAVEUR to tell COMSIXTHFLT to tell *Lib-*

7. See *Review of Department of Defense Worldwide Communications* (Washington, D.C.: Government Printing Office, 1971), reproduced here in Appendix N, pages 269–75. This report by a subcommittee of F. Edward Hebert's House Committee on Armed Services discusses in minute detail the handling and mishandling of five critical messages intended for USS *Liberty* and is the source of most of the message-handling information reported here.

8. Admiral John Sidney McCain, Jr.: born 1911; U.S. Naval Academy, class of 1931; promoted to rear admiral April 1, 1959, vice admiral, September 1, 1963, admiral, May 1, 1967. A World War Two submariner, he later spent several years in the amphibious forces. From 1965 to 1967 he was vice-chairman, U.S. delegation, United Nations Military Staff Committee, New York. In 1972 Admiral McCain retired from the Navy with forty-one years' service.

erty to remain at least one hundred miles from the coast.[9] Again, a copy was addressed to everyone concerned, including a copy addressed to USS *Liberty* for information.

Liberty would never receive her copy of this message either. Both messages were processed by the same civilian clerk, and *Liberty*'s copy (like the earlier drafted but not yet transmitted stay-twenty-miles-from-the-U.A.R. message) was misdirected to the Philippines Naval Communication Station. There it was correctly rerouted to the Pentagon for further relay to the Naval Communication Station in Morocco for delivery to *Liberty*. But the Pentagon, upon receiving the message for relay, *again* routed it to the wrong place, this time sending it to the National Security Agency communication center at Fort Meade, Maryland, where it was filed in error without action, never to be delivered.

The Joint Chiefs of Staff seem to have had less than complete faith in the ability of the communication system to convey their orders; they inserted in the second message a requirement that each addressee acknowledge receipt by message to JCS.

At 0412 USCINCEUR acknowledged receipt of the order to move *Liberty*. At 0512 CINCUSNAVEUR received the message and he, too, advised JCS of the fact. At 0830 COMSIXTHFLT received and acknowledged the JCS message (for him it was old stuff: the order to move *Liberty* had been given to COMSIXTHFLT at 0645 via a direct Teletype hookup with CINCUSNAVEUR). Apparently, no one at JCS was monitoring the acknowledgments. Had anyone been paying attention, they would have realized that something was wrong—USS *Liberty* failed to acknowledge receipt.[10]

No matter. Not content to rely entirely upon the clumsy chain of command, JCS prepared still another message. This one—according to an officer who handled it during the night—was addressed to *Liberty* for action and to the plodding commanders for information only. Like the others, this unusual, almost unprecedented message ordered McGonagle to move far out to sea. To assure expeditious handling, it was given "Immediate" precedence; like the earlier JCS message to USCINCEUR, it was classified "Top Secret" in spite of an innocuous text.

9. JCS message 080110Z June 1967. See Appendix A, page 228.
10. All times are local time aboard USS *Liberty* unless otherwise indicated or obvious in context. "Z," which indicates Greenwich mean time, is the time customarily used in military messages. Washington, D.C., on daylight-saving time, was four hours behind Greenwich mean time and six hours behind the ship's time. Therefore, for example, the attack began at 0800 Washington time, 1200Z (Greenwich) time and 1400 USS *Liberty* time.

Here was the ultimate fail-safe device. If all else failed, McGonagle could still be expected to get the word. But *Liberty* was not a subscriber to the "Top Secret" message-delivery system that the JCS communication center selected, and the message could not be delivered. The fail-safe system failed.

As we drew closer to the war, a warning to mariners was broadcast on the international distress frequency: *Warning: The attention of mariners is drawn to the possibility that lights along the Israeli coasts may be extinguished without prior notice.* This was soon followed by an even more ominous message: *Warning: All vessels are required to keep away from the coasts of Israel during darkness.* Undaunted and unaware that her orders had been changed, *Liberty* steamed on.

Chapter 5

THE GAZA STRIP

A commander must train his subordinate commanders,
and his own staff, to work and act on verbal orders. Those
who cannot be trusted to act on clear and concise verbal
orders, but want everything in writing, are useless.

Montgomery of Alamein,
Memoirs, vi (1958)

Custom in the Navy calls for relieving the watch fifteen minutes
before the hour. The 0400–0800 watch on *Liberty* was ordinarily
relieved much earlier to allow time for the off-going section to have
breakfast before morning quarters. Thus, I appeared on the bridge
shortly after seven o'clock to find Ensign John Scott, the ship's
conscientious young damage control officer, scanning the shore with
his binoculars. "Fabulous morning," John said, continuing to peer
through the binoculars as he briefed me on the watch conditions,
boilers in use, ship's course and speed, wind speed and direction,
both actual and relative to the ship, barometric pressure, readiness
condition.

"We now have ammunition at all four machine guns," John told
me. "Men are on duty in battle dress in the two forward gun mounts,
which makes our readiness condition Condition Three, modified.
The Old Man is taking no chances! The guns behind the bridge are

unmanned. In case of trouble the lookouts will man the guns while General Quarters is being set."

"Pretty scary," I said.

"There is still a lot of shooting around here. Passed Port Said during the night. Don't know what was happening, but the sky around the city was filled with smoke and fire all night long. About an hour ago," he continued, still searching the beach for an identifiable landmark, "we were circled by a flying boxcar. Real slow and easy. And every few minutes a fat little prop plane, maybe a light bomber, comes down the beach, just skimming the sand dunes. Haven't seen any fighting here, though."

I relieved John at 0720, agreeing with him as he mentioned the difficulty of accurately fixing the ship's position along this nondescript coastline. I was relieved to see the village of El Arish appear ahead of us on our left. A minaret on my navigation chart could be seen towering over the cluster of brown desert buildings, and provided the only distinctive feature in sight. By plotting the minaret's bearing and the radar-determined distances to the minaret and to the nearest beach to my left, I was able to obtain a reasonable fix. Readings from the ship's Fathometer corresponded well with what the sketchy fix told me the depth of the water should be. Acutely conscious of the international uproar that might be caused by any inadvertent penetration of the claimed United Arab Republic waters, I was particularly cautious. Compass and equipment errors, plus any errors of my own, could combine with inaccuracies in the chart to put me far from where I thought we were. (This is why navigation is known as art; it is far too inexact to pretend toward science.) I resolved to fix the ship's position every ten or fifteen minutes, instead of every thirty minutes as Captain McGonagle usually required in coastal waters.

On the bridge, everyone was alert and doing his job. On duty was a signalman; a quartermaster in charge of the men and responsible for keeping a notebook record of watch conditions and orders given, including all course and speed changes; a helmsman; an engine-order telegraph operator whose job was to relay orders to the engine room; and two lookouts. In an adjoining room was a radar operator, and on the bridge was a radar scope for my use as officer of the deck.

I noticed that the ship's five-by-eight-foot American flag was fouled, having become tangled in the lines. The flag was dark with soot and badly tattered from the high-speed steaming of the past few days. I ordered it replaced.

Soon Signalman Russell David appeared at my side, clearly agitated. "Sir, I'd like to keep that flag up there!" he said, with an insistence that surprised me. Greatly frustrated, he complained that he had only one flag left. Several had been ruined during the trip, most were worn or badly stained, and the only presentable flags left were the special oversized "holiday colors" and the one new flag that I insisted upon using.

"We must fly the new flag," I said, explaining that we were operating in a dangerous area and could afford to show only our clearest, brightest colors.

Obviously irritated, David hauled his last new flag high on the ship's mast. I watched it fly freely, then instructed David and both lookouts to check the flag regularly to assure that it remained free and unfouled. Normally composed, David seemed barely able to contain his anger. His mood seemed to me to mirror the unease that still troubled most of the crew.

On the weather decks below I could see the crew assembling for morning quarters, Philip in crisp khaki, standing apart to receive the reports of his department heads. Stan White, taking my part as division officer, reported results of the roll call to Dave Lewis, who assembled reports from his divisions and finally joined the smaller rank facing Philip while men shuffled about in ranks quietly. After receiving the usual reports, Philip advised the department heads of a General Quarters drill scheduled after lunch, returned their salutes and departed. The "word" thus received was passed along to division officers and ultimately to "the man in the back rank." Today there were also reminders to the men that we were skirting a hot, shooting war. No trouble was expected, the men were told, but anything could happen in wartime and everyone had to remain alert.

Morning quarters completed, I called the TRSSCOMM room to check on the status of the equipment. Stan White was already there and reported that all was going well. The equipment would be ready on schedule at 1400. The moon would be in a good position then to talk to Cheltenham. We felt good about it. We could control the small hydraulic leaks that remained. Now, with the electronics in shape, we were optimistic that the system would continue to operate.

When the duty quartermaster cried out, "Captain's on the bridge," I quickly reviewed the vital statistics of course, speed, weather and so forth in case he should ask. I told the captain about the bomber that had been seen near the beach, and we discussed the flying boxcar that had been seen on John's watch.

As the ship arrived at the predesignated Point Alfa from our operating orders (31-27.2N 34-00E), I changed course toward Point Bravo, fifteen miles ahead (31-22.3N 33-42E). This turn would bring the ship to her initial patrol course parallel to the Gaza Strip near the Egyptian/Israeli border and headed toward Port Said, ninety miles to the west.

"Right ten degrees rudder," I ordered the helmsman, who repeated, "Right ten degrees rudder, aye, sir," to acknowledge the order; then, "My rudder is right ten degrees, sir"; then, "Passing course one seven zero," as he reported the ship's progress swinging about in her turn. I intended to bring the ship to her new course by rudder orders, directing movement of the rudder rather than giving the helmsman the new course. As I gauged the turn on a compass repeater on the port wing of the bridge, a lookout on the open bridge above called out: "Airplane passing astern, sir!"

"Steady on course two five three," I ordered the helmsman, abandoning my sport with the rudder in order not to overshoot the new course while checking the airplane.

Together, Captain McGonagle and I watched a single jet pass down *Liberty*'s starboard side, then turn left several miles ahead of the ship and vanish, apparently toward the Gaza Strip along the coast to our left. The airplane was not close enough to make out any markings. At Captain McGonagle's direction I prepared a message report of the sighting to forward to higher authority, and had a messenger deliver it to Lieutenant Steve Toth, who was the ship's navigator and intelligence officer.

Captain McGonagle asked quietly, typically careful not to embarrass me before the men, if I had ordered the speed change from fifteen to five knots, which was to have been accomplished at Point Alfa. He knew the answer without asking, of course. Distracted by the airplane, I had forgotten the speed change. I quickly ordered the scheduled five-knot speed. The ship settled into her usual patrol posture, barely moving along a barren coastline in balmy weather, rolling gently. I checked the flag. It was standing out in eight knots of relative wind, clearly displayed for anyone who might look.

Off-duty men now occupied the forecastle, sunbathing on blankets and lounge chairs. Many commanding officers are offended by the sight of men relaxing during normal working hours, a condition that causes extreme hardship for men who happen to work irregular hours. Captain McGonagle had no such problem; through his executive officer, he encouraged off-duty men to relax. His attitude was one of the reasons for the very high morale on board.

Just before ten o'clock the bridge lookouts reported jet fighters approaching from astern. I could see the gunners lounging about, talking with swimsuited shipmates. Using a sound-powered telephone extension on the gunnery circuit, I told the men to wake up and keep a sharp lookout, warning them that unidentified aircraft were in the area.

Off the starboard side, high, I could see two sleek delta-wing jets in tight side-by-side formation, paralleling our course.[1] Although they were close enough that I could count numerous rockets hanging in clusters under each wing, I could not see any identification markings. The airplanes turned left well ahead of us, then left again and passed down our port side. I again checked the flag: still standing straight out in a light breeze, clearly visible. I watched the airplanes through my binoculars. I could see the pilots. I decided that if I could see the pilots in their cockpits, the pilots could certainly see our flag and no doubt our ship's name and number. They made three complete orbits of the ship before disappearing from view.

Since I was quite busy with coastal piloting, trying to assure our staying as close as possible to our assigned track, Steve Toth agreed to draft the sighting report. I called the captain to inform him of the armed reconnaissance.

It seemed to me that the lookouts, particularly the men in the forward gun mounts, were still not giving their job anywhere near the degree of attention it required. They were gawking, stretching, loafing and visiting with friends; they were doing everything but acting like lookouts. I called the quartermaster of the watch to the port wing of the bridge and asked him to talk individually with each lookout—four in all—to stress the importance of being alert and attentive and to ensure that they did nothing but scan the sea and sky around us for ships and airplanes. They were to have no visitors. They were to devote their full time and attention to looking for contacts.

The quartermaster returned in a few minutes to tell me that the lookouts had no binoculars, that they found it difficult to be serious lookouts without binoculars.

"Where are their binoculars?"

1. These aircraft were identified later as French-built Dassault Mirage III fighter bombers.

"Lieutenant Toth took them."

Seamen George Wilson and Larry Slavens, bridge lookouts, were on a deck above me. These men had been issued binoculars; but every hour they rotated with the forward lookouts, and when they did they left their binoculars on the bridge. I called Wilson down from his station on the starboard wing of the 04 level.

"What happened to the forward lookouts' binoculars?"

"Lieutenant Toth took them."

"Are you sure? Why would he take the lookouts' binoculars?"

"I don't know, Mr. Ennes. When we first came on watch we all had binoculars, but Mr. Toth collected them from the men in the gun mounts and locked them up in the chart house. He said we didn't need them. He said that if we kept them they'd only get banged up."

"Has anyone ever taken your binoculars away before when you were a lookout?" I asked.

"No, sir, never. I asked Mr. Toth about it myself when he was on the bridge a while ago, and he said the same thing. He told me, 'You don't need them and they'll just get banged up.' "

In a few minutes I called Steve on the bridge telephone to ask him to reissue binoculars. He refused, but promised to come to the bridge to talk with me about it. In the meantime he was busy preparing sighting reports and I was busy with control of the ship.

At about 1030 we received another visit from the flying boxcar, now more curious and coming closer. Watching the airplane through binoculars, I told the quartermaster to call the captain by telephone to inform him of the visit. The airplane paralleled our course to starboard, turning left in front of the ship in a pattern that was now becoming routine. Another left turn and he appeared on our port side. Again I checked our flag, found it flying freely as usual, and noted that the relative wind was still from dead ahead and of sufficient speed to display the colors clearly.

"Well, they certainly know who we are by now, don't they?" said Captain McGonagle, who had come to the bridge quickly in response to the telephone call. "It's good that they are checking us out this carefully. This way there won't be any mistakes. Early this afternoon they'll probably come out by boat to give us a closer look."

We stood next to a railing on the port wing of the bridge, where we could see our flag at the mast and see the airplane at the same time. As we talked, the pilot, who was now on our port quarter and headed away from the ship, suddenly executed a near 360-degree turn. Banking sharply, a wing tip of this huge, lumbering mastodon of the air threatened to dip into the sea. Completing the turn, the airplane headed directly back toward *Liberty* at a very low level, probably not more than two hundred feet above the water.

As the airplane drew closer, we could see the details of its construction: wheel wells, seams, rivets that held the airplane together, a Star of David that identified it as Israeli, large belly doors.

"Watch him," McGonagle yelled over the sound of aircraft engines. "If you see those bomb bay doors start to open, order an immediate hard right turn."

I held my breath until the airplane passed overhead. The very low altitude caused her engine noises to reverberate between ship and airplane, setting up a vibration that caused the decks to shudder. Mercifully, the doors remained closed. As the airplane passed overhead, I noticed smaller openings, which I guessed were camera ports.[2]

After the captain left the bridge, I called Steve Toth to advise him of this latest visit and of the Israeli identification markings.

The flying boxcar returned just before eleven o'clock and again thirty minutes later, each time executing the now-familiar counterclockwise orbit before completing a low-level, diagonal, direct overflight of the ship. And each time, I verified the condition of our flag.

Near the end of my watch, Steve Toth came on the bridge to return a publication that he had taken to the captain. He was upset because the sighting reports had not yet been released by the captain so that they could be sent on their way.

"Shep won't release 'em," Steve told me. "First, he wanted to see *Jane's* [*Jane's All the World's Aircraft*]. Then he wanted to see the reporting instructions. Now he's quibbling about the wording."

"At this rate we'll never get them all reported," I said. "Let's describe the boxcar as returning every thirty or forty minutes. That way we can save a few messages."

By this time we had both forgotten about the binoculars.

At 1130 the ship arrived at Point Bravo. I executed a right turn to new course 283°, heading the ship toward the point designated Charlie in our operating orders. At Charlie (31-31N 33-00E), the ship was to reverse course, retracing the dogleg pattern every ten hours until further orders were received.

2. This airplane was identified later as a French-built twin-engine Nord 2501 Noratlas. The Noratlas is a medium-range transport and does not carry bombs; the belly doors we saw were probably cargo doors.

Coastal piloting remained difficult because of the apparent chart errors and the lack of prominent features on the landscape. Radar was little help now because of the barren and indistinct beach. The duty radarman in "Combat" (the combat information center) kept a separate plot, which agreed reasonably with mine. I was satisfied with my track, but uneasy that the only positive visual landmark remained the minaret at El Arish. I hoped for a prominent rock or other feature to strengthen my fix.

Suddenly a huge explosion rocked the town of El Arish. The little bomber that had patrolled the beach all morning could no longer be seen. Did it bomb the town, I wondered. Did it crash? And how shaky will my track become if the minaret falls? I located Captain McGonagle in the wardroom to tell him of the fire and smoke ashore.

At noon, thick black smoke extending for miles along the beach, Lieutenant Painter appeared, ready to take the afternoon watch. Easygoing, always smiling Lloyd was quite relaxed about the whole thing as I told him of the bomber, the jets, the flying boxcar, the explosion ashore and the location of Point Charlie ahead.

A criminologist by training, Lloyd had the short, solid, muscular build of a bulldog. He also had the bulldog's confidence, good humor and what-the-hell outlook. Typically, he seemed already to have forgotten about the incident at Rota with the government agent. At least, he wasn't worrying about it. I promised to return in an hour to relieve him for the scheduled General Quarters drill, and headed for the wardroom for lunch.

———

During my morning watch, quite unknown to us, Vice Admiral Martin dealt with the JCS order to move *Liberty* one hundred miles from the coast, having received the order from Admiral McCain's headquarters by Teletype conference at 0645, *Liberty* time.

Admiral Martin's staff was aware of *Liberty*'s sense of danger, for *Liberty* had requested an armed escort. The Sixth Fleet staff was also aware of *Liberty*'s vulnerable position: a message to COMSIXTHFLT promised her 0900 arrival at Point Alfa, 12.5 miles from the coast.

One would suppose that staff officers would be moved to extraordinary measures to order the ship promptly to sea, since it was now obvious that *Liberty* was within sight of the fighting and was some ninety miles past the closest point of approach established by JCS. And moving her would have been simple indeed. It would have been a very easy matter to pick up a radiotelephone handset on the flagship and establish immediate voice contact with *Liberty*'s officer of the deck. But COMSIXTHFLT chose not to use that means. It would also have been simple to establish direct two-way Teletype communication between COMSIXTHFLT and *Liberty*. Privacy would have been protected by scrambler devices, and this method would have provided a written record of what was said. This was the method, after all, that CINCUSNAVEUR used when he ordered COMSIXTHFLT to recall *Liberty*. But COMSIXTHFLT chose not to use that means, either.

Liberty was an information addressee on *both* of the key JCS messages.[3] COMSIXTHFLT might have supposed that *Liberty* had received the JCS messages and had moved away from the coast without waiting for the order to be echoed by lesser commanders. COMSIXTHFLT might have supposed that, but he would not have relied upon it. Duty required COMSIXTHFLT to move *Liberty* away from the coast, and COMSIXTHFLT set about doing just that. He simply failed to attach to the matter the same urgency that JCS attached to it.

COMSIXTHFLT drafted an ordinary Teletype message for ordinary delivery through the land-based communication relay system—ignoring the more rapid means available. He treated the order, in other words, as a routine administrative detail, and tossed it into the already clogged communication system to compete with grocery orders, leave requests and spare parts requisitions. It took four hours to draft the message and deliver it to the communication center. It took another hour and eighteen minutes for the communication center to prepare the message for transmission and to transmit it. At 1235, *Liberty* time, COMSIXTHFLT's message directing the ship to move away from the coast was transmitted to the Naval Communication Station in Morocco for ultimate delivery to *Liberty*.[4]

===

After a quick sandwich and glass of milk in the wardroom pantry, I climbed down two more decks to find Jim O'Connor and Maury Bennett still hard at work in Co-ord. Most of the other officers were happily sunning themselves in deck chairs on the roof of the forward deckhouse, but O'Connor found little time for rest. "So much work," he muttered, almost as a greeting. Bennett gave me a pained look.

---

3. First described in Chapter Three, these are JCS 072230Z and JCS 080110Z June 1967. See Appendix A, pages 226 and 228.

4. COMSIXTHFLT message 080917Z June 1967. See Appendix A, page 232.

No doubt thinking of O'Connor's likely approach to nervous exhaustion, Bennett suggested that he get some fresh air and a change of scenery by taking the bridge watch during General Quarters.

"Good idea," O'Connor said. It would be his first appearance on deck in several days.

O'Connor was the regular officer of the deck for General Quarters —an assignment that put him on the bridge in charge of the ship and all shipboard operations during actual or simulated combat. I was to have relieved him of that duty in Abidjan, but the executive officer had been too busy to change the watch bill. Consequently, with Philip's blessing, I had been taking most of the assignments even though O'Connor was still officially the officer of the deck. Today, we would both stand the watch; O'Connor would take the OOD position and I would assist.

I wandered about the ship, spending a few minutes talking with technicians in the TRSSCOMM room as they conducted a careful countdown with their cantankerous patient. I found the ship's photographer, Petty Officer Charles L. Rowley, in the photo lab where he had been for most of the morning, and asked him to meet me on the bridge after General Quarters so that we could try again to get a good picture of our aerial visitors. Finally, I climbed the five decks from Co-ord to the bridge and watched Lloyd Painter work while I waited for him to sound the General Quarters alarm. During my absence from the bridge, the ship had been reconnoitered two more times by the flying boxcar.

The alarm sounded at 1310. The drill was prompted by news reports, later proving erroneous, of poison gas being used in the fighting ashore; so this was a gas attack drill. Men responded quickly, rapidly sealing all doors and other openings in order to make of the ship a gas-tight envelope impervious to the atmosphere outside. The pilothouse sealed, we saw the sea ahead only through the small peep slots cut into the heavy steel battle coverings of the pilothouse portholes. Captain McGonagle evaluated the drill promptly and shifted attention to fire and damage-control drills.

As we responded to the gas attack alarm, CINCUSNAVEUR received his information copy of the COMSIXTHFLT message that ordered *Liberty* away from the coast. *Liberty* should have received her action copy of the message at about the same time, but she didn't. That copy was now following a labyrinthine path through the communication system, which passed it about almost aimlessly, like a leaf afloat in a pond. *Liberty*'s copy of the message ultimately arrived at the Army Communication Station in Asmara, Ethiopia, for relay to the Naval Communication Station in Asmara for delivery to *Liberty* via the fleet broadcast that that station operates. But at 1348, as word was passed over the ship's general announcing system to *"secure from general quarters; secure from all drills,"* *Liberty*'s message waited its turn at a transmitting position at the Asmara Army Communication Station, which would, in a few moments, misdirect it to the Naval Communication Station in Greece, where it would remain for the next three hours.

========

On the bridge, Painter relieved O'Connor as OOD. Battle helmets made clunking sounds as men dropped them into storage racks, glad to return to cooler headgear. Telephone talkers wound long telephone cables, filthy from years of dragging over sooty decks, to stow the equipment in waterproof telephone storage boxes. On the forecastle, men lingered in the gun mounts to talk with the gunners and to examine the machine guns (usually stored elsewhere), while the sunbathers returned with towels and deck chairs.

"It's good that we have sunbathers on deck," said McGonagle. "It helps to show that we're peaceful."

Using the ship's general announcing system, McGonagle complimented the men on the fine drill and reminded them, once again, of our potentially dangerous position and of the need to respond promptly to all alarms, as one could be genuine. To illustrate his concern, he mentioned the shooting war to our left and told the men of the large fire at El Arish, whose black smoke still threatened to obscure the town from our view. In conclusion, he mentioned that the local forces knew *Liberty* was here, having made numerous aerial reconnaissance sorties during the morning, and told the men—as he had told me earlier—that we could expect boats to visit us during the afternoon for a closer look.

A bridge telephone talker, still winding his cable but not yet unplugged from his terminal, received and relayed advice from Combat of three high-speed aircraft, sixteen miles away, approaching the ship from 082°, the general direction of the Israeli capital, Tel Aviv. Then Combat corrected the report, now advising that "the contacts are fading; they appear to be weather."

Although no longer an official member of the bridge team on duty,

I told the talker to advise Combat that air contacts often look like clouds or small rain squalls when spotted on surface-search radar equipment, that Combat should continue to watch the contacts carefully. The report was then corrected again. The radar operator now described three high-speed surface contacts at the same bearing and range as the air contacts, and moving toward the ship at thirty-five knots. "Captain, you gotta look at this! I never saw anything move so fast," Lloyd Painter cried, having spotted the boats on the bridge radar repeater.

The drill over, ship's routine business resumed. Word was passed: "Stand clear of the motor whaleboat while testing engines." This was a routine test, performed daily while at sea.

I sat loosely on a wing of the bridge, perched on a cover of the starboard running light where I could best see in the direction of the expected aircraft. The captain stood nearby. Jim O'Connor, the XO and some of the men who had been on the bridge during the drill stayed to see the expected airplanes. Petty Officer Rowley, the ship's photographer, appeared, as I had asked him to.

The first to spot the visitor, I pointed to a single delta-wing Mirage jet about 45 degrees above the water, paralleling our course in the pattern that had become routine. I stayed until I was sure Captain McGonagle saw the airplane, then headed toward the open bridge on the 04 level above. Racing toward a permanently mounted telescope on the port side, I found Rowley already there with the ship's Nikon camera and a clumsy telephoto lens. Several sailors gathered for a clear view of the airplanes. As I swung the ship's telescope to starboard for a closer look at the jet, Rowley called, "Mr. Ennes, he's not there. He's up ahead!"

O'Connor, to my right, searched the sky with his binoculars as I glanced forward.

Chapter 6

AIR ATTACK

Imagine all the earthquakes in the world, and all the thunder and lightnings together in a space of two miles, all going off at once.

Description by unknown U.S. Army officer of night engagement when Farragut ran Forts Jackson and St. Philip, April 24, 1862

Searing heat and terrible noise came suddenly from everywhere.

Instinctively I turned sideways, presenting the smallest target to the heat. Heat came first, and it was heat—not cannon fire—that caused me to turn away. It was too soon to be *aware* of rockets or cannon fire.

"We're shooting!" I thought. "Why are we shooting?"

The air filled with hot metal as a geometric pattern of orange flashes opened holes in the heavy deck plating. An explosion tossed our gunners high into the air—spinning, broken, like rag dolls.

My first impression—my primitive, protective search for something safe and familiar that put me emotionally *behind* the gun—was wrong. We were not firing at all. We were being pounded with a deadly barrage of aircraft cannon and rocket fire.

A solid blanket of force threw me against a railing. My arm held me up while the attacker passed overhead, followed by a loud *swoosh,* then silence.

O'Connor spotted bright flashes under the wings of the French-built jet in time to dive down a ladder. He was struck in midair, severely wounded by rocket fragments before he crashed into the deck below.

I seemed to be the only one left standing as the jet disappeared astern of us. Around me, scattered about carelessly, men squirmed helplessly, like wounded animals—wide-eyed, terrified, not under-standing what had happened.

The second airplane made a smoky trail in the sky ahead. Unable to move, we watched the jet make a sweeping 180-degree turn toward *Liberty,* ready to resume the attack. My khaki uniform was bright red now from two dozen rocket fragments buried in my flesh. My left leg, broken above the knee, hung from my hip like a great beanbag.

The taste of blood was strong in my mouth as I tested my good leg. Was I badly hurt? Could I help the men floundering here? Could I help myself? Was it cowardice to leave here?

On one leg, I hopped down the steep ladder, lurched across the open area and fell heavily on the pilothouse deck just as hell's own jackhammers pounded our steel plating for the second time. With incredible noise the aircraft rockets poked eight-inch holes in the ship; like fire-breathing creatures, they groped blindly for the men inside.

Already the pilothouse was littered with helpless and frightened men. Blood flowed, puddled and coagulated everywhere. Men stepped in blood, slipped and fell in it, tracked it about in great crimson footprints. The chemical attack alarm sounded instead of the general alarm. Little matter. Men knew we were under attack and went to their proper places.

Captain McGonagle suddenly appeared in the starboard door of the pilothouse and ordered: "Right full rudder. All engines ahead flank. Send a message to CNO: 'Under attack by unidentified jet aircraft, require immediate assistance.' "

Grateful for an order to execute, confident that only this man could save them, the crew responded with speed and precision born of terror. Never have orders been acknowledged and executed more quickly. These were brave men. These were trained men. But these were also confused and frightened men, inexperienced in combat. An order told them that something was being done, made them a part of the effort, gave them something to take the place of the awful fear.

Reacting to habit as much as to duty, and grateful that duty required his quick exit from this terrible place, Lloyd Painter looked for his relief so that he could report to his assigned damage control station below. Finding Lieutenant O'Connor half dead in a limp and bloody heap at the bottom of a ladder, he demanded: "Are you ready to relieve me?"

"No, I'm not ready to relieve you," O'Connor mimicked weakly —aware, even now, of the irony. McGonagle interrupted to free Lloyd of his bridge duty.

I lay next to the chart table, unable to control the blood flow from my body and wondering how much I could lose before I would become unconscious. Blood from my chest wound was collecting in a lump in my side so large that I couldn't lower my arm. My trouser leg revealed a steady flow of fresh blood from the fracture site. Numerous smaller wounds oozed slowly. Next to me lay Seaman George Wilson of Chicago, who had stood part of his lookout watch this morning without binoculars. In spite of a nearly severed thumb, Wilson used his good arm and my web belt to fashion a tourniquet for my leg, effectively slowing the worst bleeding. Someone opened my shirt, ripping off my undershirt for use somewhere as an emergency bandage. Meanwhile, I wrapped a handkerchief tightly around Wilson's wrist to control the bleeding from his hand. In this strange embrace we received the next airplane.

BLAM! Another barrage of rockets hit the ship. Although the first airplane caused a permanent ringing in my ears and forever robbed me of high-frequency hearing, the attacks seemed no less noisy. Men dropped with each new assault. Lieutenant Toth, still carrying my unsent sighting reports, received a rocket that turned his mortal remains into smoking rubble. Seaman Salvador Payan remained alive with two jagged chunks of metal buried deep within his skull. Ensign David Lucas accepted a rocket fragment in his cerebellum. And still the attacks continued.

In the pilothouse, Quartermaster Floyd Pollard stretched to swing a heavy steel battle plate over the vulnerable glass porthole. A rocket, and with it the porthole, exploded in front of him to transform his face and upper torso into a bloody mess. Painter helped lead him to relative safety near the quartermaster's log table before leaving the bridge to report to his battle station.

On the port side, just below the bridge, fire erupted from two ruptured fifty-five-gallon drums of gasoline. A great flaming river inundated the area and poured down ladders to the main deck below. Lieutenant Commander Armstrong—ever impulsive, ever gutsy, ever committed to the job at hand—bounded toward the fire. "Hit 'em! Slug the sons of bitches!" he must have been saying as he fought to reach the quick-release handle that would drop the flaming and still half-full containers into the sea. A lone rocket suddenly dissolved the bones of both of his legs.

Meanwhile, heretofore mysterious Contact X came to life with the first exploding rocket. Quickly poking a periscope above the surface of the water, American submariners watched wave after wave of jet airplanes attacking *Liberty*. Strict orders prevented any action that might reveal their presence. They could not help us, and they could not break radio silence to send for help. Frustrated and angry, the commanding officer activated a periscope camera that recorded *Liberty*'s trauma on movie film. He could do no more.[1]

=====

Dr. Kiepfer, en route to his battle station in the ship's sick bay, stopped to treat a sailor he found bleeding badly from shrapnel wounds in a passageway. A nearby door had not yet been closed, and through the door Kiepfer could see two more wounded men on an exposed weather deck. Cannon and rocket fire exploded everywhere as the men tried weakly to crawl to relative safety.

"Go get those men," Kiepfer yelled to a small group of sailors as he worked to control his patient's bleeding.

"No, sir," "Not me," "I'm not crazy," the frightened men whimpered as they moved away from the doctor.

No matter. Kiepfer would do the job himself. As soon as he could leave his patient, Kiepfer moved across the open deck. Ignoring bullets and rocket fragments, the huge doctor kneeled beside the wounded men, wrapped one long arm around each man's waist, and carried both men to safety in one incredible and perilous trip.

=====

Lieutenant George Golden, *Liberty*'s engineer officer, was in the wardroom with Ensign Lucas when the attack began. A meeting had been planned for Golden, Scott, Lucas and McGonagle to discuss the drill. The captain was still on the bridge, so the meeting would be delayed. Scott was slow to arrive, as today was his twenty-fourth

---

1. This story first came to me from an enlisted crew member of the submarine, who blurted it out impulsively in the cafeteria at Portsmouth Naval Hospital a few weeks after the attack. The report seemed to explain the marks I had seen on the chart in the coordination center, as well as reports of periscope sightings that circulated in the ship on the day of the attack. Since the attack, three persons in positions to know have confirmed the story that a submarine operated near *Liberty,* although no credible person has confirmed the report that photographs were taken.

birthday and he was at the ship's store picking out a Polaroid camera to help celebrate the occasion.

Golden was pouring coffee when they heard the first explosion. "Jesus, they dropped the motor whaleboat!" he cried as he abandoned his cup and started toward the boat. Then he heard other explosions and knew even before the alarm sounded that *Liberty* was under attack.

Reversing his path, he started toward his battle station in the engine room just in time to see Ensign Scott open the door to his stateroom and slide his new camera across the floor before racing to *his* battle station in Damage Control Central.

A rocket penetrated the engine room to tear Golden from the engine-room ladder. He plunged through darkness, finally crashing onto a steel deck, miraculously unhurt. He could see rockets exploding everywhere, passing just over the heads of his men and threatening vital equipment. "Get down!" he yelled. "Everybody stay low; on your knees!"

Golden knew that the bridge would want maximum power. Already Main Engine Control had an all-engines-ahead-flank bell from the bridge that they could not answer. Flank speed was seventeen knots, but Golden had taken one boiler off the line just ten minutes earlier so that it could cool for repairs. Without that boiler the best speed he could provide was about twelve knots. He immediately put the cooling boiler back on the line and started to bring it up to pressure.

Even with both boilers on the line, the engines were limited by a governor to eighteen knots. For years Golden had carried the governor key in his pocket so that he could find it quickly in just such an emergency as this. He switched the governor off, permitting the ship to reach twenty-one knots.

As machine-gun fire and aircraft rockets battered the ship, the main engine room began to take on the appearance of a fireworks display. Most lighting was knocked out in the first few minutes, leaving flashlights and battle lanterns as the only illumination in the room except for a skylight six decks above. In this relative darkness, men worked on hands and knees, operating valves, checking gauges, starting and stopping equipment, bypassing broken pipes; and all the while above them danced white, yellow, red and green fireflylike particles. Some were small. Some were huge and burst into pieces to shower down upon them. All entered the room with a tremendous roar as they burst through the ship's outer skin.

Golden glanced at the scene above him. It reminded him of meteor showers, except for the noise, or of electric arc welding. Most of his men were here now, having safely descended the ladders through the fireworks to reach their battle stations. Boiler Tender Gene Owens was here and in charge of auxiliary equipment on the deck below Golden. Machinist Mate Chief Richard J. Brooks was here. Brooks was petty officer in charge of the engine room, and he was everywhere.

Golden realized suddenly that far above them, directly in the range of rocket and machine-gun fire, was a hot-water storage tank. Five thousand gallons of near-boiling water lay in that tank, ready to pour down upon them if it was ruptured, and it would surely be ruptured. The drain valve was at the base of the tank, so it would be necessary to send a man up more than three decks to open the valve.

Golden quickly explained to a young sailor what had to be done and sent him on his way, but the frightened man collapsed on the deck grating and refused to move.

Chief Brooks overheard the exchange. "C'mon, you heard the lieutenant. Move!" he cried, jerking the panic-stricken teen-ager to his feet.

Terror was written on the young man's face. Tears started to flow as his face contorted in a grimace of fear.

With a snarl of contempt, Brooks gave him a shove that sent him sprawling. Then Brooks mounted the ladder leading to the vital drain valve. Two decks above, perhaps fifteen feet up the ladder, a tremendous explosion occurred next to Brooks. In a shower of sparks and fire, he was torn from his place on the ladder and thrown into space to land heavily upon the steel grating below. Brooks was back on his feet before anyone could reach him. Back up the same ladder he headed until he found the valve, opened it and drained the water only moments before the inevitable rocket hit the storage tank to find it newly empty.

In a few minutes, most of the battle lanterns had been struck by rocket fragments or disabled by the impact of nearby explosions. The room was nearly dark. By working on hands and knees, men could remain below the waterline and thus below most of the rocket and gunfire, although they were still vulnerable to an occasional wildly aimed rocket and to the constant shower of hot metal particles from above.

When fresh-air fans sucked choking smoke from the main deck

into the engine rooms, Golden ordered the men to cover their faces with rags and to try to find air near the deck. When the smoke became intolerable, he sent a message to the bridge that he would have to evacuate; but just before Golden was to give the evacuation order, McGonagle ordered a course change that carried the smoke away from the fans. Fresh air returned at last to the engine room.

======

The first airplane had emptied the gun mounts and removed exposed personnel. The second airplane, through extraordinary luck or fantastic marksmanship, disabled nearly every radio antenna on the ship, temporarily preventing our call for help.

Soon the high-performance Mirage fighter bombers that initiated the attack were joined by smaller swept-wing Dassault Mystère jets, carrying dreaded napalm—jellied gasoline. The Mystères, slower and more maneuverable than the Mirages, directed rockets and napalm against the bridge and the few remaining topside targets. In a technique probably designed for desert warfare but fiendish against a ship at sea, the Mystère pilots launched rockets from a distance, then dropped huge silvery metallic napalm canisters as they passed overhead. The jellied slop burst into furious flame on impact, coating everything, then surged through the fresh rocket holes to burn frantically among the men inside.[2]

I watched Captain McGonagle standing alone on the starboard wing of the bridge as the whole world suddenly caught fire. The deck below him, stanchions around him, even the overhead above him burned. The entire superstructure of the ship burst into a wall of flame from the main deck to the open bridge four levels above. All burned with the peculiar fury of warfare while Old Shep, seemingly impervious to man-made flame and looking strangely like Satan himself, stepped calmly through the fire to order: "Fire, fire, starboard side, oh-three level. Sound the fire alarm."

Firefighters came onstage as though waiting in the wings for a

2. The jet aircraft that initiated the attack were Dassault Mirage III single-seat long-range 1,460mph (Mach 2.2) fighter bombers similar to those seen during the morning. Mirages carry 30mm cannon in the fuselage and thirty-six rockets under the wings. The follow-up jet attack was conducted by Dassault MD-452 Mystère IV-A single-seat 695mph (Mach 0.91) jet interceptors. Mystères typically carry two 30mm cannon, fifty-five rockets, and napalm canisters. None of the attacking aircraft was identified as to either type or nationality until much later, when comparison was made with standard warplane photographs.

prearranged signal. Streaming through a rear pilothouse door, they carried axes, crowbars, CO_2 bottles and hundreds of feet of fire hose. The sound of CO_2 bottles and fire-hose sprinklers added to the din as the smell of steam overtook the smell of nitrates, smoke and blood. Men screamed, cried, yelled orders and scrambled to duty as the ship struggled to stay alive.

On the forecastle, Gunner's Mate Alexander N. Thompson fought his way relentlessly toward the forward gun mount. Only moments before, Thompson had remarked to me on the bridge: "No sweat, sir. If anything happens I just want to be in a gun mount." Now he was repeatedly driven away by exploding rockets. Weakened, with duty waiting in that small gun tub, he tried again.

His radar disabled, Radarman Charles J. Cocnavitch left his post to man a nearby gun mount. "Stay back!" Captain McGonagle ordered, knowing that the gun would be ineffective and that Cocnavitch would die in a futile attempt to fire. Meanwhile, Lieutenant O'Connor, still lying near the ladder where he had fallen, was robbed of any latent prejudices by huge black Signalman Russell David, who braved fire, blast and bullets to move the limp and barely conscious officer from the bridge to safety in the now-empty combat information center.

———

The pilothouse became a hopeless sea of wounded men, swollen fire hoses and discarded equipment. Men tripped over equipment, stepped on wounded. In front of the helmsman a football-size glob of napalm burned angrily, adding to the smoke and confusion. Smaller napalm globs burned in other parts of the room, refusing to be extinguished.

Again I thought of duty. My duty was on this bridge, amid the flame and the shrapnel, driving this ship and fighting to protect her. Already I was weak from loss of blood and from the shock of my wounds. A sailor tripped over me, stepped on Seaman Wilson, and fell on other wounded as he dragged a CO_2 bottle across the room. I decided that duty did not require that we all lie here and bleed. It may even require that we get out of the way, if we can, so that others may fight. Relinquishing Wilson's tourniquet to Wilson, he released mine. Acutely conscious of my retreat from the heart of battle, I raised an arm toward some sailors huddled nearby. Seaman Kenneth Ecker pulled me to my feet and I resumed my one-legged hopping.

I need a place to plug my wounds, I told myself, a place to find the holes and stop the flow of blood.

I hopped out of the room. Ecker stayed with me, adding to the guilt I felt for leaving the bridge. Bad enough that I should leave, but to take the bridge watch with me! "Go back!" I insisted. Ecker stayed. The ladder leading from the pilothouse was thick with fire hoses. Somewhere beneath the hoses were solid ladder rungs, but my foot could find only slippery fire hoses. With one hand on each railing and with my beanbag catching awkwardly on every obstruction, I hopped clumsily down the ladder. Once I stood aside to let a man pass in the other direction with a CO_2 bottle. He stopped to stare at me with a startled look, his mouth open. "Hurry!" I said. I reached the level below to find Ecker still with me. "Go back!" I protested again.

Lightheaded from loss of blood, I searched for a place to examine my injuries and to treat my wounds. The search became urgent as I became increasingly dizzy. More airplanes pounded our ship as I discovered that the captain's cabin offered no refuge. Through his door I could see a smoke-filled room with gaping holes opening to the flame outside, and frantic napalm globs eating his carpet.

Around a corner I found the doctor's stateroom. The room was dark, the air free of smoke. His folding bunk was open from a noontime nap, his porthole closed with a steel battle plate. Strangely concerned that I was soiling his sheets with blood, I pulled myself onto his clean bed. My useless left leg hung over the side in a sitting position. Ecker, still nearby, wanting to help but afraid to touch the leg, finally laid it gingerly alongside the other. I thought of the tissue being abused and wondered how close the sharp bone ends were to the artery.

What happens if I cut the artery? I wondered. *Maybe I have already.* A thousand questions begged for answers: Did we get our message off? Will they never stop shooting? When will our jets arrive? And who is shooting at us, anyway?

We still had no idea who was attacking. Although the Arab countries largely blamed the United States for their problems and falsely charged that American carrier-based aircraft had assisted Israel, we knew that the Arab air forces were crippled and probably unable to launch an attack like this one. And to increase the confusion, a ship's officer thought he saw a MIG-15 over *Liberty* and quickly spread a false report among the crew that we were being attacked by the Soviet Union. Probably no one suspected Israeli forces.

I took a few still-painful breaths to clear my head before tending my wounds. Ecker hovered nearby, forcing my conscience to remind me that I should be on the bridge; worse, that an able-bodied man was away from his battle station to help me.

With each movement I could feel the tear of sharp bone end against muscle. I was only abstractly aware of pain; instead, I was conscious of fear, of duty abandoned on the bridge, and of an urgent knowledge that, no matter what else might happen, I would almost surely die if I didn't soon stem the flow of blood, particularly from the leg wound.

I reached for Dr. Kiepfer's sheets to make a more effective tourniquet when suddenly four deadly rockets opened eight-inch holes to tear through the steel bulkhead into the room. Blast, fire, metal passed over my head and continued through an opposite wall. Ecker, standing in the open doorway, was startled but unhurt; several thumb-size holes at forehead level verified the utility of his battle helmet as he raced away to answer a call for firefighters.

My bare chest glowed with a hundred tiny fires as burning rocket fragments and napalm-coated particles fell on me like angry wasps. Desperately I brushed them away. As the tiny flames died, the hot metal continued to sear my chest. The room filled with smoke as the carpeting near me and the bedding around me burned with more small fires.

Through the fresh rocket holes I could see a tremendous fire raging on deck outside and I could hear the crackle of flames. The motor whaleboat burned furiously from a direct napalm hit while other fires engulfed the weather decks and bulkheads nearby. Directly above me on the next deck, I realized, were a gun mount and a radio antenna. Both were obvious targets. I would have to leave this place.

My leg pinned me to the bunk. It blocked my movement, weighed me down, prevented my escape from the additional rockets that were sure to come. I considered and quickly dismissed sliding under the mattress for protection. With the last of my strength I used my good leg to evict the useless broken limb from the bunk. Would this open the artery? I had to take the chance as the sharp bone ends again sliced through muscle. With great effort I forced myself up, rolled out onto my good right leg, and hopped away once more toward what I hoped would be safer ground, closing the door behind me.

The door, closed by habit, shielded me from a new blast and probably saved my life as a rocket penetrated the room from above, blasting through the heavy deck plating and air ducts in the overhead to explode with such force that the heavy metal door was torn from its frame. I fell to the deck outside.

=====

On the bridge, the helmsman fell wounded as another assault sent rocket fragments through steel and flesh. Almost before he fell, his post was taken by Quartermaster Francis Brown. The Quartermaster of the watch is the senior enlisted man on duty and is responsible for the performance of the men. Friendly, hard-working, cooperative, Brown was a popular member of the bridge team. I was always pleased when Brown was on duty with me. He never needed to be told what to do. When Brown was on watch, if a helmsman was slow to respond to an order or if a man had trouble with bridge equipment, he spotted and corrected the problem without being told. Now, typically, he saw his duty at the unattended helm.

The gyro compass no longer worked. It was disabled by three rockets that rode in tandem through the gyro room, passing harmlessly between a group of sailors, smashing the equipment and leaving a three-foot hole in a steel door on the way out. The magnetic compass, meanwhile, spun uselessly, like a child's toy.

=====

Gunner Thompson finally reached Mount 51 to find the gun partially blocked by the body of Fireman David Skolak. Skolak had been assigned to Repair Two, but after Seaman Payan was wounded, leaving the gun unmanned, Skolak left his repair party to take Payan's place. He was quickly dismembered by a direct rocket hit. Very weak now, Thompson forced himself toward Mount 52, some forty feet away on the ship's port side. With luck he would be able to fire at the next attacking jet.

=====

Long before our arrival in the area, most secret documents had been placed in large weighted bags, ready to be thrown overboard if necessary to keep them from an enemy. This was a precautionary measure, frequently taken by ships operating in dangerous areas. Now, defenseless and under attack, everything classified but not actually in use was to be destroyed. The bags proved useless, as they were too large and heavy to carry, and the water wasn't deep enough for safe disposal, anyway. The ship's incinerator couldn't be used, as it was on the 03 level within easy range of the airplanes. As a last resort, Lieutenant Jim Pierce, the ship's communication officer, ordered his men to destroy everything as best they could by hand. Acrid smoke soon filled the room as he and Joe Lentini dropped code lists, a handful at a time, into a flaming wastepaper basket; nearby, Richard Keene and Duane Marggraf attacked delicate crypto equipment with wire cutters and a sledge hammer.

In the TRSSCOMM room, equipment finally in full operation, operators had just begun to talk with their counterparts at Cheltenham, Maryland, when rockets suddenly undid all their work to disable the system forever. A shower of sparks cascaded from high-voltage wires overhead, bathing the men and equipment below in melted copper and filling the room with the smell of ozone. Operators at Cheltenham did not learn until much later why *Liberty* stopped talking in mid-sentence.

A code-room Teletype operator on *Liberty*'s third deck pounded desperately on a keyboard, trying to send the ship's cry for help. Getting no answer, he tried other equipment until someone finally noticed that a vital coding device had been removed for emergency destruction, disabling the machine. The operator tried again. Still nothing. Vividly aware of the nearness of death, the man was speechless with terror. His voice came in senseless gasps and his body shook; he wet his pants in fear, but he remained at his post and continued to hammer his message into the keyboard. Still no answer. In the rush to reinsert the coding device, the wrong device had been used. "Forget the code," cried Lieutenant Commander Lewis when he saw the problem. "Go out in plain language!"

Still the message failed to leave the ship. No one knew that all our antennas had been shot down.

From where I fell outside the doctor's stateroom I could hear the flames, the loud hiss of CO_2 bottles, the rush of water from fire hoses and the sharp crunch as water became steam against hot steel. Smoke was everywhere.

A young sailor plummeted hysterically down a ladder, crying, "Mr. O'Connor is dead! He's in combat and he's dead!" then disappeared on his grim mission, informing everyone of the death of my roommate and long-time friend. I thought of Jim's wife, Sandy, pregnant; his infant son; their pet schnauzer. Who will tell Sandy? My wife, Terry, will console her, help her. Maybe they'll console each other.

A sailor arrived with a pipe-frame-and-chicken-wire stretcher. Judging my rank from the khaki uniform, Seaman Frank McInturff assured me as he laid the stretcher at my side, "Don't worry, Chief, you'll be all right." Then, startled when he noticed my lieutenant's bars, he apologized grandly for the oversight. We both laughed as I assured him, "That's okay. You can call me Chief."

I saw no point in moving from where I was. Surely there was no time to treat wounded. If there was time, certainly there were enough men near death to keep the medical staff more than busy. McInturff insisted that the wardroom was in operation as an emergency battle dressing station and that I should go there. He and his partner rolled me onto the stretcher, my leg twisting grotesquely in the process. Then he tied me in place with heavy web belting and hoisted the stretcher. The first obstacle was not far away. The ladder leading down to the 01 deck inclined at a steep angle. *I will fall through the straps and down the ladder,* I thought. With my stretcher in a near-vertical position, we started down. My arms ached as I held the pipe frame to keep from slipping; chicken wire tore my fingers; as I slid deeper toward the foot of the stretcher I could feel the broken bone ends grinding together. Suddenly all such concern was forgotten as another rocket assault battered the ship. The now-familiar, ear-shattering, mind-destroying sound of rockets bursting through steel raced the length of the ship.

I braced for the plunge down the ladder as holes opened in the steel plating around us. Then, except for the flames, the machinery and the firefighting equipment, silence.

Following each rocket assault, the silence seemed unearthly; slowly we would become aware of the other sounds, but the immediate sensation was relief and a strange silence. In silence we found ourselves still alive, still standing on our ladder and still breathing deeply. The next ladder was no less steep, but passed easily without the rocket accompaniment.

We arrived next at the door of the wardroom, our destination, where we were greeted by more rockets, entering the room through an opposite wall. White smoke hung in the air. A fire burned under the empty dinner table.

"Where should we go?" McInturff asked. Nothing could be seen of the battle dressing station that was supposed to operate here. Clearly, the wardroom could not be used.

"Just put me down here," I told him. My stretcher was eased to the ground at the open door as the two men returned to the bridge to retrieve more wounded. "Move me away from the door!" I cried as more rocket fragments hurtled through the open door and over my stretcher to spend themselves on the nearby bulkhead. I was quickly moved; the door was closed. The narrow passageway soon filled with wounded, frightened men. A battle dressing station, I learned, had been set up in the chief petty officers' lounge around the corner and was already filled with wounded. Dr. Kiepfer was operating the main battle dressing station in the enlisted mess hall one deck below while this auxiliary station was being operated by a lone senior corpsman, Thomas Lee VanCleave.

If we can hold out for a few more minutes, I thought, Admiral Martin's jet fighters will be overhead. This hope quickly passed as a sailor kneeled at my side to inform me that all our antennas had been shot away. "They put a rocket at the base of every transmitting antenna on the ship," he said, "but there is one that I think I can repair. Do you think I could go out there and try to fix it so we could get our message off?" I assured him that he would be doing us all a great service, but asked him to be careful.

Soon the radio room pieced together enough serviceable equipment to send a message that would alert the Navy to our predicament. An emergency connection patched the one operable transmitter to the hastily repaired antenna. But as Radiomen James Halman and Joseph Ward tried to establish voice contact with Sixth Fleet forces, they found the frequencies blocked by a buzz-saw-like sound that stopped only for the few seconds before each new barrage of rockets struck the ship. Apparently, the attacking jets were jamming our radios, but could not operate the jamming equipment while rockets were airborne. If we were to ask for help, we had to do it during the brief periods that the buzzing sound stopped. Using *Liberty*'s voice radio call sign, Halman cried, "Any station, this is Rockstar. We are under attack by unidentified jet aircraft and require immediate assistance!"[3]

---

3. See Appendix B. *Liberty* appealed for help commencing 1158Z (1358 ship's time) and continuing for more than two hours, remaining silent only when the ship was without electrical power. At 1400Z, two hours after the commencement of the attack, *Liberty* Radioman Joe Ward transmitted: "Flash, flash, flash. I pass in the blind. We are under attack by aircraft and high-speed surface craft. I say again, Flash, flash, flash. We are under attack by aircraft and high-speed surface craft." At 1405Z (1605 ship's time) Ward came on the air again to say, "Request immediate assistance. Torpedo hit starboard side." These times are important, as *Liberty* was under fire until 1315Z, was confronted by hostile forces until 1432Z, and was in urgent need of assistance the entire time.

Operators in USS *Saratoga,* an aircraft carrier operating with Vice Admiral Martin's forces near Crete, heard *Liberty's* call and responded, but could not understand the message because of the jamming.

"Rockstar, this is Schematic," said the *Saratoga* operator. "Say again. You are garbled."

After several transmissions *Saratoga* acknowledged receipt of the message. The Navy uses a system of authentication codes to verify the identity of stations and to protect against sham messages.

"Authenticate Whiskey Sierra," demanded *Saratoga.*

"Authentication is Oscar Quebec," Halman answered promptly, after consulting a list at his elbow.

"Roger, Rockstar," said *Saratoga* at 1209Z. "Authentication is correct. I roger your message. I am standing by for further traffic."

Saratoga relayed *Liberty's* call for help[4] to Admiral McCain in London for action and, inexplicably, only for information to Vice Admiral Martin and to Rear Admiral Geis (who commanded the Sixth Fleet carrier force).[5]

Several minutes later, having heard nothing from COMSIXTHFLT, the *Liberty* operator renewed his call for help.

"Schematic, this is Rockstar. We are still under attack by unidentified jet aircraft and require immediate assistance."

"Roger, Rockstar," said *Saratoga.* "We are forwarding your message." Then *Saratoga* added, quite unnecessarily and almost as an afterthought, "Authenticate Oscar Delta."

The authentication list now lay in ashes a few feet away. Someone had destroyed it along with the unneeded classified material. Frustrated and angry, the operator held the button open on his microphone as he begged, "Listen to the goddamned rockets, you son of a bitch!"

"Roger, Rockstar, we'll accept that," came the reply.[6]

4. *Saratoga* misidentified the ship as USNS *Liberty.* USNS ships are civilian-manned and operate under contract with the Navy; USS ships are manned by American sailors and are commissioned by the United States.

5. Rear Admiral Lawrence Raymond Geis: naval aviator; born 1916; U.S. Naval Academy, class of 1939; promoted to rear admiral July 1, 1965; was commanding officer, USS *Forrestal* (CVA 59) 1962–63; would be assigned to duty in September 1968 as Chief of Naval Information. The Office of Naval Information has long played a leading role in the cover-up of the USS *Liberty* story.

6. *Saratoga's* repeated demand for authentication, coupled with errors and possible delay in forwarding *Liberty's* messages, contributed to confusion at CINCUSNAVEUR headquarters. *Liberty's* first appeal for help, received by *Saratoga* at 1209Z, was forwarded at Immediate

Operators in the Sixth Fleet flagship *Little Rock* and in the carrier *America,* meanwhile, had long since received *Liberty*'s message. *America*'s Captain Donald Engen[7] was talking with NBC newsman Robert Goralski when the message was brought to the bridge. "This is confidential, Mr. Goralski!" Engen snapped. And Goralski respected the warning.

Aircraft-carrier sailors know that certain airplanes are always spotted near the catapults where they are kept fueled, armed and ready to fly. They are maintained by special crews, they are flown by carefully selected pilots, and they are kept under special guard at all times. These are the "ready" aircraft. To visitors, they are almost indistinguishable from other aircraft, but they are very special aircraft indeed, and their use is an ominous sign of trouble. They carry nuclear weapons.

No one in government has acknowledged that ready aircraft were sent toward *Liberty,* and no messages or logs have been unearthed to prove that nuclear-armed aircraft were launched; moreover, there is no indication that release of nuclear weapons was authorized under any circumstances—only that ready aircraft, which normally carry nuclear weapons, were launched toward *Liberty,* and that the Pentagon reacted to the launch with anger bordering on hysteria. Widely separated sources have described the launch and subsequent recall of those aircraft in detail, and the circumstances are compelling.

According to a chief petty officer aboard USS *America,* the pilots were given their orders over a private intercom system as they sat

---

precedence to CINCUSNAVEUR headquarters. Immediate precedence, however, is entirely inadequate as a speed-of-handling indicator for enemy contact reports; more than 30 percent of the messages glutting the communication system are Immediate precedence or higher. *Liberty*'s second appeal was appropriately forwarded at the much faster Flash precedence, overtaking the initial report to arrive at CINCUSNAVEUR at 1247Z with the damning notation that it was not authenticated. Thus the first Teletype report of *Liberty*'s attack arrived in London with the misleading caveat that the transmission could be a hoax. The earlier report, arriving eight minutes later, failed to mention that *Liberty*'s initial transmission *was* authenticated. Not until 1438Z, as the attack ended and Israel apologized, did CINCUSNAVEUR learn from *Saratoga* (USS *Saratoga* message 081358Z June 1967) that the initial report was indeed authenticated.

7. Captain Donald Davenport Engen: naval aviator; born 1924; first commissioned 1943; University of California at Los Angeles, class of 1948; holds nation's second-highest award for bravery, the Navy Cross. Would be promoted to rear admiral in 1970 and to vice admiral in 1977.

in their cockpits. A United States ship was under attack, they were told, and they were given the ship's position. Their mission was to protect the ship. Under no circumstances were they to approach the beach.

Two nuclear-armed F-4 Phantom jets left *America*'s catapults and headed almost straight up, afterburners roaring. Then two more became airborne to rendezvous with the first two, and together the four powerful jets turned toward *Liberty,* making a noise like thunder. All this activity blended so completely into the shipboard routine that few of the newsmen suspected that anything was awry; those who asked were told that this was a routine training flight.

=====

"Help is on the way!"[8]

This short message was received by a *Liberty* radioman and quickly passed to nearly every man aboard. Messengers ran through the ship, calling, "They're coming! Help is coming!" Litter carriers and telephone talkers passed the word along. I remembered Philip's warning of the night before: "We probably wouldn't even last long enough for our jets to make the trip."

=====

Meanwhile, Navy radio operators at the Naval Communications Station in Morocco worked to establish communications for the emergency. Lieutenant James Rogers and the station commander, Captain Lowel Darby, came immediately to the radio room, where Petty Officer Julian "Tony" Hart quickly set up several circuits, including voice circuits with the aircraft carriers and COMSIXTHFLT, and established a Teletype circuit with CINCUSNAVEUR in London. When the men tuned to the high-command voice network, they could hear USS *Liberty,* her operators still pleading for help, and in the background the exploding rockets.

A Flash precedence Teletype message from COMSIXTHFLT coursed quickly through the Morocco communication relay station, destined for the Pentagon, State Department and the White House:

8. COMSIXTHFLT message 081305Z June 1967 (Appendix C, page 236) promises: SENDING AIRCRAFT TO COVER YOU. This message, released on the flagship about fifty-five minutes after *Liberty*'s first call for help, was not the first such message. *Liberty* crewmen, including the writer, recall reports of help on the way at about 1220Z while the ship was still under air attack.

USS LIBERTY REPORTS UNDER ATTACK BY UNIDENTIFIED JET AIR-
CRAFT. HAVE LAUNCHED STRIKE AIRCRAFT TO DEFEND SHIP.

It seemed only seconds later that a new voice radio circuit was
patched into the room that was now becoming a nerve center for
Liberty communications. This was a high-command Pentagon circuit manned by a Navy warrant officer, but once contact was established the voice on the circuit changed. Every man in the room
recognized the new voice as that of the Secretary of Defense, Robert
S. McNamara, and he spoke with authority: "Tell Sixth Fleet to get
those aircraft back immediately," he barked, "and give me a status
report."

A few minutes later the Chief of Naval Operations himself came
on the air. The circuit was patched through to the Sixth Fleet flagship, and Admiral David L. McDonald bellowed: "You get those
fucking airplanes back on deck, and you get them back *now!*"

"Jesus, he talks just like a sailor," said one of the sailors listening
on a monitor speaker at Morocco.

Soon four frustrated F-4 Phantom fighter pilots returned from
what might have been a history-making mission. They might have
saved the ship, or they might have initiated the ultimate holocaust;
their return, like their departure, blended smoothly into the ship's
routine and raised no questions from the reporters who watched.

Another Flash message moved through the Morocco Teletype
relay station: HAVE RECOVERED STRIKE AIRCRAFT. LIBERTY STA-
TUS UNKNOWN. At about the same time, Hart relayed the same
message to the Pentagon by voice radio. *Liberty* was silent now. No
one at Morocco knew whether the ship was afloat or not, but they
knew that if she still needed help she would have a long wait.[9]

McInturff returned to the bridge to find Lieutenant Commander
Philip Armstrong, wounded but coherent and strong, sprawled on
the floor of the chart house. His trousers had been removed to reveal
grave damage to both legs just below the level of his boxer shorts.
Two broken legs kept him off his feet, but he remained in control.

9. Months later Hart was visited by an agent of the Naval Investigative Service—armed with
notebook and tape recorder—who sought to "debrief" him on the events of June 8; that is,
to record for the record everything that Hart could recall of the attack and the communications
surrounding it. Hart refused to discuss the attack and the man went away. Hart never heard
from him again.

"No more stretchers, Commander," McInturff advised, still winded from his journey with me. "We'll have to take you down in this blanket."

"No, get a stretcher!" Philip insisted.

"No more stretchers," McInturff repeated as he laid the blanket next to Philip, ready to roll him onto it.

"I'm not going anywhere in any goddamned blanket. Go get a stretcher!"

"But sir, I—"

"Go! I *know* there are enough stretchers on this ship!"

"Yessir."

Certain that every stretcher had a man in it, usually a man too badly injured to be moved, McInturff raced through the ship, frantically searching for the required stretcher. He opened a door to the main deck, remembering that he had once seen some stretchers stowed near a life-raft rack. A cluster of rockets crashed to deck around him with a deafening roar, showering the area with sparks. Shaken but not slowed, McInturff knew only that he must find that stretcher and get it back to the XO in the chart house. Finally, precious platform in hand, he struggled back toward the sick and impatient executive officer. Up ladders, around corners, tripping over discarded CO_2 bottles and the near-solid mass of fire hoses covering the last ladder to the bridge, he arrived again in the pilot-house to find Philip Armstrong waiting not too patiently on the deck of the chart house. Although the battle still raged outside, one-sided as it was, although the ship was still being hammered every few seconds with aircraft rockets, Philip was not involved and he was furious about it. He wanted desperately to be on the bridge. He wanted to fight. If he could do nothing more, he would throw rocks and shake his fist at the pilots as they hurtled past. But Philip was rooted to *two* beanbags and could only lie there and rage. Someone gave him a cigarette and he turned it into a red cinder almost in one long drag. He asked for another.

He didn't complain as he was lifted, rudely, painfully, onto the chicken-wire bed. He muttered something as the two sailors lifted the stretcher and started away with him, but McInturff didn't understand as all voices were drowned out by exploding rockets. McInturff dreaded another trip down that treacherous ladder. He was afraid he would slip on the fire hoses, dropping the XO and blocking the ladder. He was exhausted. His heart pounded loudly in his chest, complaining of the exertion until he thought it must rebel; but he had no time to think, certainly not to rest. With Philip and his stretcher nearly on end, Philip's fingers clawing the pipe frame to keep from abusing the fractures, they made the left turn at the bottom of the steep ladder, passed through the narrow door, and found themselves in a passageway next to the captain's open cabin door.

"Put me down!" Philip ordered.

"But—"

"Put me down!"

"Sir, I—"

"Get me a life jacket!" Philip demanded loudly.

"But, sir, they're still shooting and—"

"Goddamn it, get me a life jacket!" Philip insisted. "I'm not moving from here until I have a life jacket."

An unusually heavy barrage hit the ship. McInturff pushed the XO's stretcher to relative safety against a bulkhead, and ducked into the burning, smoke-filled captain's cabin. Quickly driven out by the arrival of still more rockets, he heard Philip demand, more firmly: "Damn it! I told you to get a life jacket!"

"Jeezus! There's shit comin' in everywhere, Commander!" he pleaded as an explosion tore open a nearby door, but Philip still insisted upon having a life jacket.

Disbelieving, McInturff obediently left Philip in the care of his partner while he made another desperate trip through the ship, searching wildly for the required life jacket. Finally, he located a discarded jacket in the CPO lounge emergency battle dressing station and forced himself back to where he had left the XO.

Gone! He was gone. During the insane search for a life jacket, someone had taken the XO below. Certain that his heart would burst, McInturff struggled back up the ladder, back to the carnage in the pilothouse, to retrieve more wounded.

————

Most of the wounded had been removed from the bridge. It was possible once again to walk across the pilothouse. Quartermaster Brown stood at the helm. Captain McGonagle, suffering from shrapnel in his right leg and weakened by loss of blood, remained in firm control of his ship as he directed damage control and firefighting efforts. Ensign David Lucas, the ship's deck division officer, had been "captured" by the captain to serve as his assistant on the bridge. Now Lucas wondered if he would ever see the baby girl born to his wife a few hours after *Liberty* sailed from Norfolk. He quickly pushed such thoughts from his mind; three motor torpedo boats were sighted approaching the ship at high speed in an attack formation.

McGonagle dispatched Seaman Apprentice Dale Larkins to take the torpedo boats under fire from the forecastle. Larkins was an apprentice not because he was new to the sea, but because, for reasons of his own, he had refused to take the examination for advancement. He was a large man and a tough fighter. He had already been driven first from Mount 54, then from Mount 53. Now he charged down the ladder and across the open deck to take the boats under fire from Mount 51.

Captain McGonagle, looking through the smoke of the motor whaleboat fire, saw a flashing light on the center boat. He called for the gunners to hold their fire while he attempted to communicate with the boats using a hand-held Aldis lamp. The tiny signaling device was useless. It could not penetrate the smoke surrounding the bridge.

Larkins, who had not heard McGonagle's "hold fire" order, suddenly released a wild and ineffective burst of machine-gun fire and was quickly silenced by the captain. Immediately, the gun mount astern of the bridge opened fire, blanketing the center boat. McGonagle called for that gunner, too, to cease fire, but he could not be heard above the roar of the gun and the loud crackle of flaming napalm. Although less than twenty feet apart, McGonagle was separated from the gun by a wall of flame. Lucas ran through the pilothouse and around a catwalk, trying to reach the gun. Finally, when he could see over a skylight and into the gun tub, he found no gunner. The gun mount was burning with napalm, causing the ammunition to cook off by itself. The mount was empty.

Heavy machine-gun fire from the boats saturated the bridge. A single hardened steel, armor-piercing bullet penetrated the chart house, skimmed under the Loran receiver, destroyed an office paper punch machine, and passed through an open door into the pilothouse with just enough remaining force to bury half its length in the back of the neck of brave young helmsman Quartermaster Francis Brown, who died instantly.

Ensign Lucas, seeing Brown fall and not knowing what had hit him or from which direction it had come, stepped up to take his place at the helm.

A torpedo was spotted. It passed astern, missing the ship by barely seventy-five feet.

Chapter 7

TORPEDO ATTACK

Nobody can actually duplicate the strain that a commander is under in making a decision during combat.

Admiral Arleigh A. Burke, 1901–

The ship's general announcing system came alive to warn, *"Stand by for torpedo attack, starboard side."*

Lieutenant Golden, in the engine room, had heard such warnings before. In October 1942, Golden was seventeen years old and in the Navy for less than three months when his ship, destroyer USS *Lamson,* fought off Japanese air attacks to help sink a pair of enemy picket boats. A month later, with Task Force 67 during the battle of Tassafaronga, he saw an American cruiser go down. Nearby, a Japanese destroyer sank. Hundreds of men were lost, and Golden knew that many of the casualties were in the engine rooms. Low, large, difficult to evacuate, the engine rooms usually flooded first. Blast easily snapped high-pressure steam lines. Pipes, machinery, oil and steam prevented escape. Always before he had been in other parts of the ship, but now he was in the very heart of the engine room.

Golden was a professional. He could perform every job here, and if pressed he could do several jobs at once.

"Evacuate the engine rooms!" he ordered.

Greasy, sweat-soaked enginemen raced up the steep ladders, eager to leave the 120-degree room before the sea rushed in. Golden did not move. Orders from the bridge had to be acknowledged; gauges had to be watched; the plant had to be operated. He could do it alone.

Chief Brooks stayed too. It would never have occurred to Brooks not to stay.

Fireman Benjamin Aishe also stayed. "You'll need help, sir. If you stay here, I'll stay."

Together these men ran the engineering plant while they waited for the torpedo to arrive.

=====

"Where are those goddamned jets?" someone near me begged.

I thought of the ship's thin steel skin, bowed between each rib and frame like the paper covering of a model airplane. I thought of the water outside, of sharks, of swimming with a broken leg. I wondered if the water would feel warm. Someone put an inflatable life jacket around my neck, but the swelling on my left side was now so great that the straps would not reach, could not be tied. I kept the life jacket. It would keep me afloat as long as I could hold on to it. Would the shock of hitting the water wrench it from my hands? What about the stretcher? I was still tied to the stretcher!

Twenty men crowded together around me. One man cried. He was not ashamed, and cried loudly; his body shook with sobs. Someone called for his mother. Men really do that, I thought, surprised; men really do call for their mothers. "Hail Mary, full of grace . . ." someone murmured as he knelt on the linoleum floor. Several men prayed silently, hands tightly clasped, lips moving in unintelligible murmur.

"Stand by for torpedo attack, starboard side!" a messenger repeated as we huddled in our starboard passageway. How dumb, I thought. We could move to a *port* passageway, maybe near a door; that would be safer than a starboard passageway. I should tell these men to move, I thought. No. They would pick me up and take me along. No. I'll take my chances right here.

=====

"Stand by for torpedo attack, starboard side," spoke the announcing system in Co-ord and in the adjoining Crypto and Communication spaces.

The men in these rooms were calm. The sounds of warfare were muffled and unreal in these third-deck spaces below the waterline. These men routinely spent hours at a time waiting out the drills elsewhere in the ship, so today's ordeal was not unlike the drills they knew so well. They had been told that this was not a drill, and they heard the sounds of gunfire above them, but for the most part they assumed that things were under control and that most of the firing was our own.

Men sat, as they had been trained to do, on the deck, along the edges of the room. They wore battle helmets. Sleeves were rolled down, collars turned up, trousers tucked into socks to protect against flash burn. This had all been done so many times before that it seemed routine.

Petty Officer Ronnie Campbell stretched, got up and placed fresh paper in a typewriter. "You guys can stay there if you want. I'm gonna write a letter home."

Dear Elizabeth, You won't guess where we are, he wrote to his Scottish-born wife. He continued to hammer away, ignoring the gunfire above him.

Meanwhile, Petty Officer Jeffery Carpenter, concerned about preparing classified material for destruction, organized a team to collect things to be destroyed. Carpenter realized that some sensitive material remained in Lieutenant O'Connor's desk. The desk was locked and O'Connor was not there, so Carpenter called Seaman Lenau in the typewriter repair shop on the deck below, and asked him to bring a sledge hammer.

Lenau appeared promptly, and Carpenter used the sledge to deliver one smart underhand blow that neatly popped the top from O'Connor's desk, laying bare all the material within. It was not until this moment that many of the men in these rooms seemed to fully realize that the ship was in serious danger.

Stan White heard the torpedo attack warning and thought of Lenau alone in the fourth-deck repair shop. A week ago he would have been with Lenau, but now Lenau was alone. White started below to reassure him, but all compartments were sealed to control possible flooding. No doors could be opened until the danger passed. White called by telephone, reaching Lenau just as he returned from the sledge-hammer assignment. Lenau was frightened, but in good control of himself. "No sweat, Chief, I'm okay," he said.

Petty Officer Joseph C. Lentini, working nearby in crypto, saw a small hole open in the bulkhead next to him. He felt a blast of air push through the hole and brush his leg. Then, as his shoe filled with blood, he realized that what he felt was not air at all: a bullet had grazed his leg, opening a wide gash in the left thigh.

Lieutenant Commander Lewis, in an adjoining room, removed a large bandage from a battle-dressing kit at his feet to cover the sailor's wound. As Lentini stepped toward him, Lewis's attention was drawn to his right, through a door, to the exterior bulkhead of the coordination center. Looking past Chief Melvin Smith in the doorway, Lewis was transfixed by a slow-motion scene that few men have lived to describe. As he watched, the seaward bulkhead bulged toward him; the light-green standard Navy interior paint crackled into bright flame, then became black ash along with hundreds of decorative pinups; the now-bare steel beneath turned red with heat, then white. Blackened paint particles flew across the room as the bulkhead dissolved to admit the sea.

With a great crunch, flesh and steel were compressed into a distant corner as the blast hurled men and equipment the width of the ship. Steel walls vanished to make large rooms of smaller ones. Typewriters and staple machines moved with such force that some continued through the ship's opposite side and into the sea beyond.

Lewis, blinded by burnt paint chips, deafened by the blast of a thousand pounds of high-energy explosive packed into the head of an Italian-made torpedo, floated in neck-deep water admitted through a forty-foot hole opened in *Liberty*'s starboard side. Smith, a mere arm's length away, was thrown to his death.

Ronnie Campbell died at his typewriter.

The terrified Teletype operator died at his Teletype machine.

Jim Pierce died while burning code lists.

Dick Keene and Duane Marggraf died together as they destroyed a crypto machine.

Chief Raymond Linn died a few feet from where he had discussed with me the irony of dying this way in this place. Jim Lenau, alone in the Teletype repair shop, died quickly and still alone. Civilian Technician Allen Blue died suddenly, never to hold the new baby that waited for him in Rockville. In an instant, the torpedo had killed twenty-five men.

The single exit from this flooded room was a narrow ladder leading through a hatchway to the deck above. The hatch was closed, as was a manhole in the hatch cover. Lewis was thrown to the top of the ladder and found himself waist-deep in swirling water, hanging on to the quick-release wheel for the manhole. He couldn't see or hear. He didn't know where he was or what he was hanging on to. He was simply trying not to be swept away in the water that was around him.

With Lewis were roly-poly Robert "Buddha" Schnell and John Horne. Horne pried Lewis loose from the handle so that the door could be opened. Schnell exited first and joined the group around the hatch. Then he helped Lewis, Horne and the others through.

Jeff Carpenter, a self-described fatalist, found himself trapped under water by an overturned desk. Unable to break free, he soon ran out of air. Certain that he would drown and true to his philosophy, Carpenter relaxed to accept his fate; but before death could claim him, the heavy desk shifted in the churning water and he drifted to the surface, unhurt.

Lentini, stunned, pinned under water at the base of the escape ladder, with a broken leg, clawed wildly, straining to hold his head above the oily and rapidly rising water to cry for help. The ship was rolling and, as it did, ever-larger portions of the room went completely under water. A single battery-powered battle lantern burned under water near the ladder, and men moved toward that light, trying to get there before the water covered the manhole to block their only chance of escape.

Douglas C. "Doug" Ritenburg, Jeff Carpenter and some others came upon Lentini in the darkness, helped free him from the twisted steel that held him, and pushed him toward the manhole where shipmates above helped pull him through.

The battle lantern burned out, leaving only the dim light coming through the hatch to guide scores of men out of that compartment. Men swam, climbed and clawed their way through an impossible jumble toward the single manhole. Where moments before had stood a wall, now hid jagged metal beneath black water in a dark room. Men fought their way toward the hatch and were blocked by cables, by equipment, by misshapen steel, by upended desks.

Lean, tough Marine Staff Sergeant Bryce Lockwood felt flesh underfoot, then movement, and ducked underwater to find a man pinned under a section of doubled-back plating that had been the third deck. Lockwood found the time and the strength to free him. He pushed the lucky survivor toward the hatch, then stopped to help someone else.

As he turned toward a man who seemed to be in trouble, water finally reached the manhole. Lockwood was too busy to realize that his only exit was now covered with water. Water gushed through the hole in a great torrent onto the deck above. It took three men fighting the flow of water to force the cover shut, but Lockwood knew of none of this. He knew only that the man he had hoped to help was already dead and that the room was suddenly dark.

In blackness, he tried to remember the direction toward the light. As he moved toward the hatch, sometimes swimming, often pulling himself hand-over-hand along the pipes and cables that spanned the ceiling, the ship completed her roll back toward the starboard side, once again placing the hatch above water. Finally, Lockwood's leg struck a rung of the warped but still-familiar heavy steel ladder. From there it was easy to find the manhole in the darkness.

He reached it quickly, but the handle would not turn. Was it locked? Stuck? Water churned around him as he cursed the devil sailors who had closed the manhole and who doubtless stood over it. Where other men might be afraid, Lockwood reacted with rage. Was the ship sinking? Would he go down with it? He could only guess as he pounded on the heavy door. And as he pounded, his rage increased.

Finally, white light shone around the heavy rubber gasket as the manhole opened. Pulled through, he yelled angrily at everyone near: "Who was the stupid son of a bitch who closed the hatch? Couldn't you hear me yelling? Didn't you see me coming? Didn't you hear me knocking? Stupid son of a bitch!" He bellowed until, catching his breath, he ordered a sailor to keep the manhole open and reentered the terrible room. Water covered much of the overhead as he searched for life in the treacherous water. Men shone battle lanterns through the hatch and Lockwood continued his search with the aid of a waterproof light that he took into the water with him, but he could find no one in need of help. Finally, he crawled back through the manhole for the last time to testify in a sick whisper, "No one is alive down there."

———

Captain McGonagle was almost alone on the bridge when the torpedo struck. His navigator was dead, the executive officer dying; the officer of the deck and junior officer of the deck were both badly wounded and out of the action; the helmsman was wounded; the quartermaster dead; lookouts, messengers, signalmen, all were dead or wounded, all below, all away from the holocaust on the bridge.

Except for Ensign David Lucas and telephone talker John LaMar, Old Shep was alone.

> "But Old Shep was right there, to the rescue he came.
> He jumped in and helped pull me out."

He didn't see the torpedo coming, but he would never forget the sound it made. It exploded with a muffled roar, like rolling thunder; then it covered the scene with a blanket of smoke. Impenetrable black smoke hid the ship, spread over her length, and extended up her mast. Through the smoke came a torrent of water, thrust up by the explosion to fall as dirty rain upon Old Shep and his ship. McGonagle and Lucas clung to a starboard rail while *Liberty* rolled away from the blast.

"Shall I pass the word to prepare to abandon ship?" Lucas asked.

McGonagle, not yet aware of the extent of flooding, knew that he was lucky to be afloat in a torpedoed Victory ship. *Liberty* might sink, he knew, but he remembered shoal water was nearby and he resolved to run her aground first if necessary.

"No," he told Lucas, "we're not going to sink."

====

I shuddered as the torpedo explosion directly below quieted the murmur around me and briefly overcame the sound of machine guns. *Liberty* rolled heavily to port, away from the explosion. The roll increased. Someone cried louder for help from his God as it seemed we would roll onto our side. Near me a sailor lost his footing and tumbled headlong down a wildly slanted athwartships passageway.

Ensign John Scott was one deck above the torpedo and perhaps sixty feet forward of it. As damage control officer, he was responsible for all of the damage control effort everywhere in the ship, and to accomplish this he worked in Damage Control Central where, with the aid of two telephone talkers, he kept in touch with the bridge, main engine control and several repair parties. As damage occurred, it was reported by telephone to Scott who assessed its seriousness and the urgency of need to repair it, and dispatched men to repair it whenever that was called for.

The telephones were manned by Yeoman Stephen Gurchik and by the ship's red-haired barber, Thomas Moulin. These three men received and acted upon all of the damage reports, and they knew better than anyone else that the situation was not good, even before the torpedo explosion. For these men, the torpedo attack warning came over the general announcing system first, and was confirmed by Seaman John Lamar on the bridge telephone circuit.

Gurchik recited the Lord's Prayer.

Fireman John Beattie called by telephone from the emergency fire room, where he was standing by the emergency fire pump, and asked permission to come out of that vulnerable lower-deck space. Permission was quickly granted.

Ensign Richard P. Taylor, the supply officer, appeared suddenly in a doorway, bleeding and dazed, on his way to a battle dressing station. Chief Harold Thompson had taken charge of Repair Two, he reported, so that Taylor could dress his wounds and try to stop the bleeding; then he stumbled on down the passageway and out of sight, leaving a trail of blood. Scott called Painter and asked him to send help, as Taylor didn't look as though he could go much further on his own.

A stray bullet, the only shot to penetrate this space, struck a sanitary discharge vent on the outboard bulkhead, neatly breaking off a valve and rupturing a pipe to add the smell of sewage to the smells of warfare. The machine-gun fire was louder now, heard through the opening made by the bullet.

The impact of the torpedo sent all three men sprawling across the room.

"Our Father, who art in heaven . . ." The prayer grew louder and more urgent.

As the ship rolled sharply away from the torpedo, Scott, Gurchik and Moulin scrambled to get back on their feet. The ship's roll increased. Helplessly, they slid against the inboard bulkhead in a jumble of men, telephone equipment, telephone cables, a stool, charts, publications. As the ship's roll increased, they tried to regain their footing. Now, on a wildly canted and rapidly moving deck, frightened and almost helpless, they saw the lights go out.

Scott knew that the emergency generator located in a forward deckhouse had already been disabled by a rocket, so it would never serve its intended purpose; but battery-powered emergency lights did switch on automatically, and as the ship recovered from her roll, Scott found his footing.

Above his desk was the ship's inclinometer, a device that measures the degree of roll, and Scott's eyes were glued to this as *Liberty* completed her initial reaction to the blast and rolled back toward the starboard side. Eight . . . ten . . . eleven degrees . . . Slowly, the ship stopped rolling at twelve degrees starboard list, hung there a moment, then settled back to nine degrees starboard list.

"Thy kingdom come, Thy will be done . . ."

The bridge telephone circuit came alive. "Repair Three, this is the bridge. The torpedo has wiped out Damage Control Central. You are to take charge of damage control."

Scott quickly advised the bridge that Damage Control Central was still in operation. Meanwhile, he dispatched runners throughout the ship to report to him on the extent of flooding so that he could keep the bridge informed and at the same time do whatever could be done to repair the damage.

———

In the forward deckhouse, Petty Officer John Randall was knocked off his feet by the impact of the torpedo. His battle station was here, in the electrical shop. The lights had gone out early in the attack and he had no working intercom or telephones, so he had only a vague idea of what was happening. But it was clear that the ship had been torpedoed.

Randall burst out of his shop and onto the main deck in time to see torpedo boat *Tahmass* drift slowly down the ship's starboard side, her guns trained on *Liberty*'s bridge. Impotent with rage, Randall extended the middle finger of his right hand in a universal gesture of contempt—and then watched the 40mm cannon swing around until it came to bear squarely on his chest. But Randall was too angry to be frightened and too proud to move; he stared defiantly at the gunner while the boat drifted past. Luckily for him, that gunner had no stomach for firing at such an easy target. Moments later all three boats commenced circling *Liberty* at high speed while firing at the waterline and at any men they could see moving.

———

When Scott found he could not reach Research by telephone, he dispatched Shipfitter Phillip Tourney from the forward repair locker to check Research for damage. And Tourney found damage. At first the men who worked in Research weren't going to let him in, as he lacked the required security clearance, but cooler heads prevailed and Tourney was admitted in time to see the last of the survivors crawl, wet with seawater and black with dirty bilge oil, through the tiny scuttle to the safety of the still-dry second deck.

"Bridge, this is Damage Control Central. Flooding is confined to the third deck and below, frames fifty-two through seventy-eight. The Research spaces are totally flooded below the second deck. No other serious flooding is reported. The ship appears to be in no present danger of sinking, but we cannot take another torpedo and stay afloat."

"Roger, DCC," responded a telephone talker from the bridge. Inexplicably, the same talker then announced, "All stations, bridge. Prepare to abandon ship." Other telephone talkers received that advice and repeated it on other circuits.

"Prepare to abandon ship!" spoke the general announcing system, now working only in parts of the ship.

"Oh, goddamn," a sailor near me cried as he looked out through a rocket hole at the torpedo boats. "We can't go out there. They'll kill us out there."

A messenger paused briefly at the end of our passageway to yell, "Prepare to abandon ship! Prepare to abandon ship!"

No one moved. The ship might be sinking, but it was a lot safer aboard a sinking ship than in front of those machine guns.

An engineman brought the news that bullets were whistling over the ship's boilers: "The boats are firing at the waterline. They're trying to explode the boilers!" he yelled. But most of the bullets were passing harmlessly through the ship.

We had no way of knowing that "our" jet fighters waited lifelessly on the flight decks of the Sixth Fleet aircraft carrier force, crippled by diplomacy and inept planning.

"Where are our jets?" we asked each other. We were promised help and we were told that help was on the way, but no friendly forces were anywhere near us while an enemy—we still didn't know who—machine-gunned us. Through tightly clenched teeth men called for help as though they were playing cards or dice: "Come in, jets! Now, Phantoms! Right now! Come in here and get these bastards before they sink us," they begged.

Although carriers *America* and *Saratoga* carried more than 150 aircraft between them, this potent force found itself incapable of coming promptly to our aid with conventional weapons. Having recalled the ready aircraft that might have defended the ship, the administration in Washington eventually granted permission to send conventionally armed aircraft. But, incredibly, nearly every aircraft was disabled, was restricted to a nuclear mission, was reserved for some other mission (protection of the force, air-to-ground strikes, antisubmarine warfare, reconnaissance) or was otherwise grounded. In any case, before aircraft could be sent to defend *Liberty*, it was necessary to replace the nuclear bomb racks with conventional bomb racks, gun pods and air-to-air missile racks, and to bring up conventional weapons from the magazines far below decks. All this takes an interminable amount of time.

While carrier sailors began the tedious job of changing bomb racks, two more messages arrived from *Liberty*. *Saratoga* relayed, GUNBOATS ARE APPROACHING NOW,[1] followed moments later by, HIT BY TORPEDO STARBOARD SIDE. LISTING BADLY. NEED ASSISTANCE IMMEDIATELY.[2] Then silence. Nothing more was heard from the ship. An hour later CINCUSNAVEUR in London would order *Liberty*, ESTABLISH IMMEDIATE COMMUNICATIONS . . . CONFIRM REPORT OF ATTACK.[3] Three Naval Communication Stations listened on every frequency, but *Liberty* was no longer on the air.

=====

I heard the steady *thu-runk, thu-runk, thu-runk* of the feed pump as it drew water from the feedwater storage tanks and fed it to the always-thirsty boilers. The sound never stopped while the ship was underway. *Thu-runk, thu-runk* was an ever-present musical background to wardroom meals, to the evening movies. Now the sound changed. *Thur-runk, thuur-runk.* Slower. *Thuur-ruunk. Thunk.*

The ship was still shuddering from the torpedo blast when the pump stopped. The boilers, lacking water, ceased to produce steam, and the engines, lacking steam, ceased to turn. A great cold wave of nausea swept over me as, one by one, vital equipment ceased to operate. The engines stopped. Lights dimmed and went out; emergency lights switched on. Fire main pressure failed. A firefighter swore loudly as his hose went limp, forcing him to retreat quickly from a barely under control river of flaming napalm. Air blowers and air-conditioning equipment stopped. Silence. We heard only footsteps, voices and the incessant clatter of the torpedo boat's machine guns as they relentlessly punched holes in our sides.

1. USS *Saratoga* message 081245Z June 1967.
2. USS *Saratoga* message 081254Z June 1967.
3. CINCUSNAVEUR message 081340Z June 1967.

Petty Officer Jeffery Carpenter emerged from the flooded research compartment to find the passageways filled with choking black smoke. Having been spared the force of the explosion, having escaped from drowning, still dripping with water, and with the voice of the torpedo ringing in his ears, Carpenter groped his way along a dark passageway. *Stay low, there's air near the deck,* he remembered from firefighting school, and he tried to stay low, but the deck slanted precariously, moved treacherously, was slippery with oil tracked by the men ahead of him, and he couldn't make good time staying below the smoke anyway, so he plunged on toward the ladder he knew to be ahead of him somewhere. Finally, he emerged on the main deck, just forward of the bridge, and stood alone under a blue sky that he had thought he might never see again. Above him, leaning over the forward railing on the starboard wing of the bridge, was McGonagle.

"Hey, we need more firefighters up here," McGonagle yelled. Carpenter, choking from the smoke, spitting the taste of oil and explosives from his mouth, charged up the congested ladders toward the fires that needed to be fought.

He found flames everywhere. The port-side gasoline fire raged out of control, and napalm burned in gun mounts and in the motor whaleboat. Carpenter found "J" "C" Colston and James Smith on the port side, fighting fires with water and with CO_2. He quickly carried another CO_2 bottle to the inferno, and almost immediately had to retreat under machine-gun fire from the still-circling torpedo boats. This time the machine guns punctured the fire hose in several places, sharply reducing the flow; and a few minutes later the hose went completely limp as Lieutenant Golden in the engine room, unable to communicate with the bridge and forced to choose between supplying water to the boilers and to the fire mains, chose to supply the engines in the hope that he could get them to operate. Water wouldn't extinguish a gasoline fire, but it would cool down the area, helping to prevent flashbacks and protecting the men. Now the fires radiated heat like a blast furnace. There were plenty of CO_2 bottles, but the men couldn't get close enough to use them. The best they could do was lay a blanket of foam around the periphery.

Carpenter had an idea. Opening the valve on a new bottle of CO_2, he locked the valve in the open position and heaved the entire bottle into the middle of the inferno. It worked. For the first time the men were able to make headway against the flames.

Again the word "Prepare to abandon ship" was circulated. Lieutenant Golden in Main Engine Control had heard that before too. During the invasion of Okinawa in April 1945, Golden was in destroyer USS *Hazelwood* when three Japanese kamikazes dove out of low cloud cover. *Hazelwood* maneuvered to avoid two, but a third, coming from astern, hit the number-two stack on the port side and crashed into the bridge. Flaming gasoline spilled over the decks and bulkheads as the mast toppled and the forward guns were put out of action. Ten officers and sixty-seven men were killed, including the commanding officer, and thirty-five were missing. *Hazelwood* rolled over on her side and had to be abandoned.

Golden remembered being plucked out of the water that day. *Hazelwood*'s engineer officer took command and led a crew that went back aboard to extinguish the remaining flames, pump out the flooded spaces and save the ship. Golden was one of that group. Now Golden was *Liberty*'s engineer officer. He was *Liberty*'s third-ranking officer, and he was a "plank owner," having been aboard since the ship was commissioned.

"Disable the main engines and scuttle the ship," Golden was now told by sound-powered telephone from the bridge. The order seemed to come in the captain's voice, but Golden wanted confirmation. All of the crew should be removed before anything was done to scuttle the ship, and Golden had not heard any orders to go over the side. Men had been told only to *prepare* to do so. He asked the bridge to confirm the scuttle ship order, but got no answer. He called again. Finally he decided to ignore it.

Men everywhere now reacted with enthusiasm to a *"demolish ship"* order, which echoed over the announcing system. Equipment that had not been destroyed by the attackers fell to "demolition" teams. In the radar room, a sailor threw a heavy coffee cup through a cathode-ray tube, which burst with a satisfying sound. Aft of the bridge someone attacked a cluster of electrical cables with a fire ax. Elsewhere, men took fire axes to the already disabled gyro compass.

In Damage Control Central, Ensign John Scott received the prepare-to-abandon-ship order over his telephone circuit from the bridge, and relayed it to the repair parties. Repair Three, headed by Lieutenant Painter and located in the crew's mess hall, was now the main battle dressing station and was crowded with wounded and dying men. Scott suggested that Painter start moving some of the wounded up to the next deck, closer to the life rafts. Painter checked the situation topside, saw no attackers, and began the difficult task of moving wounded men up the steep ladder. Many of the wounded could walk with help, and these were no problem. The more seriously wounded, those who had to be moved in their stretchers, required backbreaking effort as two, three or four men hauled each of the awkward stretchers up the narrow and nearly vertical ladder leading to the main deck.

Painter organized a reasonably orderly exodus from this place, under the circumstances, and in a few minutes had assembled most of the wounded in and around the after deck house near the abandon-ship stations. As the men caught their breath they, too, realized that they would not be able to abandon ship. They were still being machine-gunned by the torpedo boats. Armor-piercing projectiles were passing easily through the ship. *Liberty* didn't seem to be sinking. Her heavy list to starboard was getting no worse. No word was coming from the bridge. Nothing had been heard from the bridge since the orders to prepare to abandon ship, to disable engines, and to demolish and scuttle ship, and those orders were still in effect; the order to go over the side had not been given. Painter elected to return the men to the mess deck. There would be time enough to move them when the abandon-ship order came, if it came. In the meantime, there would be more protection from the bullets that continued to whistle so easily through the upper decks.

———

Thomas Smith, the ship's laundry operator, heard the orders to prepare to abandon ship, and with a group of seamen began making preparations. Smith hoped that he would not have to go over the side; but this order was to *prepare* to abandon ship—it required men to assemble at their assigned life-raft stations with their equipment and life jackets and to be prepared to go into the water if it became necessary.

Smith waited for the sound of the machine guns to stop. When the torpedo boats finally pulled back, he raced to his abandon-ship station where he was alarmed to see sticky rubber sealant leaking from the life rafts. All of the rafts in his area had been charred by fire or punctured by bullets or rocket fragments. Finally, at a life-raft rack on the ship's port quarter, Smith found several apparently sound rubber rafts. When he pulled cords on the CO_2 cylinders, only three rafts held air. These he secured with heavy line and dropped over the side, where they would be ready if the abandon-ship order came.

Lurking lazily a few hundred yards away, patiently waiting for *Liberty* to sink, the men on the torpedo boats watched the orange rafts drop into the water. Smith saw someone move on the center boat as her engine growled and her stern settled lower in the water. The boat moved closer to *Liberty*. When within good machine-gun range she opened fire on the empty life rafts, deflating two and cutting the line on the third, which floated away like a child's balloon on the surface of the water.

Smith cursed helplessly as a torpedo boat stopped to take the raft aboard. Then the boats added speed, taking the raft with them, and turned toward their base at Ashdod, sixty-five miles away.

======

As the torpedo boats faded in the distance, helicopters could be seen approaching the ship. *"Stand by to repel boarders!"* barked the announcing system while messengers ran through the ship crying, "Helicopters are coming! Helicopters are coming! Stand by to repel boarders!"

"Oh, shit!" a sailor near me cried as men raced off to previously assigned repel-boarder stations. "Repel boarders" is a frequently drilled shipboard exercise, reminiscent of wooden sailing ships, in which the crew man the sides with rifles and side arms. The men who responded to the call found themselves facing two large Israeli Hornet assault helicopters, each heavily loaded with armed men in battle dress. A sailor broke away from his station and ran screaming through the ship. "They've come to finish us off," he yelled. But the helicopters did not attempt to land and made no effort to communicate. Clearly marked with a blue or black Star of David on a white circular field, Israeli helicopters H4 and H8 circled the ship several times at a comfortable distance, then came in for a closer look, and departed.[4]

Men used the lull in the shooting to fight fires, repair damage, string emergency telephone lines, care for the wounded and, as time permitted, collect the dead. Nothing more was heard from the bridge about the order to abandon ship, and at one point

4. A witness would later describe these helicopters to the Court of Inquiry as "Russian Sikorsky" models; Sikorsky is, of course, an American aircraft company, but the helicopters were neither Russian nor American. Photographs taken by McGonagle reveal that these were French-built Aérospatiale SA321 Super Frelon (Hornet) helicopters, designed for heavy assault and antisubmarine operations. This model is the largest helicopter made in France and can carry thirty armed troops; it has a boat-type hull and stabilizing fins to permit amphibious operations.

Captain McGonagle leaned over a bridge railing to order some men to leave the life rafts alone. The various doomsday orders were soon forgotten as full attention was paid to staying alive and remaining afloat.

Lieutenant Golden and Chief Brooks in the engine room fought to keep the ship's engines on the line, but it became a nearly impossible job as machinery surrendered to combat damage and vital gauges rendered false readings. These men supervised an eager and able force. Engines growled, started, ran for a few minutes and then died; lights and auxiliary equipment went on and off. By 1520 the engines were back on the line, but McGonagle could not control the rudder from the bridge. In another oft-drilled and ancient procedure, men were dispatched to the after steering station to manipulate the rudder by hand. More emergency telephone wire was strung to keep these men in communication with the bridge, as the regular telephone circuit was out of order. Ordinarily, the men would have been given a course to steer; but the compass was out of order, so McGonagle was reduced to giving rudder orders. With great effort, the men were able to force the rudder through an arc of about ten degrees. "Right five degrees rudder," the bridge ordered. Slowly the rudder responded. Even more slowly the ship began to turn. "Rudder amidships," the bridge ordered. In this manner USS *Liberty* commenced a zigzag movement toward deeper water.

At 1530, more than an hour and a half after the first strike, it began to look as though we would survive. For the moment, at least, no one was shooting at us. The crew was advised by messengers and, where it worked, by the general announcing system that *"the attack appears to be over. The attack appears to be over."*

We still didn't know who was shooting at us or why; only a few men had seen the Israeli markings on the helicopters, and no one was certain that the helicopters were associated with the aircraft or torpedo boats. One officer gave me his solemn opinion that the Soviet Union was responsible and that World War Three would surely follow. Others were certain that the attackers were Egyptian. Hardly anyone suspected Israeli forces.

———

Word of the attack finally reached President Johnson in the White House about two hours after it all began. Pentagon officials had apparently been aware of the situation for nearly forty minutes when National Security Advisor Walt Rostow telephoned the President to tell him that a U.S. Navy ship was in trouble.

Johnson ordered an emergency meeting to be held within the hour in the White House Situation Room. He called Rostow and McNamara personally; his staff summoned Secretary of State Dean Rusk, Foreign Intelligence Advisory Board Chairman Clark Clifford, Under Secretary of State Nicholas Katzenbach and Special Consultant McGeorge Bundy. Then, because the President feared that the Soviet Union might be responsible for the attack, he summoned our ambassador to the U.S.S.R., Llewellyn Thompson, who happened to be in Washington.

Unruffled, the President went about his ordinary business while he waited for his advisers to assemble. "Get me in twenty minutes how many states I have been in since I became President," he told his secretary on a private line. That report took just fifteen minutes to prepare; he had visited all but four states.

———

Meanwhile, near Crete, Sixth Fleet sailors completed the rearming of *Liberty*'s much-delayed air support. *"General Quarters! General Quarters! All hands man your battle stations. This is not a drill,"* cried the general announcing systems as pilots raced to their airplanes. Four F-4B Phantoms armed with Sparrow and Sidewinder missiles and four A-4 Skyhawks with air-to-ground missiles were launched from *America.* Four piston-driven Douglas A-1 Skyraider "Spad" bombers were launched from *Saratoga.* As before, the pilots were instructed to clear the air and water around the ship, but under no circumstances to approach the nearby land. They were reminded, however, that *Liberty,* 400 miles from the carrier task force, was beyond the ordinary combat range of the aircraft and that it would be necessary to refuel. One tanker was in the air and would provide fuel for four of the defending airplanes. Another tanker might be launched in time, the pilots were told. But at least four aircraft and possibly eight could not be refueled and would necessarily ditch at sea when their fuel was exhausted.

Aircraft from three squadrons were involved. Because of the danger of the mission and the prospect of losing the aircraft, each squadron commander elected to fly.[5] Thus—"a day late and a dollar short"—help finally streaked toward *Liberty.*

———

5. A squadron of carrier aircraft is comprised of about twenty aircraft under a commanding officer, usually a Navy commander. The squadron commander does not routinely lead each mission. In this case the squadron commanders were later chastised by the air wing and carrier

By this time, the Israeli government had hastily summoned the U.S. naval attaché to report that an unidentified "maybe Navy" ship had been erroneously attacked. At 1614, *Liberty* time, a Flash precedence message from the American embassy reported the Israeli apology to everyone concerned, including COMSIXTHFLT, the White House and the Department of State.

Admiral Martin received the message only moments after his twelve jet aircraft vanished in the distance and well before they were due to arrive over *Liberty*. No doubt influenced by the "ditch at sea" contingency order given to the pilots, he promptly recalled them—all twelve of them. Not one—not even one of the few that *could* have been refueled—was permitted to approach *Liberty* to verify her condition and reassure her crew.

President Johnson received the Israeli apology just as his emergency meeting was getting started; he took time to dispatch a message to Premier Kosygin on the Moscow/Washington hot line to advise the Soviets that our aircraft were en route—and, presumably, that they were being recalled. Then, with much of the tension relieved, he made a quick trip to the Oval Office with Press Secretary George Christian before popping into the Situation Room just six minutes behind schedule.

Christian was left to fend off a hungry Washington press corps. Reporters sensed trouble when they learned that Rusk had been called away from a committee hearing—an unprecedented event— and they descended immediately upon the press secretary for answers. They found him close-mouthed.

Q. George, is Secretary Rusk in the building?
A. Yes.
Q. Seeing the President?
A. Yes.
Q. . . . he was called away from the Hill for an "emergency meeting." Is that true?
A. Secretary Rusk is here.
Q. There is some grumbling on the committee . . .
A. The Secretary is here in the White House seeing the President.
Q. Can you say anything more?
A. No, I cannot.
Q. Are you aware of any emergency, George?
A. I am not going to comment on it.

---

air group commanders for having exposed themselves to risks that could have been taken by junior and presumably more expendable pilots.

Q. . . . you can't give us any help on this situation?
A. No.

The immediate White House reaction to the attack, I am told by a former staff member, was to accept Israel's apology at face value even though there was considerable skepticism that the attack was entirely accidental. The feeling was strong that Israel had nothing to gain and much to lose in attacking a United States ship; consequently, it was felt that if the attack *was* deliberate, it resulted not from a premeditated act of the Israeli government, but rather from a tactical decision of some local military official—and no evidence supported even that suspicion. Besides, the President could ill afford a confrontation with Israel. His major concern was to bring about an end to the war before the Soviet Union stepped in; a confrontation with Israel would likely destroy the leverage he needed. After some discussion, Johnson detailed Clark Clifford to head an investigation into the circumstances of the attack, and the White House resolved to bite its collective tongue until the Clifford report came in.

Johnson and his advisers drafted two more hot-line messages to Premier Kosygin—one concerning *Liberty* and one concerning cease-fire negotiations. Then the President went off to a long diplomatic luncheon and upon his return consulted briefly with Bundy and Rostow before sending still another hot-line message concerning *Liberty.* In all, the hot line was activated five times during the day: three times to convey messages to Kosygin concerning the *Liberty* attack and twice for messages concerning cease-fire negotiations.[6]

When the Clifford report eventually came in, it contained no evidence that the attack was deliberate, and White House tolerance of the affair as a "feasible" error of war thus became permanent.

In *Liberty*'s main battle dressing station Corpsman VanCleave administered first aid to the many wounded. Dr. Kiepfer checked all of the men and left orders for several to be given morphine or for intravenous solutions to be started. He assigned men to stay with some of the most seriously wounded, keeping a close watch for

6. The National Security Council has released two of these messages, but declines to release the text of a message intended for relay to President Nasser of Egypt.

changes in pulse or respiration, and then headed for the bridge to check on the captain's condition.

A messenger ran through the ship shouting that "friendly fighters are in the area," but the report was wrong. The aircraft, reconnoitering from a distance, were soon identified as the same swept-wing jets that had been attacking us.

Lieutenant Painter was helping VanCleave hang an i.v. bottle from an overhead fluorescent light fixture when the general announcing system suddenly cried: *"Aircraft and torpedo boats approaching, starboard side. Stand by for torpedo attack, starboard side."*

Pandemonium broke loose in the room as men raced for the ladder. Every table bore a wounded man, and those who had the strength burst from their tables, lurching, falling, stumbling toward the ladder. Men tore freshly inserted i.v. tubes from their arms in a wild effort to leave the place before it filled with water as they knew the Research spaces were filled. Men too sick to move, men too weak to be driven to their feet even by the fear of instant death, cried out: "Help me!" "Please, oh, please help me!" "Mama, Mama!"

Lieutenant Painter, fearing the panic as much as the torpedo, reached the ladder ahead of most of the men. With a great leap he landed on the third rung, then turned to face the fear-crazed throng behind him.

"Stop it, goddamn it, knock it off!" he screamed as a wall of frightened sailors piled up against him. Someone grabbed at his foot in trying to pull him from his perch, but he sent the man flying with a kick to the neck.

Having slowed the momentum, he ordered the men to move away from the ladder. "No one leaves here until every wounded man is safe! No one leaves!" he bellowed.

He was afraid they would tear him apart, but they moved back. With haste, but this time without panic, men helped other men leave the space that they were all certain would collapse at any moment. The strain was everywhere. Men trembled. Their voices cracked. But they controlled their panic. A senior petty officer with more than fifteen years in the Navy, a man who had long instructed others in the use of life-saving equipment, trembled uncontrollably as he realized that he had forgotten how to inflate his life jacket. He was embarrassed as a younger man reminded him to twist the air tube to open the valve.

A flight of Israeli jets passed over the ship at low level without releasing ordnance. Men who had braced for the arrival of more rockets exhaled slowly. Perhaps it was over, they hoped. Perhaps the torpedo boats that were approaching at such high speed would not attack. Maybe, just maybe, it was over.

As before, the three boats arrived with signal lamps flashing. The signals, unobstructed by smoke this time, were clearly seen; but no one on the bridge could read the flashing light. Word was passed for a signalman or a radioman to report to the bridge. Although several men reported, none could read the signals.

Petty Officer Jeffery Carpenter was on the bridge now, serving as messenger, steward, hospital corpsman, lookout and jack-of-all-trades as needed. Soon he became combat photographer, taking pictures of the torpedo boats with the ship's 35mm Canon that I had selected and placed on the bridge only a few days before. "Take pictures as long as you can," McGonagle directed. "If you have to, destroy the camera and try to hide the film."

A small flag with the Star of David could be seen. "They seem to be Israeli," commented McGonagle.

At 1632, more than two and a half hours after the first rocket was launched against *Liberty,* radarman Cocnavitch entered in his log the first identification of the attacking force: "1632—Boats flying Israeli ensign. 'Torpedo boats seem to be Israeli' Captain's statement."

Radioman Chief Wayne L. Smith regained power in the radio room and quickly raised Commander Sixth Fleet. "The torpedo boats are flying the Star of David. They seem to be Israeli," he reported.

The boats came closer.

McGonagle strained to read the hull numbers, partially obscured by bow waves. "Two oh four one seven," he read aloud to a quartermaster, who recorded the numbers that would be reported to Admiral Martin and to newspaper reporters around the world. Israel had no boats numbered 204-17. McGonagle misread as Arabic numerals "17" the Hebrew letter "T" of Israeli motor torpedo boat *Tahmass,* hull number 204T, which now stood close to *Liberty.*

Chief Thompson came up from the forward repair locker. Harry Thompson had once been trained as a signalman, so he tried to help, but the lights from the boats made no sense. He tried semaphore. Standing in the open with semaphore flags, he tried to talk with the boats. Still there was no response.

The *Tahmass* commander came closer in order to use a bullhorn.

Slowly, enunciated carefully, the message came across the water in English: "Do you need any help?"

Enraged, McGonagle specified to his quartermaster the particular profanity that he thought most appropriate for reply under the circumstances and that short message, uncharacteristic of McGonagle, was obediently relayed to *Tahmass*. The torpedo boats withdrew in silence and resumed their observation from a safer distance. A few minutes later they turned away for the last time and disappeared over the horizon.

Listing heavily to starboard, canted toward the bow, most of her vital equipment destroyed, two thirds of her crew wounded, thirty-two men dead and others dying, a quarter of the ship flooded, and with her captain severely wounded, *Liberty* traced an oily serpentine path upon the water.[7]

7. See Appendix D, pages 237–41, for a discussion of efforts to send aircraft to *Liberty*'s defense.

Chapter 8

RECOVERY, REPAIR AND RENDEZVOUS

You can squeeze a bee in your hand until it suffocates, but it will not suffocate without having stung you. You may say that is a small matter, and, indeed, it is a small matter. But if the bee had not stung you, bees would have long ago ceased to exist.

Jean Paulhan, 1884–1968

Recovery of the dead and collection of the wounded continued as the shipfitters, enginemen and damage control parties fought to keep control of the heavily damaged ship. Ensign Scott in Damage Control Central received dozens of reports of flooding from bullet and rocket holes near the waterline. Men packed these with rags, then hammered cone-shaped pieces of wood into the openings to force a tight fit. Larger holes were sealed by using giant timbers to force blocks of wood or waterproof boxes against the holes.

Scott received a report of a large leak just aft of Damage Control Central in the crew's gym and weight-lifting room. Two feet of water swirled through the room in a great torrent admitted through a huge underwater hole. The usual methods would not work here. Men raced through the ship to gather mattresses from the crew's sleeping compartment. Three mattresses were stuffed into the hole, where they slowed but failed to stop the flooding, then were swept away and into the sea.

The list of the ship kept the flooding contained within the one room. Water, which was at shoe-top level near the door, became more than two feet deep in other parts of the compartment. Using large plywood panels to hold mattresses against the opening, forcing these into place with jacks and braces, and holding the whole arrangement in place with timbers, Scott and his men plugged the hole. Pumping the room dry, they found only a small and controllable trickle of water coming through the apparatus.

———

Not far from where I lay in the passageway outside the wardroom was the chief petty officers' lounge. This room, never intended as a battle dressing station, was relatively safe from rockets, bullets and napalm due to its location near the ship's centerline. It became a collection station for the wounded. Painter found the XO in the passageway outside—bleeding, coherent and angry. Painter lit a cigarette for him, then broke the seal on a bottle of Johnny Walker that he had brought down from the XO's stateroom. Armstrong poured a comforting quantity down his throat, then tucked the bottle under his brown Navy blanket where it nestled alongside his left arm. The bottle remained there as, a few minutes later, a group of men lifted the stretcher for the arduous journey to the main battle dressing station in the crew's mess hall. Philip complained bitterly as the stretcher stood nearly on end to make a sharp turn in the narrow passageway, but he didn't let go of the bottle.

Soon it was my turn. My leg was grotesquely swollen now as I was carried, none too gently, through circuitous passageways. It was dusk as I was lifted over a section of the main deck alongside the after deck house. Above me at very low level hovered a small green helicopter with two men visible in the bubble that was its nose. Then the green bird disappeared from my view as someone covered my face with a blanket to protect me from the strong prop wash.

———

On the bridge, one of our sailors appeared at the captain's side with an M1 .30 caliber rifle. "Captain," he said, "I can pick off the pilot easy."

"No," McGonagle answered quickly, "they'd only return to finish us off."

As the helicopter continued to hover near the bridge, its occupants attempted to signal by gestures and hand signals that they wanted to land. In no mood for visitors, McGonagle waved them away.[1]

Moving closer to the forecastle, the men continued to signal their wish to land, and McGonagle remained firm in his refusal. Finally, a message packet dropped from the helicopter. Retrieved and brought to the bridge to be opened, it was, McGonagle found, the calling card of the naval air attaché of the United States embassy at Tel Aviv—Commander, U.S. Navy, Ernest Carl Castle. Written on the back of the card was the terse query, "Have you casualties?"[2]

"Yes," replied McGonagle, again using the hand-held Aldis lamp. But Commander Castle seemed not to understand, and in a few minutes he, too, departed toward Tel Aviv. "The entire helo trip," he reported later by message, "was a frustration."

===

I finally arrived at the main battle dressing station to find a bloody scene that seemed somehow reminiscent of the American Civil War. Eased out of my stretcher and onto the cold Formica of a table top, I could see other wounded men lying on top of other tables. About two dozen mess-hall tables, each welded to the deck as is customary for tables aboard ship, now served as hospital beds. From fluorescent light fixtures hung glass bottles, which dripped vital fluids through plastic tubes into the arms of the men below. Thin mattresses from the crew's sleeping compartments had been placed on deck between and under the tables, and these held still more men.

Everywhere were wounded men. Most lay silently staring at the overhead. Some chatted quietly with friends. Several were in obvious distress as they awaited the arrival of Dr. Kiepfer or a corpsman, and these were being comforted by shipmates. Bandages, slings, compresses of all sizes and shapes cluttered the room.

Men filtered through the room offering water, fruit juice or coffee. Medicinal whiskey had been authorized for issue, we learned, and brandy, wine or bourbon was available. I accepted a quart can of chilled grapefruit juice and drained it without stopping for breath.

"Anything else, sir?" asked a startled sailor.

1. Commander Castle later described McGonagle's gesture as a thumb-up signal, apparently meant to convey the message that the situation was under control. An officer who was on the bridge reports that the extended digit was not a thumb, but a defiant middle finger. Castle, in civilian clothes aboard an Israeli helicopter, was assumed to be an Israeli.
2. See Appendix F, page 243.

"Yes, more juice, please," I said, as surprised at my own capacity as the sailor was at my performance.

On a table near me I could see Lieutenant Commander Dave Lewis, my department head. No wounds were visible, but Dave's face was the color and texture of fresh asphalt paving. "Dave!" I called, but got no answer.

"He's deaf," I was told, "and he's blind. He was in the room with the torpedo. Saw it coming through the side of the ship. The explosion burnt his eyes and burst his eardrums." I thought of the story of Medusa.

Chief Benkert sat with me and brought my first detailed news of casualties. "Your roommate is over there," he said, pointing over my left shoulder with obvious pleasure.

"No, he's dead," I insisted. But O'Connor was alive. He was clearly very ill, lying on a blood-soaked mattress between two mess-hall tables. When I caught his eye he smiled and waved.

Across the room I could see the XO atop a table near the serving line. Pale but alert, Philip lay on his side and raised himself on one elbow to survey the room. He, too, had just arrived, and he wanted to know who had survived with him. I waved. Philip waved back.

"Thank God the XO is okay," I said.

The serving line, where men ordinarily carried meal trays, was now stocked with bandages, drugs, i.v. bottles, syringes and a host of other medical supplies. Dr. Kiepfer stopped to see me a few minutes after I arrived.

"How do you feel, Jim?" he asked.

Calm, unhurried, seemingly unflustered by the chaos and carnage around him, Kiepfer projected self-assurance. He reminded me of a hospital physician making routine rounds.

"I feel pretty lucky. I'll be okay, Dick."

"Let me know if you need any help," he said, moving on to look after men who obviously were in trouble.

"How do you feel, XO?" he asked Philip Armstrong.

"I'm okay, Doc," he lied as the doctor started to examine the bleeding near Philip's groin. "Some of the guys are a lot worse off than I am. Cup of coffee and I'll be fine."

"Okay, XO," the doctor promised after examining his wounds and checking pulse and blood pressure. "I'll be back to see how you're doing."

Moving to Seaman Salvador Payan, Kiepfer found him unresponsive and apparently dying. Gray matter dribbled into Payan's left ear as he stared at the ceiling, hearing nothing, seeing nothing, but with a grimace of distress on his face.

Kiepfer knew he couldn't save the man. If Payan lived, it would not be Kiepfer who saved him. Kiepfer could only help to make him more comfortable. With that mixture of science and sixth sense that came to characterize the doctor this day, he guessed that much of Payan's distress came from a simple need to urinate. Inserting a catheter to drain the bladder that Payan's own system could not control, he heard a giggle of pleasure that confirmed the diagnosis. Prescribing morphine, Kiepfer moved on.

Steward's Mate Troy Green sat with Armstrong now. Green was the XO's room steward, but he was also his friend, a drinking companion and a confidant. Green brought the coffee that Armstrong asked for, and stayed to comfort him.

McGonagle, unaware of the extent of his executive officer's injuries, came on the general announcing system to ask, *"Will the executive officer please come to the bridge?"*

Enjoying the irony of his position, Armstrong laughed. "Tell the captain that I can't come to the bridge right now," he said, swallowing more coffee. Green laughed with him. Others who heard the exchange chuckled. One simply doesn't send word to the captain that one can't come to the bridge. One goes.

Abruptly Armstrong began to cough, then to vomit. Green was alarmed at the deep red color of the vomit; Armstrong was calm.

"I'll get the doctor," Green said. "Doctor! *Corpsman!*"

"No, no, no," Philip cautioned. "I'm okay. A little blood. No big deal. Now, look," he said, removing his wristwatch, "look, I want you to have this. No. Please. Keep it. And this," he said, removing his wedding band. "See that Weetie gets this."

"C'mon, XO," Green begged. But Armstrong was gone.

Looking across the room a few minutes later, I found his table empty and sobbed for the first time that day. Philip Armstrong was an enigma. We all loved him. Probably even McGonagle loved him. Now he was gone.

We learned much later that a tiny shrapnel wound in Armstrong's back had caused severe internal damage and extensive bleeding near his heart; finally, the pressure around the heart became so great that the heart could no longer pump.[3]

3. A pathologist who examined Philip's body told me later that his throat, bronchial passages, lungs, kidneys and liver were all in poor shape from his abuse of alcohol and to-

McGonagle worried about running aground in shallow water. His bleeding was under control, thanks to a tourniquet that had been applied by Petty Officer Carpenter, and now the leg was numb. The tourniquet should have been loosened every few minutes to maintain circulation, but too much was happening.

He was headed toward open sea. The gyro compass was out of order and the magnetic compass was not reliable, but he headed the ship toward where he thought deeper water should be. The Fathometer was one of the few items of auxiliary equipment that continued to work, and the reports it gave were not reassuring. Where he expected to find fifty fathoms of water, he found forty. As he slowed the ship from eight knots to four, the depth of water dropped to thirty-five fathoms.

Summoning the deck department officer, Ensign David Lucas, McGonagle directed Lucas to set the anchor detail. He knew that several of the men who had been assigned to this detail were dead or wounded. "Just round up as many of the men as you can," he said, "and hurry!"

In less than five minutes Lucas reported by sound-powered telephone from the forecastle that the anchor detail was set. Golden reported from Main Control that power was available to the anchor windlass. McGonagle waited.

"Thirty fathoms," reported a quartermaster who stood near the Fathometer.

"All engines stop," ordered McGonagle.

"Twenty-eight fathoms."

"All engines back one third!" cried McGonagle.

"Twenty-eight fathoms," repeated the quartermaster as the ship shuddered from the sudden exertion of trying to reverse her direction in the water. Water in the flooded spaces added to the strain by resisting the change. Bulkheads bordering Research heaved and bulged as they threatened to give way under the pressure. In the supply department, behind a small-parts stowage cabinet in number-four storeroom, a small crack admitted a stream of water from the adjacent room.

"Twenty-eight fathoms."

---

bacco. It was likely, the doctor told me, that Philip would have died within two years, as he had prophesied, even without help from Israel.

On the forecastle, Lucas had prepared the anchor for letting go. The anchor windlass friction brake gripped the heavy chain only lightly, as the main weight was taken by a large pelican hook. A boatswain's mate stood with a sledge, ready to knock the retaining shackle from the pelican hook upon command.

"Let go the starboard anchor," directed McGonagle.

"Let go the starboard anchor," repeated Lucas by sound-powered telephone from the forecastle.

The boatswain's mate hoisted the heavy sledge.

"Belay that," snapped McGonagle over the phones as he countermanded his order. Catching the sledge in mid-swing, too late to stop, the boatswain's mate directed the blow against the steel deck, missing the shackle. The blow, sounding to those in the area like the report of a rocket, caused some to wince, others to duck for cover. The anchor stayed in the hawsepipe.

McGonagle had decided against anchoring and to attempt instead to back out of the ever-shallower water in which he found himself. For twenty minutes the ship backed. Rudder control while backing is poor under the best of conditions; now there was almost no control at all as the rudder reacted slowly within the narrow arc the men could manually move it. Still, the ship did move generally in the direction that McGonagle wanted it to go.

"Thirty fathoms," repeated the quartermaster. "Thirty-eight."

Finally, McGonagle found deeper water. Resuming forward motion and changing course to the right, he maneuvered around the shallow water.

"Forty-eight fathoms."

One emergency seemed only to lead to another: the ship's engines stopped.

"Lost lube-oil pressure," came the report from Golden in the engine rooms. The sudden loss of momentum again caused water to surge wildly through the flooded compartments and to pound heavily against the weakened forward bulkhead. The steel bulkhead plating showed a decided bulge now from the weight of water pushing against the other side. Seamen described the movement as "panting" as the steel rippled like thin paper from the relentless push of the churning water. The small crack enlarged; the trickle of water became a small, but ominous, spray.

Golden quickly brought the engines back on the line, and the ship continued to move toward deeper water. Within minutes she was in more than eighty fathoms of water and McGonagle determined that there was no longer a danger of grounding. The engines were performing well now and responded to his call for ten knots.

====

At 1725, the COMSIXTHFLT order to move *Liberty* away from Gaza was broadcast to the ship from the Naval Communications Station in Asmara. The message was now more than six hours old and had long since been overtaken by events. The receivers that would have received the message were out of order; the decoding equipment that would have unscrambled it was underwater; the men who would have processed the message were dead. But the ship seemed to be relatively free of danger for the first time in several hours.

In Main Engine Control, Golden allowed himself to relax. Fireman Aishe brought a large pitcher of cold water, which he slowly poured over Golden's head. Then he handed Golden a towel and a lighted cigarette.

On the bridge, McGonagle moved to the port wing where he lay on deck and propped his injured leg on part of his "captain's chair." Identical chairs—large, comfortable and elevated for good view— were permanently affixed to each wing of the bridge. From his supine position, McGonagle could see aft over the fantail, where he could judge the ship's progress from the wake she left and could easily give orders to the men on watch in the pilothouse a few feet away.

A plain-language voice radio message from COMSIXTHFLT told him to steam almost due north for a hundred miles, where he would be met by two destroyers with medical aid. Nearly everyone aboard was wounded to some extent, and about a third of the crew were more or less seriously wounded. McGonagle was proceeding toward a rendezvous with friendly forces, but with only tenuous control of ship's equipment and with a weakened bulkhead whose collapse would almost certainly cause the ship to sink.

When Lieutenant Bennett appeared on the bridge, McGonagle dictated a report of the attack for *Liberty*'s seniors in Washington and London and in the Sixth Fleet. Bennett transcribed the captain's words, then typed the message himself in the ship's office, returned the completed message to the bridge for the captain's signature, and delivered it to Chief Smith in Main Radio for transmission.[4]

---

4. USS *Liberty* message 081715Z June 1967 (Appendix G, page 244).

Next, the captain summoned Ensign Malcolm "Patrick" O'Malley and directed that a report of personnel casualties be sent to the Bureau of Naval Personnel. Finally, he called Dr. Kiepfer, assured himself that everything possible was being done for the wounded and that the dead were being properly cared for, and at last permitted the doctor to examine his wounds. These things completed, McGonagle succumbed to fatigue.

He had lost a large amount of blood. He had wounds in his right arm and leg and over much of his body from flying rocket fragments, mostly aluminum and magnesium particles. The leg was numb. He was exhausted. Soon he was barely conscious.

When Kiepfer asked his name, McGonagle could not answer. He could not tell who he was, where he was, what had happened, where he was going. Kiepfer considered declaring the captain physically unable to retain command and consulted with Lieutenant Golden. The captain had lost so much blood that he could no longer think clearly. Certainly he was in no condition to make important decisions concerning the ship. Kiepfer and Golden decided that since he was in no condition to make any decisions at all, he was unlikely to make any dangerous ones. Most of his problem, the doctor decided, was caused by fatigue and great loss of blood, and this would soon start to correct itself with rest and the passage of time. Kiepfer left the captain unconscious on the deck and sent Signalman David to locate an officer who could come to the bridge and take control of the ship.

Just before dusk, Signalman David found Lieutenant Painter helping look after the wounded in the after battle dressing station.

"You're it for tag, sir," he said.

"Huh?"

"Mr. Golden's busy in Main Control. You're the next senior line officer. Captain's alone on the bridge and needs help."

Painter went directly to the bridge, where he found a lightly manned watch. McGonagle was unconscious. Painter assumed the "conn," advised the pilothouse watch that he was in control of the ship, and thus took over for the stricken captain. When no new emergencies arose immediately, he dispatched a messenger to his stateroom to bring his Instamatic camera, which he used to take several pictures in the remaining rays of light from the setting sun, including a view of the unconscious commanding officer.

During the evening, Commander Sixth Fleet advised that he was sending an airplane to provide navigational support,[5] and lookouts were instructed to search carefully for such an airplane, but it failed to arrive. Once, a light was seen at great distance, but it came no closer and did not respond to calls by radio. We never learned what happened to the airplane, but the search for it helped keep the conning officer and lookouts occupied.

Meanwhile, Dr. Kiepfer worried about Seaman Gary Blanchard, a very young sailor who had suffered serious wounds from the full force of an exploding rocket at his midsection. Kiepfer had several patients whom he could do nothing for. Blanchard's injuries were to his kidneys. Although the damage was serious, surgery might save him.

"How is it? Will I die, Doc?"

"It's not good, Gary," Kiepfer said. "If I don't operate, I'm sure you'll die. If I do operate, you may die anyway. Your chances are not good either way, but if I operate we may be able to save you."

Lieutenant Painter, who had been relieved on the bridge and was again helping with care of the wounded, turned away from the poignant scene and tried to hide the emotion he felt. Young Blanchard showed no fear.

"Well, then, I guess we better operate," he said.

An hour later Kiepfer performed major surgery under emergency conditions on the wardroom mess table. Blanchard, both kidneys riddled with rocket fragments, never regained consciousness.

═══

Lieutenant Maury Bennett stopped to see me quite early in the evening. I knew that his battle station was in the flooded space, and I had been told that he had died there. I had been thinking of his wife, Joy; his son, Maurice III; and his unforgettably named daughters, Heidi, Holly, Heather and Hilary. And as I mourned for them, Maury appeared in front of me.

"My God, Maury, I thought you were dead!"

I don't think he ever understood how glad I was to see him, or why my voice cracked, or why I wiped my eyes.

"I just sent the battle report on this thing to the Chief of Naval

5. COMSIXTHFLT message 081953Z June 1967.

Operations," he told me. "I hope you get to see it. You won't believe what Shep said."

"What did he say?"

"From reading the report, you'd think almost nothing happened at all. The report says there were just one or two airplanes that made a total of maybe five or six strafing runs over a period of maybe five or six minutes. Then, bam, the torpedo, and it was all over. Clean. Simple. Just like that."

"For Christ's sake! Who wrote the goddamned report?"

"Well, I did. Shep dictated it to me."

"Jesus Christ, Maury, what did you let him send a crazy report like that for? He's pretty sick. Doesn't he know what really happened?"

"What do you mean, 'let him'? He's the captain. I couldn't sit up there and argue with him about the details of his battle report. He told me what to say and I said it."

"For Christ's sake, Maury!"

I didn't see Maury again that night. When I mentioned the report to Lloyd Painter and others during the night, they reacted with bewilderment. No one could understand why the report so minimized the incident. But that message was the first detailed report to leave the ship, and it was subsequently released by the Pentagon, essentially verbatim, to the press.

———

Pat O'Malley compiled the casualty report. He drafted the message in three headings: KILLED IN ACTION; MISSING IN ACTION; WOUNDED IN ACTION. A few hours later he told me the story.

Pat was a small man. Only a few weeks out of Officer Candidate School, he was *Liberty*'s most junior officer and consequently the butt of every ensign joke ever known. "You'll always be an ensign to me, Pat," he was told, as are all ensigns, and he took the kidding well, but now he was angry.

"Goddamned stupid Bureau," he said. "They got my casualty report okay. And do you know what they said? They sent a message back, and they said, 'Wounded in *what* action?' 'Killed in *what* action?' They say it wasn't 'action,' it was 'an accident.' I'd like to tell 'em to come out here and see the difference between 'action' and 'accident.' Stupid bastards!"

Pat stayed with me for a while, brought me yet another chilled can of grapefruit juice, which I drained, and filled me in further on what was happening in the ship and in the Sixth Fleet and how the world was reacting to the attack.

Finally, he wandered off, still angry over having to respond to what seemed an insane query from the Bureau of Naval Personnel.

=====

When Damage Control Officer John Scott received reports of the weakened and leaking bulkhead in number-four storeroom forward of the flooded research compartment, he made a personal inspection. Alarmed, he mobilized the most experienced members of his damage control teams to "shore up" and support the weakened steel plating, but he was less than comforted with the result.

The flooded compartment was like a giant swimming pool, nearly filled, being hauled over rough ground by drunken teamsters. With each roll, water crashed crazily against the ship's sides, increasing her roll, delaying her return to equilibrium. Tons of water moved freely throughout this large compartment that had been "number-three hold" when the ship was a merchantman; and with the water moved heavy desks, radio receivers, filing cabinets, battered doors and bulkheads, and the bodies of friends. All crashed relentlessly against the ship's sides and the already weakened and leaking forward bulkhead.

Scott did all that could be done. Heavy plywood was braced against the straining steel, and everything was held in place with timbers. The fury inside still howled to get out, but the barrier was now, if not secure, at least more equal to the task.

It was necessary to station a man near the shoring to warn by telephone of any shifting of the shores or of any new leaking. Ordinarily, men would have been assigned to such duty in four-hour shifts; because of the hazard and the terror of this task, volunteers were sought to rotate for ten minutes at a time. Typical of the *Liberty* crew, there were ample volunteers.

=====

Chief Joe Benkert and Senior Chief Stan White spent most of the night with me, keeping me informed of what was going on and looking after my health and comfort. Although compresses had been applied to every important wound, blood continued to ooze through the bandages and to collect in a sticky mess in my clothing. The stuff collected under my body; it pooled on the table top and under the small of my back; and it dripped from the table onto the deck below.

"Be still, damn it," I remember Benkert saying. "I want you to be around for the next trip."

It didn't seriously occur to either of us that *Liberty* would not be making another trip. I was still high enough on morphine and on the happy accident of being alive that I was not terribly concerned about the continued bleeding, and my confidence was maintained by an occasional visit by Dr. Kiepfer or a corpsman who, after taking pulse and blood pressure, reported that these vital signs were within normal limits.

=====

On the bridge, men continued to scan the sky and to search the horizon for American ships or airplanes. No American forces were sighted. The first sighting was not American, but Russian. Soviet-guided missile destroyer 626/4 arrived after midnight—hours ahead of Martin's forces—to send a flashing-light message in English.

DO YOU NEED HELP? asked the Russian.

NO, THANK YOU, the conning officer replied.

I WILL STAND BY IN CASE YOU NEED ME, the Russian answered.

Thus the Soviet skipper celebrated his achievement discreetly by remaining near *Liberty* to wait with her for the arrival of American ships.

The night went slowly. The few officers who were able took turns on the bridge with the captain, who, regaining some strength, moved into the pilothouse at about 0200. He spent the rest of the night in a special captain's chair fashioned long ago from a discarded helicopter pilot's seat. The seat, comfortable yet small, fitted neatly next to the disabled bridge radar repeater and in front of a porthole. In it, the captain could see through the porthole, and he could lean on the radar repeater for support.

When Kiepfer found him here and gave him a report on the condition of the wounded, McGonagle remained incoherent and seemed not to understand what was being said to him.

Toward morning Benkert informed me that two destroyers from Destroyer Squadron 12, USS *Davis* and USS *Massey,* were approaching on schedule and would be alongside with additional medical help soon after sunrise. A few hours behind the destroyers were the Sixth Fleet flagship USS *Little Rock*; our newest carrier, USS *America*; carrier USS *Saratoga*; and other ships. Helicopters would begin transferring wounded to the carriers during midmorning.

Seaman Nathan Coleman had worked all night. He had helped plug rocket holes and had repaired damage wherever he could. He had helped man the rudder from the after steering station. He had raced through the ship, carrying messages. And he had helped look after the wounded. Now, with Navy ships on the way, he remembered his new 35mm Canon camera in his locker in the sleeping compartment. He was a serious amateur photographer in the midst of a great drama, and his new camera had yet to be loaded with its first roll of film.

He had not been in the sleeping compartment at all during the night. The room looked as it had never looked before. Usually spotlessly clean, it now had greasy footprints tracked everywhere. Bunks, suspended three-high from steel stanchions, were usually neatly made up, with clean white towels hanging near each pillow. Today, greasy rags hung in their place. A few men dozed in their bunks, half-dressed, shoes abandoned to the jumble on deck along with unrecognizable denim that had been clothing. Fully half of the bunks in this room were now stripped, the mattresses having been borrowed for the wounded.

Coleman found the camera undamaged in his tiny locker, loaded it with his only roll of Kodachrome II, and headed forward. Pausing in the battle dressing station, he took two quick shots by existing light.

"Hey, Nat, I don't think we're supposed to be taking any pictures."

He moved forward toward the bridge.

The pilothouse on a Navy ship at sea is almost a sacred place. One doesn't go there unless one has business there. One doesn't joke or speak loudly. Idle chatter is discouraged. And on *Liberty,* McGonagle tolerated smoking on watch only by the conning officer.

Coleman entered the room through a rear door. He had preset the camera so that he would be ready to shoot, even though he didn't know what he might find here. He knew he should not be here at all, but there were pictures that had to be taken. The men on watch said nothing, seemed not to see him as he stood next to a chart table to the left of the helm. Steering control had been restored, and a helmsman stood behind the wheel, feet apart, learning that a heavy list and a belly full of water cause a ship to respond differently. Fully occupied with a very difficult task that had once been second nature, he seemed not to notice Coleman.

In silence, Coleman sensed that the captain now occupied his chair on the port wing of the bridge, perhaps ten feet from the pilothouse door. Moving to the door, he raised the camera to eye level and focused carefully. McGonagle sat stubbornly in the chair, a paper cup in his left hand, drinking black coffee. His khaki trouser leg had been torn away above the right knee to reveal the abuse it had suffered.

Clack, reported the single-lens reflex camera as shutter clicked, mirror moved.

Coleman saw the captain stiffen, but so far he had not been seen. He wound and snapped again. *Clack.*

"Hey, stop that man!" cried McGonagle.

Coleman spun, dashed past the startled helmsman, and nearly fell through the rear door. Holding the camera to his chest with his left hand, he bounded down the ladder to the 02 level. All ladders were slippery now with fuel oil tracked from the ruptured tanks. He lost his footing as he crossed the landing outside the captain's cabin, but his right hand caught a railing. He recovered his balance without damage to himself or his camera. Behind him he could hear a shipmate, dispatched by McGonagle. Coleman was faster and more determined. On the 01 level he made a top-speed dash down a long corridor through "officers' country," and burst through an open door onto a landing leading to the main deck. Two giant steps put him on the main deck, and a few more steps put him inside the after deck house near the barber shop.

He paused to listen for his pursuer and to catch his breath. "What have I done?" he asked himself, wondering what charges would be lodged against him when he was caught. Although he was no longer being chased, the men on watch knew him. It was only a matter of time before someone would report him. No matter. He had his prize and he would not give it up. He had a latent image, two latent images, of a U.S. Navy commanding officer on the bridge of his ship during a historic incident at sea.

He removed the film from his camera and hid it. He might be caught and punished, but he would never give up the film.[6]

=====

"Surface contact dead ahead," cried a bridge lookout. "Two contacts, sir, hull down on the horizon."

6. The pseudonymous Seaman Coleman declines permission to reproduce his photograph of McGonagle. Despite the several years that have passed, he fears Navy or U.S. government retaliation for any apparent connection with any published material concerning the attack.

Forgetting the phantom photographer, McGonagle left his chair to scan the horizon with binoculars. He was on a westerly course now, with the rising sun at his back. In the distance he could see the superstructures of two ships, the hulls hidden by the curvature of the earth. Untrained eyes would have seen nothing at all. McGonagle, sick as he was, recognized the distant gray shapes as United States Navy destroyers.

More than sixteen hours after the onset of the attack, destroyers *Davis* and *Massey* came alongside. The ships nestled together, dead in the water, as Commodore Lehy of Destroyer Squadron 12 came aboard from his flagship, *Davis,* along with Navy doctors Peter Flynn from USS *America* and Joseph Utz from USS *Davis.* Also sent over were two medical corpsmen, fifteen damage control technicians and a host of other specialists.

Commodore Lehy was escorted to the bridge, where he found McGonagle conscious and on his feet, but sick and exhausted. Clearly, it was time for McGonagle to go below, to rest, to look after his own wounds. Gently, the commodore offered to assume command of *Liberty.* Even though McGonagle was so weary that he slurred his words, he refused to relinquish command. Lehy held a quick conference with Dr. Kiepfer and Lieutenant Golden, then resumed his conversation with McGonagle.

The two men leaned on the bridge railing for several minutes while they talked. Finally it was agreed: McGonagle would go below to his cabin to rest and recuperate. Lieutenant Golden, now *Liberty*'s second-ranking officer, would handle the ship's business, keeping the captain informed and executing his orders, and Lieutenant Commander William Pettyjohn from Lehy's staff would come aboard to assist with navigation and ship handling.

Retiring to his cabin, McGonagle found the place a shambles. Fire from napalm had scorched the furniture and melted portions of his nylon carpet. Rockets had torn more than a dozen jagged eight- and ten-inch holes in his bulkheads. Portholes were shattered. A rocket had exploded in his pillow, and an unexploded eight-inch projectile lay quietly in his shower. Taking time only to have the projectile removed, McGonagle retired.

—————

During midmorning, the first helicopter from USS *America* arrived to begin the slow job of removing the dead and wounded. I was slated to make the trip, along with about fifty others. Once again, the tireless *Liberty* crew started the muscle-wrenching job of hauling stretchers up the impossibly steep ship's ladders, and once again my stretcher stood nearly on end as men struggled to move me toward the helicopters.

The fresh air on the main deck was refreshing. The sky was blue and the weather mild as I waited in a row of identical stretchers to be hoisted into the air. Finally, my turn came. As the big blue Navy helicopter hovered over the forecastle, a wire and hook descended from a winch, grasped my stretcher, and hauled me into the sky. Although it couldn't have been more than twelve feet, it seemed higher as I was pulled into the heat, noise, oily exhaust, smoke and pressure of the helicopter's prop wash. A few minutes later we were deposited on the flight deck of USS *America.*

I was met on *America* by a civilian agent from the Office of Naval Intelligence, who walked alongside my stretcher as it was carried away from the helicopter and past a group of reporters and cameramen. "Don't answer any questions," the man warned as he hunched over the moving stretcher to show me his identification. "Don't talk to the press or anyone else until you are told it's all right."

More than an hour passed before the carrier reached *Liberty.* The ship was a pathetic sight. Her list could be seen from miles away. Her bow was several feet lower in the water than her stern. She was blackened with smoke, oil and blood, and punctured with hundreds of rocket and bullet holes. She was afloat and moving under her own power. And she flew her American flag.

As the ships came closer, every man not on watch was on deck. From my bunk in *America*'s sick bay I heard the cry of several thousand men. "Hip, hip, hooray! Hip, hip, hooray! Hip, hip, hooray!" they cheered to honor our ship.

Petty Officer Jeffery Carpenter, weakened finally from loss of blood, occupied a stretcher on *Liberty*'s main deck, where he waited for a helicopter. Stan White lifted the stretcher by one end so that Jeff could see the tribute being paid by the carrier.

"Now I know we'll be all right," he said.

The most seriously wounded were aboard the carrier now and in the hands of an expert and well-equipped medical team. The entire medical department sprang to life. The ship's senior medical officer, Commander John J. Gordon, spent more than twelve hours continuously in surgery, where he was assisted by Drs. Donald Griffith and, when he returned from *Liberty,* Peter Flynn. Drs. Frank Federico and George Lussier made ward rounds. The very seriously ill were attended constantly by corpsmen. Off-duty men from other departments volunteered to help with feeding, bathing, changes of bedding and other details. Carpenter's faith was well placed. Although doctors identified several men as probably beyond help, not a single man died.

An alert corpsman with the unlikely nickname "Smokey the Bear" adjusted a special splint that the *America* team made for my leg. For the first time I was relatively free of pain, thanks to Smokey. Recognizing that my primary need now was for sleep, he posted a sign over my bunk: DO NOT DISTURB. THE LIFE YOU SAVE MAY BE YOUR OWN. [signed] SMOKEY THE BEAR, MASTER-AT-ARMS IN CHARGE OF WARD. As long as that sign hung, I was never disturbed.[7]

In Norfolk and elsewhere throughout much of the United States, friends, family and sweethearts of *Liberty* crewmen reacted to the news that *Liberty* had been mauled at sea. Most received the news first on radio or television. All lived through at least twenty-four hours of anxious misery before learning whether their particular man had survived.

My wife, Terry, received the news before noon on Thursday as she worked at home in the kitchen of our rented Norfolk townhouse. A neighbor, a Navy wife whose husband was at sea in a submarine, appeared at the patio door to tell of the news report she had heard on the radio.

Terry went straight to Sandy O'Connor, who lived half a block away, but Sandy was at Weetie Armstrong's. She called Weetie. The rest of the day was spent at one *Liberty* wife's house or another, listening to news reports, hoping for information, knowing that messages of death or injury would come before reports of survivors. And as they waited, the news reports became more grim.

Initial reports listed ten dead, a hundred wounded. Soon reports were broadcast of fifteen *seriously* wounded. Then came a report that twenty-four were missing, trapped in the flooded space. Everyone knew that these men were almost certainly dead. Finally, later in the afternoon, the wives decided that they should go home and keep the telephone lines open so that they could receive any news that might come to them from Washington.

Paula Lucas was in Corriganville, Maryland, visiting her mother

7. Smokey dropped from sight a few months after the attack. If he reads this, he is invited to write to the author in care of Random House, as he is remembered fondly by many of his former patients, who would like to hear from him.

with the new baby when she heard Paul Harvey report on his news show that "a communication ship in the Mediterranean" had been torpedoed. Paula knew that *Liberty* was the only communication ship in the Mediterranean. A call to a friend at the radio station confirmed that *Liberty* had been hit. In a few minutes Paula's stockbroker cousin called to report that he had seen the story on the Dow-Jones ticker.

Pauline Pierce was en route to New York when she heard the report on her car radio. She telephoned Weetie Armstrong from a motel. Unsure of what to do, she waited for more news on the radio. Finally, she reversed her direction on the turnpike and returned home to await whatever news was coming.

Retired Navy Captain Joseph C. Toth heard the news while waiting for a traffic light. He went directly home and waited with Mrs. Toth. Steve was their only son, and Captain Toth was proud that Steve had chosen to follow in his footsteps, had graduated from the Naval Academy just as his father had, and was now a Navy lieutenant and *Liberty*'s navigator and operations officer. Captain Toth didn't move from the television. Between television newscasts he scanned the dial of a portable radio. Long after midnight Mrs. Toth went to bed. Captain Toth finally fell asleep in his chair.

He awoke shortly after 0600 to the sound of his doorbell. The front door had a translucent fiberglass curtain, and through the curtain Captain Toth could see two figures. With mounting fear he rose from the chair. He could see that the visitors were naval officers. One was a chaplain.

Captain Toth told me much later that it was not necessary for the officers to speak. He had served as a commanding officer during his military career, and he had made such calls himself. He tried to wish them away, but they wouldn't go. He had a flash of hope that he was still asleep and the men were part of a very bad dream, but the vision remained. Finally, he opened the door, accepted the message in silence, thanked the officers for their courtesy, and closed the door very slowly.

———

Meanwhile, the officers and men of *Liberty* were fully occupied with keeping the ship afloat and keeping Washington informed of what was going on. Necessary reports were still being made; vital repairs were being accomplished; urgent messages from Washington and London were being answered.

Early Friday afternoon, while several ships of the Sixth Fleet stood by, Vice Admiral Martin came aboard. He was escorted by Ensign Lucas, who gave him a brief tour and then took him to the captain.[8] McGonagle, thoroughly drained, received the admiral in his cabin.

John Scott and his damage control crew by now had a satisfactory feel for the extent of damage and the size of the torpedo hole. They could *see* much of the hole through the clear Mediterranean water, and by probing the opening with a long fire nozzle they had determined that it was at least thirty feet wide. Clearly, such an opening could not be repaired at sea. Nevertheless, senior officers in the other ships pestered Golden and Pettyjohn with demands to have divers measure the hole and report what might be done to patch it.

Lieutenant Bob Roberts, commanding officer of the fleet tug *Papago,* donned scuba gear and led a small group of divers. Stretching nylon rope from one edge of the opening to another, they knotted each end, then cut the rope to the length of the opening and sent it up to the main deck to be measured. Several such lengths were cut, and they all told the same story: the opening in *Liberty*'s side was more than forty feet wide. They didn't have to measure the height. They could see that it extended from above the waterline to the bilge keel twenty-four feet below. Any remaining hopes for patching the hole were quickly abandoned.

Golden was becoming increasingly concerned about an apparently undiscovered major leak in the forward part of the ship. The ship, already noticeably low in the water forward, was getting lower. Although her sharp starboard list was getting no worse, now she seemed to be sinking by the bow, and no flooding or other reason for this condition could be found. Golden pumped ballast around to try to improve the ship's trim; still, every hour she was a few inches lower. He resolved to jettison anchor chain if necessary to lighten the forward part of the ship, and continued to search for undiscovered flooding.

After borrowing a circular saw from *Davis* (to replace the ship's saw, which an officer had borrowed and failed to return), Ensign Scott rounded up a crew to replace the temporary shores that had been erected to support the panting bulkhead in number-four store-

8. So severe was Lucas's exhaustion and such was his state of mind that he has no recollection of Admiral Martin's visit. The story of Admiral Martin's visit came from other officers and from letters in which Lucas described escorting the admiral, but days later he could not recall ever having seen Admiral Martin in person.

room. This job took up most of the afternoon, required every available man and several *Davis* men as well, and used every remaining piece of shoring on the ship, all of the adjustable shoes and all of the plywood. Duilio Demori helped, as did Richard Neese, James Smith, Phillip Tourney and others, and when they were finished the bulkhead looked reasonably secure. Although it still leaked, the leak was small. The shoring was a sturdy complex of professionally fitted timbers that looked as though it would do the job. The men were proud of their work, and several of them posed proudly by the scaffoldinglike structure to have their pictures taken.

Golden never did find the reason for the ship's poor trim. Luckily, the condition stabilized during the afternoon, and it was not necessary to take any drastic action.

Chapter 9

COVER-UP

The barrier of rank is the highest of all barriers in the way of access to the truth.

B.H. Liddell Hart,
Thoughts on War, xi (1944)

In Washington, apparently while the ship was still under attack and fighting for her life, Pentagon officials struggled with the first news report of the attack. Immediately, they were faced with the vexing problem of how to describe her mission.

Phil G. Goulding, assistant secretary for public affairs, argued that the ship was an intelligence collector and should be identified as such. "This ship collects intelligence," said Goulding. "We should take the public affairs initiative, leveling with our people from the beginning."

But the United States government had never declared officially that any of its peacetime ships were in the intelligence-collection business, and the intelligence and diplomatic authorities argued against making such a declaration now. Goulding tells us in his book *Confirm or Deny* that they made three points: first, Defense Department employees are taught never to discuss intelligence matters under any conditions, and nothing must be done to change this policy or to suggest a change to it. Second, although *Liberty* would be called a spy ship by the press, this was not the same as an official government admission. A neutral country may accept a Technical Research Ship in its port regardless of how the press describes it, but may not accept an acknowledged United States intelligence vessel. Third, they argued that Israel and Egypt might be offended if the United States openly admits it had sent an intelligence ship to eavesdrop on their radio conversations.

Secretary McNamara listened carefully before finally yielding to the security and diplomatic arguments. The Pentagon, he decided, would use the official unclassified description of *Liberty* as a Technical Research Ship and would elaborate upon her duties somewhat to describe a specific communication mission. Goulding prepared the initial statement, adding two more paragraphs as new information poured in. Soon this report was cleared with the State Department and the White House, and was handed to the press:

A U.S. Navy technical research ship, the USS LIBERTY (AGTR-5) was attacked about 9 A.M. (EDT) today approximately 15 miles north of the Sinai Peninsula in international waters of the Mediterranean Sea.

The LIBERTY departed Rota, Spain, June 2nd and arrived at her position this morning to assure communications between U.S. Government posts in the Middle East and to assist in relaying information concerning the evacuation of American dependents and other American citizens from the countries of the Middle East.

The United States Government has been informed by the Israel government that the attack was made in error by Israeli forces, and an apology has been received from Tel Aviv.

Initial reports of casualties are 4 dead and 53 wounded. The LIBERTY is steaming north from the area at a speed of 8 knots to meet U.S. forces moving to her aid. It is reported she is in no danger of sinking.[1]

Although the carrier *America* teemed with newsmen—twenty-nine of them, including representatives from every major wire service, the television networks and several large newspapers, plus newsmen from England, Greece and West Germany—Admiral Martin somehow managed to keep these men in the dark about the *Liberty* attack for more than five hours. These were some of the best news-

1. Phil G. Goulding, *Confirm or Deny—Informing the People on National Security* (New York: Harper & Row, 1970), p. 102.

men in the business, but they might have received more information if they had been ashore. Admiral Martin told them only what the Pentagon wanted told, and apparently he waited for instructions from the Pentagon before telling them of the attack at all.

WE UNLEARNED ABOUT [the *Liberty* attack] UNTIL SAW WX STORY AT 5:30 P.M., GMT, correspondent Bob Horton complained to his home office. When Sixth Fleet briefing officers finally did talk, they revealed very little, and what they did say was cloaked in security restrictions.

Frustrated by inability to promptly file their stories, Neil Sheehan of the New York *Times,* Bob Horton, writing for the Associated Press, and Harry Stathos, writing for United Press International, sent urgent messages to their home offices asking to "immediately work on Pentagon Public Affairs to spring [the stories] loose." The stories were being filed not to their home offices, but as classified traffic to the Pentagon.

Other reporters, chafing at the restrictions placed upon them, interfered with ship's routine as they schemed to conduct forbidden interviews and plotted to file uncleared stories. One particularly enterprising reporter, after earning the enmity of dozens of ship's officers, attempted to file his ill-gotten and uncleared story by disguising it as a personal letter, which he asked a helicopter pilot to mail. The pilot forwarded the letter, not to the reporter's newspaper, but to the Navy's Chief of Information in the Pentagon, who returned it, unfiled.

Confusion grew. Captain McGonagle's original report, dictated to Lieutenant Bennett while McGonagle was sick, delirious and nearly unconscious, was soon released to the press. ATTACKED WITH UNIDENTIFIED JET FIGHTERS BELIEVED ISRAELI, McGonagle's message said. APPROX SIX STRAFING RUNS MADE ON SHIP. . . . TOOK TORPEDO HIT STARBOARD SIDE.[2] This mild, understated report eventually became the nucleus of the official story of the *Liberty* incident. No one asked whether it was possible to inflict in six strafing runs the damage that *Liberty* suffered, or how many aircraft would be required to put on target the hits that *Liberty* received. When a group of the Navy's most senior admirals were briefed on the incident, they agreed among themselves that at least ten aircraft would be required to do the job, but their professional opinions were never reconciled with the official report.

2. See Appendix G, page 244, for full text of McGonagle's message.

One of Israel's first public responses to news of the attack was to issue
a news release asserting that Israel had specifically asked our government for the location of any American ships near the Israeli coast,
and had not received a reply. This caused some consternation in the
State Department until officials realized, after an urgent exchange of
messages, that no such question had been asked at all—that the news
release was simply a public relations ploy.

Next, Israeli newspapers reported that the American flag was not
flying. Pentagon officials added that there was little wind in the area
and that our flag "may have hung limp and unrecognizable at the
mast." The public was now convinced that the flag either was not
flying at all or was hanging limp at the mast on a windless day.

The news stories from Washington seemed torn in two directions.
On one side was the need to tell the story as quickly and as accurately
as possible without revealing classified information, and on the other
side was a diplomatic and political need to give Israel the benefit of
reasonable doubt.

"This would be called 'keeping everything in perspective,' " Philip
Armstrong had said a few hours before he died.

On Saturday, two days after the attack, this wire-service story appeared:

WASHINGTON JUNE 10 (UPI)

US MILITARY OFFICIALS SAID SATURDAY THAT THEY WERE SATIS-
FIED ISRAEL'S ATTACK THURSDAY ON THE U.S. COMMUNICATIONS SHIP
LIBERTY WAS ONE OF THE TRAGIC MISTAKES OF WARFARE.

THEY SAID THEY STILL DID NOT HAVE A COMPLETE ACCOUNT OF
THE ATTACK FROM THE LIBERTY'S CAPTAIN, BUT WHAT THEY HAD
LEARNED SO FAR SHOWED NO INTENT ON ISRAEL'S PART TO DELIBER-
ATELY DESTROY AN AMERICAN VESSEL.

PENTAGON OFFICIALS SAID THE CIRCUMSTANCES OF THE ATTACK, SO
FAR AS THEY WERE KNOWN, MADE HUMAN ERROR A PLAUSIBLE EX-
PLANATION FOR IT.

THE LIBERTY WAS MOVING SLOWLY AND THERE WAS LITTLE WIND
AT THE TIME OF THE AIR AND SEA ASSAULTS, THEY SAID, MAKING IT
QUITE POSSIBLE ITS AMERICAN FLAG WAS HANGING LIMP AND UNI-
DENTIFIABLE AT THE MOMENT THE ISRAELI JET PLANES FIRST AP-
PROACHED.

SHORTLY AFTER THE ATTACKS, WHEN THE SHIP'S AMERICAN IDEN-

TITY BECAME KNOWN TO THE ISRAELI GOVERNMENT, A STATEMENT
WAS ISSUED IN TEL AVIV CLAIMING THE VESSEL HAD DISPLAYED NO
FLAG, BUT U.S. OFFICIALS INSISTED IT WAS FLYING THE AMERICAN
FLAG, CARRIED ITS NAME ON THE STERN AND BORE ITS NUMERICAL
DESIGNATION ON ITS BOW.

IN DESCRIBING THE EVENTS OF THE ENCOUNTER, THE PENTAGON
SAID FRIDAY, THERE WAS A 20 MINUTE INTERVAL BETWEEN THE SIX
STRAFING RUNS OF THE ISRAELI JETS AND THE SUBSEQUENT ATTACK
BY THREE ISRAELI TORPEDO BOATS.

BUT OFFICIALS NOW BELIEVE THAT TIMING SEQUENCE TO BE INEX-
ACT SINCE IT WAS NOT YET KNOWN WHETHER THE PERIOD WAS
CLOCKED STARTING WITH THE FIRST PASS OF THE JETS OR SOMETIME
LATER. THE INTERVAL BETWEEN THE PLANE AND NAVAL ATTACKS
COULD HAVE BEEN SUBSTANTIALLY SHORTER, THEY BELIEVE.

THERE WAS ALSO THE POSSIBILITY THE TORPEDO BOATS WERE SOME
MILES FROM THE U.S. VESSEL WHEN THE JET ATTACKS BEGAN, SAW
THE ACTION FROM A DISTANCE, AND LOOSED THE TWO TORPEDOES
FIRED AT THE LIBERTY AS THEY CAME RACING UP TO JOIN THE EN-
GAGEMENT, OFFICIALS SAID.

ONE TORPEDO STRUCK THE LIBERTY, A LIGHTLY ARMED WORLD
WAR II VICTORY SHIP OUTFITTED WITH THE LATEST ELECTRONIC
EQUIPMENT. IT REPORTED "EXTENSIVE BUT SUPERFICIAL DAMAGE
TOPSIDE AND SOME LOWER-DECK SPACES FORWARD DESTROYED," THE
PENTAGON SAID. IT WAS IN NO DANGER OF SINKING.[3]

President Johnson read the story almost as soon as it appeared
on the White House ticker and immediately called Secretary
McNamara. There was nothing plausible about the attack. The attack was an outrage. Thirty-four Americans were dead. Many
wounded. The attack was inexcusable and was not to be brushed off
lightly by anyone in the United States government.[4]

Phil Goulding dictated and quickly cleared the following statement:

We in the department of Defense cannot accept an attack upon a clearly
marked noncombatant United States naval ship in international waters
as "plausible" under any circumstances whatever.

The implication that the United States flag was not visible and the
implication that the identification markings were in any way inadequate
are both unrealistic and inaccurate.

3. See Goulding, *Confirm or Deny,* p. 123, for an account of the circumstances of the story.
4. Goulding, p. 123, and wire-service stories.

The identification markings of U.S. Naval vessels have proven satisfactory for international recognition for nearly 200 years.[5]

The ship's mission became an issue in Washington when the press quoted an officer on *America* as saying: "To put it bluntly, she was there to spy for us. Russia does the same thing. We moved in close to monitor the communications of both Egypt and Israel. We have to. We must be informed of what's going on in a matter of seconds."[6]

Messages came out of the Pentagon telling everyone to pipe down. "No comment" was the only acceptable answer to questions about spying.

Somehow failing to get the word, Vice Admiral Martin, when asked about *Liberty*'s mission, gave the answer that governments always give to such questions: "I emphatically deny she was a spy ship," he said.[7]

Finally, in an effort to maintain some credibility and to avoid conflicting stories, McNamara clamped a news lid on all *Liberty* stories until the official Court of Inquiry report could be published. He asked the Navy to expedite the report and issued a statement that read as follows:

> Many rumors and reports about the attack have been circulating. The Department of Defense has no evidence to support some of these rumors and reports. Others appear to be based on partial evidence. Some appear to be accurate on the basis of present information here, which is incomplete. Until the Court has had an opportunity to obtain the full facts, the Department of Defense will have no further comment.[8]

This "intriguing piece of prose," as it was described by Fred Farrar of the Chicago *Tribune*, was issued to everyone in or near the Sixth Fleet. It became an order to be followed. Nothing was to be said to the press. And with that order went the last hope of countering the wildly inaccurate stories that were being circulated and widely accepted.

On Sunday, Rear Admiral Isaac C. Kidd[9] came aboard *Liberty*

---

5. Goulding, p. 124, and wire-service stories.
6. Goulding, p. 124, and wire-service stories.
7. Goulding, p. 125; Norfolk *Virginian-Pilot*, June 11, 1967, p. A6; and wire-service stories.
8. Goulding, p. 130; SECDEF message 141747Z June 1967.
9. Rear Admiral Isaac Campbell Kidd, Jr.: born 1919; U.S. Naval Academy, class of 1941; promoted to rear admiral September 1, 1964. A rapidly rising star, he would be promoted to

with a small staff to head the Navy Court of Inquiry assigned to investigate the incident. I had seen this exceptional man operate and knew him for the tough, brilliant, personable and ambitious genius that he was. I remembered the blizzard of 1965, when the Pentagon was snowed in and virtually nothing moved in or around Washington. Isaac C. Kidd reported to his office as usual; he drove in behind a Navy snowplow.

The admiral came to *Liberty* from the destroyer USS *Barry* before dawn on Sunday morning. He moved into Lieutenant Commander Dave Lewis's now-empty stateroom, next to the captain's on the 02 level and, after meeting Captain McGonagle and discussing the incident briefly with him, removed the intimidating stars from his collar, as was his custom, and circulated among the crew.

He had, of course, been instructed by his seniors to "keep everything in perspective." Modern diplomacy simply does not permit one to embarrass a "friendly" nation, even when that nation is caught red-handed with its torpedo in one's ship. There are indications that Admiral Kidd did not accept those orders easily, and there are reports from an officer in Norfolk that he complained of the restrictions placed upon him, but he was too much a part of the system not to follow orders. And after all, this order came from the Commander-in-Chief, the President of the United States, Lyndon B. Johnson.

One can suppose that President Johnson was also tormented by the order, having so recently and so strongly reacted to the question of the attack being "plausible." By now, though, the Department of State had entered the picture, and the question of diplomacy and "perspective," as Philip Armstrong had so clearly prophesied, overcame the facts.

Admiral Kidd would be required to collect evidence, to screen witnesses, to complete a report for the record; he would not be expected to collect or publish a lot of embarrassing detail about wind speed, identification markings, extent and duration of reconnaissance, or intensity of attack, and he would not be expected to discuss the fleet's failure to provide air protection. Such details would cause untold diplomatic and political problems. So, before the formal court interviewed *Liberty* sailors, it would be prudent for the admiral to talk privately with the potential witnesses to learn what they might

---

vice admiral October 1,1969, and to admiral December 1, 1971. He retired from the Navy in 1978.

be expected to say and to decide who should be called to testify and what questions they should be asked in court.

This process went on until the ship arrived in Malta. "Just think of me as some old chief," he told the crew as he worked his way quietly through the ship, chatting informally with small groups of men. A few men were invited to the admiral's state-room for extended conversation. At this point the investigation was casual and informal; all conversations were unofficial and quite off the record.

=====

In Washington, meanwhile, officers and senior civilians who had participated in *Liberty*'s scheduling were summoned to an almost-unprecedented Saturday afternoon meeting. McTighe, Fossett, Raven, Brewer and others were ushered into a smoke-filled room occupied by shirt-sleeved men.

Walter G. Deeley stared grimly from behind a pile of documents at the head of the table. Deeley was a senior Defense Department executive of "supergrade" rank, and he was clearly impatient with the task that had been suddenly thrust upon him. "Can you write?" he snarled. His eyeglasses hung askew on broken frames, giving him a wild and cockeyed look, but Deeley seemed not to know or care. "Well, damn it, write down some reasons for sending that ship out there."

Fossett wrote. "*Liberty* was sent to the eastern Mediterranean in order to provide VHF and UHF communication coverage," he said.

"Good. Good. Line-of-sight comms. That makes sense," said Deeley. "Now write *why* you needed that kind of coverage. Who needed it? What for? Write it all down."

Deeley's group spent the weekend questioning everyone they could find who had any connection with the decision to ask the Joint Chiefs of Staff to divert *Liberty* to Gaza. When they were finished, they had compiled a report more than two inches thick consisting of statements, charts, background information, fold-outs and multicolored transparent overlays. Prominently displayed on page one was the message to JCS asking to have the ship moved away from the contested coast.

Deeley's masterpiece discusses the technical reasons for sending *Liberty* to Gaza in the first place and explains the decision to move the ship away from the coast. The report establishes that Deeley and his organization were not at fault; it does not discuss a cover-up of the circumstances of the attack—and Deeley's group seems unaware of any cover-up effort.

A few hours after the group finished its work, the report was reproduced on a rush basis in a Department of Defense print shop manned by specially cleared lithographers, and was distributed on a strict need-to-know basis to a small number of senior officials. Despite repeated Freedom of Information Act inquiries, the government has resisted acknowledging even the existence of this report.

=====

Captain McGonagle was regaining his strength and, while Admiral Kidd slept, entertained a small group of visitors in his cabin. Recalling that Dr. Kiepfer's supply of medicinal alcohol had been an important morale booster in the hours following the attack, McGonagle decided that his guests might appreciate some of the same spirits.

Locating Dr. Kiepfer by telephone in the wardroom, he asked, tongue in cheek, "Do you have any more of that medicinal alcohol? I think you could prescribe some for our visitors to help them recuperate from the rigors of their journey."

"Certainly, Captain," Kiepfer said. "Give me five minutes. I'll bring it up to your cabin."

Kiepfer knew that the medicinal alcohol had long since been consumed. Not one to be caught unprepared, he quickly rounded up the empties (which he had been careful to preserve) and brought them to a stateroom that had become a collection point for the many *un*medicinal spirits that had been turning up. Breaking the seal on an imperial quart of brandy, Kiepfer carefully filled the tiny medicinal alcohol containers. Then he restored the larger bottle to its hiding place and gathered up the smaller ones, which the captain and his guests could consume with clear conscience.

Only as he prepared to leave did he notice that the bunk was occupied. Kiepfer had forgotten that this room was now assigned to Admiral Kidd, who—driven suddenly to bed with a severe bronchial infection—had quietly watched the entire operation.

=====

On Saturday, *Papago* recovered the body of a *Liberty* sailor that had been swept through the hole in the ship's side. Other bodies were lost, along with a more or less steady flow of paper, much of it presumed to contain sensitive information. Men on both ships were detailed to watch for bodies or for paper, and at night *Papago* swept the water with a searchlight. Although no more bodies were found, every so often a large amount of paper would be seen leaving the ship, and this would be reported to *Papago* by flashing light. *Papago* would retrieve what it could, and what it could not retrieve it would try to destroy by backing over it with the ship's screws.

On Sunday it was decided that if the hole could not be patched, at least it should be possible to control what passed through it, and for this effort the deck department officer, Ensign Lucas, and the damage control officer, Ensign Scott, worked together. Four cargo nets were located, each twenty feet square. Boatswain's mates laid them out on *Liberty*'s main deck and tied their edges together to form one huge net forty feet square. Then the net was lowered over the side and tied in place, with the top edge just below the water. Finally, Bob Roberts and his divers from *Papago* spread the net so that it covered most of the torpedo hole, and held it in place with long lines that they carried under the ship and passed up to men who waited on the port side.

With lines girdling the ship to hold the netting in place—already nicknamed a "brassiere" by the crew—the ships resumed their slow journey toward Malta. The netting was swept away almost as soon as the ship reached speed, and it was cut loose to avoid catching in the screws. No further attempts were made to cover the hole.

———

Numerous musters of the crew were held, and somehow each muster was different from every other muster. Men who had been reported missing turned up hard at work in some distant repair party. Jeff Carpenter, now aboard *America* for treatment, missed the list of those transferred. No one remembered seeing him, and he was reported missing, presumed dead; and in due course his wife received a telegram from Washington, advising her of his presumed demise. At about the same time she received another telegram, this one sent by her husband from *America,* assuring her of his good health. Confused and frightened, she placed a call to her congressman, asking that he find out what was going on.

Presumably, other confused wives called their congressmen also. Soon *Liberty* was besieged with angry messages from the Navy in Washington, advising the ship of insistent congressional inquiries and demanding a prompt and correct muster report.

Golden had had enough. Now he would take the most careful,

complete muster in the history of the Navy. After advising the captain of his intentions and obtaining his concurrence, Golden stopped the ship in mid-ocean. He secured the main engines. He secured every piece of equipment that required a man near it. He called every man on the ship, assembled them in ranks on the main deck, and had them kept there while he personally searched the entire ship for the inevitable ignoramus who wouldn't otherwise get the word. Finally satisfied that every man alive and aboard *Liberty* was standing in rank on the main deck, he walked from man to man with a clipboard and checked off each name.

=====

While *Liberty* steamed toward Malta, the Naval Hospital at Naples was told to prepare for fifty wounded *Liberty* survivors. The hospital staff promptly discharged all but the most needy patients in order to make room for the new arrivals; except for two maternity cases and one officer with jaundice, the hospital was emptied. Leaves were canceled as doctors and nurses were put on special alert to await the *Liberty* wounded.

America, however, had decided that most of the wounded could be treated on board after all, and—without informing the hospital—kept all but six men in the ship. Four men with brain injuries were sent to an Army hospital in Landstuhl, Germany, while a man with a broken arm and I were sent to Naples for treatment; the rest stayed in the carrier. Electronic Technician Barry Timmerman and I arrived after dusk to find a fully staffed and nearly empty hospital eager to care for us.

Separated from my traveling companion, I was placed in a private room where I was fed, bathed and powdered, and introduced to Barbara, Joyce and Felicity, who would be my nurses. The doctor prescribed whiskey, which I drank. Lovely Australian-born Felicity provided tender care. And my outlook began to improve.

=====

Tuesday evening, just hours before the ship's arrival in Malta, McGonagle summoned Dr. Kiepfer to his cabin. "I'd like you to read the statement I have prepared for the Court of Inquiry," he said.

Several pages long, the statement elaborated upon the report that McGonagle had recited to Bennett on the day of the attack and that had been sent by message to Washington. It contained the same errors, the same omissions.

Although Kiepfer was unaware of the extent of preattack reconnaissance, he clearly remembered numerous strafing runs extending
over a considerable period of time, and he knew the ship was fired
upon after the torpedo explosion. He knew that McGonagle had been
under incredible strain, that he was still sick and distraught—that he
was, in fact, still in pain and quite weak from wounds and from loss
of blood. No one man could be expected to recall the details of this
attack, least of all McGonagle, who was too busy reacting and
fighting to accurately report such abstract particulars as duration,
time, number, sequence and intensity.

Gently, Kiepfer tried to explain the discrepancies that he saw. And
McGonagle seemed not to hear. McGonagle did not take advice well
anyway, particularly from junior officers, and he did not accept
Kiepfer's version of the attack. After all, Kiepfer spent most of the
battle below decks, treating wounded men. McGonagle had already
reported his version of the incident by message, and he was not going
to change the story now. Kiepfer wondered why he had been called.

In the ensuing conversation it became clear that McGonagle was
worried: "I want you to remember that Admiral Kidd is not coming
here to give us medals," he said. "I don't know what we did wrong,
but if they look hard enough they can find something. We don't have
to help them. I'm going to answer their questions and no more, and
I don't expect you to do any more than that."

During the evening he had a similar conversation with Lieutenant
Golden. Like Kiepfer, the engineer officer suggested tactfully that
the attack had involved more than the six strafing runs and single
torpedo that McGonagle described, but the captain insisted that his
report was accurate. He would acknowledge no errors and would
consider no changes in his report.

During the next few days, McGonagle cautioned officers and key
enlisted men who might testify before the court. Once he assembled
a group of officers and chief petty officers in the wardroom and told
them, "Our best course of action is don't volunteer a thing. Answer
their questions, but don't tell them anything you don't have to tell
them."

McGonagle seemed tormented by the idea that he was somehow
responsible for the agony his ship and crew had suffered. Where had
he gone wrong? Should he have moved away from shore? Did the
presence of men in battle dress in the gun mounts cause *Liberty* to
appear hostile? Did the ship stray into Egyptian waters? Had he
trained the crew properly to handle emergencies? Had the crew

responded properly to *this* emergency? Had he? Could he have *saved* those men?

Thirty-four of his men were dead, but nearly three hundred were alive despite an encounter with a force hellbent on murdering every last man; and McGonagle's training, example, leadership and inspiration had kept them alive.

This brave man, who had defied bullets, shrapnel and napalm, now seemed worried that he might not have done enough. This man, who had remained at his post under impossible conditions in a performance that had saved his ship, now seemed concerned that he might have done more. And apparently he feared the court that had come to investigate.

=====

On Wednesday, the day *Liberty* arrived in Malta and the day the Court of Inquiry convened in formal session, the hospital's executive officer brought me a message from the Department of State. Israel's ambassador to Italy wanted to talk with me. Would I consent to see him?

I was the first *Liberty* officer ashore. The others were all either still aboard the ship, or wounded and aboard *America,* or dead. I considered the alternatives. If he came, he would no doubt convey condolences and an apology. It would be inappropriate for me to accept or reject an apology. Anyway, I was convinced that the attack was deliberate, premeditated murder. And as a junior officer, I certainly could not allow myself to be rude or angry to this man whose visit, no doubt, was offered in good faith and in ignorance of the background for the attack.

"No," I said.

=====

On Thursday, Jim O'Connor, Dave Lewis, Ensign Dick "Slippery" Taylor (*Liberty*'s supply officer), Seaman George Wilson and twenty others arrived in Naples from USS *America.* Higher authority had finally directed the carrier to send *Liberty*'s wounded to shore-based hospitals. Although the ship was probably capable of handling most of them, the presence of a large number of wounded men in her medical department impaired the ship's combat readiness, she was told, so the men would have to go.

Now Naples became a battle scene. The hospital staff manned the operating room more or less continually for two days as they extended the treatment of our scraggly group. Most of the men were ambulatory. Many were in pain. Some wanted to return to our ship, but few were allowed to do so. And three men with large bleeding wounds who had convinced *America*'s doctors that they were in good health had been ordered back to duty. These men were intercepted at the local airport by the Naples Hospital medical staff, and were reexamined and rehospitalized.

To prevent unauthorized contact with the outside world, guards were stationed at each door of the *Liberty* men's ward. If it became necessary for a man to leave the ward, a guard went along.

Jim O'Connor became my roommate again. He was walking now and feeling chipper. The large wound in his side was healing, and he found that if he moved carefully, he could take a shower. With a look of satisfaction, he walked gingerly from the room, toward the showers.

He returned in pain, face ashen, biting his lower lip to control the screaming. He leaned against the doorway, holding his side, then lurched toward his bed, where he pulled his knees up toward his chest and groaned. I called for a nurse.

"No, I can't call a doctor in surgery. No, I can't get anything for the pain," announced an officious nurse, not Barbara, Joyce or Felicity. The doctors were all in surgery and the nurses would not call them.

Jim was in agony, and it seemed that nothing could be done until all of the day's scheduled surgery was completed. Finally, after more than four hours of unnecessary misery, a surgeon stopped to see him. Recognizing the problem immediately, the doctor called a local Italian urologist in for consultation. This man confirmed the diagnosis. Jim's kidney was riddled with shrapnel and probably would have to be removed.

A few minutes later a Navy helicopter settled near a rear door of the hospital, where Jim was loaded aboard for the short trip to the local public airport. A military airplane was waiting. Later that afternoon he joined other *Liberty* survivors at the Army hospital in Landstuhl, West Germany, where, as predicted, the kidney was removed. As at Naples, guards stood at each door of the *Liberty* men's ward.

———

Meanwhile, *Liberty* had arrived in Valletta, Malta, shortly after sunrise on Wednesday, six days after the attack. She was accom-

panied by the destroyer *Davis* and fleet tug *Papago,* and spent most
of the day standing in the harbor. During the afternoon she was
moved into a dry dock.

The grim task of removing the remains of friends and shipmates
could only be done by the men who had worked there. That left
perhaps fifty men for the initial cleanup of the torpedoed spaces. For
security reasons, no one else was admitted to the compartment.

As water was pumped from the dry dock, *Liberty* settled heavily
on huge blocks previously placed on the dry-dock bottom; and as the
water level around her dropped, so did the water level within the
ship. From outside, nothing could be seen, as a previously placed
canvas awning effectively screened the torpedo hole in *Liberty*'s side.

A group of sailors crouched in awe around the single interior
access to the space, the second-deck hatch through which so many
had so narrowly escaped only a few days before. For days they had
imagined what they would find here; now they saw, and no one was
prepared for the experience.

The ladder was still in place, but little more was recognizable. The
ladder these men had descended so many times had ended in a small
corridor, and leading from the corridor had been a number of doors
to the surrounding offices. No longer was there a corridor. The doors
and supporting bulkheads were gone. The several offices were now
one oversized compartment, and strewn wildly about were the
twisted sheet-metal bulkheads, desks, file cabinets and communication equipment. All this was covered with a thick film of black oil
from ruptured tanks nearby. The smell of oil mixed with the stink
of death to suggest the horror within, but only the hardware could
be seen as the men surveyed the room from above. A body had been
pulled through the hatch shortly after the attack; another had floated
free and had been found by *Papago* in *Liberty*'s wake. The men knew
that twenty-three of their friends were still here.

The odor was overwhelming. "Oh, bloody shit!" announced a
pink-faced seaman as he decided that he didn't want to be here.

"Oh, wow!" said another.

A man threw up. Another cried.

The group fell silent until a young sailor, more brazen than most,
stepped forward. "The longer we wait, the harder it will be," he said,
mounting the ladder.

"Careful! Slippery."

"No sweat," he said.

He wore overalls and gloves and his boot-camp marching shoes.

Descending the ladder, he found firm footing near the bottom. Clipped to his belt was a Navy-issue flashlight, which he now removed to help survey the dimly lighted room, otherwise il-luminated only by light from the hatch and from the canvas-covered torpedo hole.

He kept up a running commentary as he swept the room with his flashlight. "This is gonna be hell! Oil is everywhere. Bulkheads all down. Looks like half the stuff here is pushed into one corner. No bodies that I can see. Must be under the equipment. Here's a desk. On its side. Oh! OW! OH!"

He dropped the flashlight.

The men above could not see what frightened him as he stepped back, slipped on the oily metal, scrambled to get his footing, slipped again, and finally got a handhold on the ladder. Whining in uncon-trollable gasps, he scrambled up the ladder, hands and feet slipping on oil in wild panic until he came within reach of the many arms that extended from the hatch to help him.

Hoisted through the hatch, he stammered helplessly, unable to speak. Finally, he crouched on deck with his head between his knees and shivered. Then he cried.

"What the hell is down there?"

He couldn't answer. He could only sob.

It was a long time before anyone else braved the slippery black hole to find out what was down there. The next man to try found a shipmate, six days dead, fully clothed and impaled on some stray pipe that held him, with toes just touching the ground, eyes and mouth open, guarding the ladder. And overhead, caught in the pipes and electrical wiring, a long-dead officer blankly surveyed the scene.

For several days these men worked continuously at their terrible task. Secret papers and publications had to be sorted from the wreck-age and destroyed. Twisted steel plates, aluminum sheets and sup-porting beams had to be cut away—usually by hand, because power tools could not be used amid the inflammable oil. And the bodies of shipmates had to be located, identified and, too often, assembled.

Officers and men worked together—the stink growing ever worse in the June Maltese heat—and when it was done, three men, appar-ently swept away and into the sea, could not be accounted for. Three others could not be identified. These were eventually buried, along with stray limbs and other unidentifiable parts, in a mass grave at Arlington National Cemetery.

Newsweek, meanwhile, published the following story:

SINKING OF THE LIBERTY: ACCIDENT OR DESIGN?

The Israeli attack on the naval communications ship U.S.S. Liberty has left a wake of bitterness and political charges of the most serious sort. First of all, the Liberty was no ordinary vessel but an intelligence-gathering ship on a "ferret" mission. It carried elaborate gear to locate both Israeli and Egyptian radio and radar and to monitor and tape all military messages sent from command posts to the battlefield. Although Israel's apologies were officially accepted, some high Washington officials believe the Israelis knew the Liberty's capabilities and suspect that the attack might not have been accidental. One top-level theory holds that someone in the Israeli armed forces ordered the Liberty sunk because he suspected that it had taken down messages showing that Israel started the fighting. (A Pentagon official has already tried to shoot down the Israeli claim of "pilot error.") Not everyone in Washington is buying this theory, but some top Administration officials will not be satisfied until fuller and more convincing explanations of the attack on a clearly marked ship in international waters are forthcoming.[10]

This report, circulated even before Kidd's court convened in formal secret session, seemed to indicate that the administration was not entirely complacent about the "mistaken identity" claims coming from Israel and echoed in the Pentagon. *Liberty* officers rejoiced when they read it. It seemed to us to be the most perceptive paragraph yet written on the subject. It personally rankled Israel's General Yitzhak Rabin ("General Rabin has never been so angry," a senior Israeli officer informed the U.S. naval attaché), and it drew an immediate reaction from the government of Israel:

Such allegations are just malicious. Such stories are untrue and without any foundation whatever. It was an unfortunate and tragic accident which occurred in an area where fierce land and air fighting took place in recent days.

Philip Goulding *(Confirm or Deny)* describes the final sentence of that reply as "typical of Israel's casual attitude toward the episode, an attitude which suggested from the beginning that it was really our

10. *Newsweek,* June 19, 1967.

fault for being there in the first place." Indeed, it was more than a suggestion. As we shall see, messages from Israel directly charged that a share of the blame was McGonagle's for being there at all—a presence which, Israel said, demonstrated a "lack of care" and contributed to *Liberty*'s identification as an enemy ship.

A few days after the *Newsweek* story, the Shreveport *Times* suggested in an emotional editorial that our government was involved in a cover-up and—in a fresh slant on the motive of the attackers—that the attack itself may have been conducted to prevent the ship (and the United States) from prematurely detecting the pending invasion of Syria:

> The tragic and vicious attack is becoming more and more shocking daily as hitherto covered-up details become public. What adds to the shock is that much of the coverup has been made more by Washington than by Israel.
>
> Almost as shocking as the attack itself has been the manner in which Washington—especially the Defense Department—has seemed to try to absolve Israel from any guilt right from the start. Some of these efforts would be laughable but for the terrible tragedy involved.
>
> But there are some 34 American mothers and fathers, perhaps also wives and children of those 34 American sailors who died in a reckless tragedy for which not an iota of *logical* excuse has been made public so far by Israel or Washington. Yet, in the Pentagon, various so-called excuses have been "slipped" to the communications media reporters, ranging from "the sun was in the eyes of the torpedo boat captain"; "it was mistaken identity"; "it was a still day and the flag may have hung limp" (the Liberty captain says it was unfurled) to "they probably thought the Liberty was Egyptian."
>
> When the Pentagon announced the attack on June 8, it stated without qualification that the attack was by mistaken identity, that Israel had apologized, that the U.S. had accepted the apology. In other words, it was all over. Too bad about the dead and their families. Just forget it all.
>
> There may be significance to the timetable of what was going on in Tel Aviv, in Washington and in the United Nations at New York as the Liberty arrived at its East Mediterranean post, and on the day it was attacked, and on the day after it was attacked. For example:
>
> June 7: The Liberty took up its post off the Sinai Peninsula. In New York, Foreign Minister Abba Eban of Israel, who has rushed to New York from Tel Aviv to tell Israel's case to the world through the U.N., was proclaiming that "only Israel has accepted the U.N. cease fire mandate." Later developments showed that even as Abba Eban spoke, Israel was massing columns of tanks, sizable forces of mechanized infantry, and

squadrons of jet warplanes on the Syrian border *for invasion of Syria.*

Israel had shut down Government House in Jerusalem, the U.N.'s Middle East headquarters for its observers. Thus, the U.N. Security Council was barred, by Israel, from getting the truth from its own Middle East observers about cease fire progress or observance. There was no normal way for the U.S. or the U.N. to learn of the military buildup at the Syrian border; except that the Liberty now was only 15 miles offshore from Egypt and Israel and only 90 miles from Tel Aviv.

June 8: The Liberty was put out of action by Israel.

June 9: Israel invaded Syria, an act that was almost as big a shock to the world as the war itself.

Whether this timetable is meaningful or meaningless we do not know. Only Washington and Tel Aviv can say. But the American people— especially the families of American sailors so pitifully and ruthlessly slain —have a right to know who ordered the attack on the Liberty. The ship's senior crewmen testified they believed the attack was by intent in full knowledge that the ship was American.[11]

The Shreveport *Times* editorial was typical of widespread demands for a better explanation of what happened to the ship. What set the *Times* apart (aside from its choleric tone) was that this was the first public speculation on a specific motive for the attack.

As we shall see, evidence suggests that the Shreveport *Times* was correct: *Liberty* was indeed attacked to prevent her from detecting and reporting preparations for the Syrian invasion. For that aspect to be explored, *Liberty* crewmen would have had to talk freely and openly with the press. And few *Liberty* crewmen ever got that chance.

Sailors were reminded daily—by their division officers, by notes in the ship's Plan-of-the-Day, and personally by Admiral Kidd in meetings he held before arrival in Malta—that *nothing* could be said to the press: "Refer all questions to the commanding officer or executive officer or to Admiral Kidd. Answer no questions. If somehow you are backed into a corner, then you may say that it was an accident and that Israel has apologized. You may say nothing else."

When reporters approached the ship for interviews, they were told that nothing could be said until the Court of Inquiry had completed its work. Once the report was published, the Navy said, the blackout would end and the men would be free to talk to the press. But this was not to be.

11. The Shreveport *Times,* July 18, 1967.

Chapter 10

THE COURT OF INQUIRY

While COMSIXTHFLT supposedly had [*Liberty*] under his operational control, this was a misnomer. Her movements were not being directed by COMSIXTHFLT but by the JCS in view of her recognized high risk mission.

Statement for Court of Inquiry by Deputy Chief of Staff, Commander-in-Chief, U.S. Naval Forces, Europe

A Navy Court of Inquiry is a formal fact-finding body convened to investigate an incident involving substantial loss of life or possible significant international or legal consequences. Its purpose, says the Navy's governing directive, is to "formulate clearly expressed and consistent findings of fact [in order to] inform authorities of the Department of the Navy fully and concisely as to the incident, its causes, and the responsibility therefor." It is an administrative, not judicial, body; its report is purely advisory.

The Court of Inquiry into the USS *Liberty* attack was convened at the direction of Vice Admiral McCain at his headquarters in London. Admiral McCain, in a letter to Admiral Kidd dated June 10, 1967, charged Kidd to "inquire into all the pertinent facts and circumstances leading to and connected with the armed attack; damage resulting therefrom; and deaths of and injuries to Naval personnel."

The court consisted of Kidd as president and Captains Bernard J.

Lauff and Bert M. Atkinson as members. Assigned as counsel to the court was Captain Ward M. Boston, Jr., a Navy legal officer. Assistant counsel was Lieutenant Commander Allen Feingersch, a thirty-four-year-old surface-warfare officer. Chief Petty Officer Joeray Spencer was assigned as recorder.

The first crew member was examined in the *Liberty* wardroom immediately after breakfast on June 14 while the ship rested at anchor in the Malta harbor. Ensign David Lucas testified for nearly three hours, providing vivid recollections of events on and around the bridge during much of the attack, but his recollections grew hazy and seemingly contradictory when questioned about the *sequence* of events. Despite persistent questioning by Kidd, Lucas was unable to estimate how much time passed between the torpedo explosion and the offer of help, and could not recall whether or not the ship had been fired upon during that period. To Lucas, much of the chaos on the bridge was a timeless, disordered blur; although he recalled the details, he could not fit them into an orderly chronology.

Next to appear was McGonagle, who testified for about six hours on June 14 and 15, filling thirty-seven pages of legal-size transcript in the official record of the proceeding. McGonagle described the ship's mission, her operating orders, her location in international waters and the navigational situation. He told the court of the ship's hasty departure from Abidjan and of her transit across the Mediterranean Sea. He described the normal operating routine of the ship, told of the type of reconnaissance ordinarily experienced, and alluded to an incident in which a minor African dictator had once attempted to board the ship by force. He described the preattack reconnaissance in some detail. Like Lucas, he provided lucid descriptions of the situation as seen from the bridge during battle; unlike Lucas, he professed nearly total recall. Inexplicably, many of his key recollections were wrong.

In direct examination by the court, McGonagle testified:

During the 0800 to 1200 watch on the morning of 8 June, at about 1030, a flight of two unidentified jet aircraft orbited the ship at about 10,000 feet, three times at a distance of approximately two miles. It was not possible to identify any insignia on the aircraft and their identity remains unknown. [McGonagle also described a small patrol plane seen during the morning flying along the coast at an altitude of about 500 feet.] At about 1056 . . . an aircraft similar to an American flying boxcar crossed astern of the ship at a distance of three to five miles, [then] circled the ship . . . and headed back toward the Sinai Peninsula. This aircraft continued to return in a somewhat similar fashion approximately at 30 minute intervals. It was not possible to see any markings on the aircraft and [its] identity remains unknown. This aircraft did not approach the ship in any provocative manner.[1]

Portions of a statement I signed in Naples were read to the court in the presence of Captain McGonagle:

The flying boxcar was usually close enough that I could see the pilot. It had a Star of David under one wing. On at least one occasion the Captain was on the bridge as the airplane passed directly overhead at very low level. We stood together as we saw it approaching. The Captain said, "If you see those bomb bay doors start to open, order an immediate hard right turn."[2]

"Captain McGonagle, can you account for the differences between your testimony and the statement by Lieutenant Ennes?" the court asked.

"No, sir, I cannot, except that I would like to point out that the statement is inconsistent with my own testimony before this court, and it is not confirmed in the ship's logs."

This ambiguous reply went unquestioned. Lookouts, gunners and bridge personnel who could have described the preattack reconnaissance were not asked to testify, and I was never advised of the challenge to my story or asked to explain the discrepancies.[3]

McGonagle described the onset of the attack:

About 1400 lookouts . . . reported . . . jet aircraft . . . in the vicinity of the ship. . . . I went to the starboard wing of the bridge . . . and there observed one aircraft . . . similar . . . to the two aircraft which were sighted earlier in the day and upon which a sighting report had been submitted. The relative bearing of this plane was about 135, its position

1. All of McGonagle's testimony (here condensed) is taken from the twenty-eight-page officially released *Unclassified Transcript of Testimony and Summary of Proceedings of Navy Court of Inquiry into the Attack on USS LIBERTY.*

2. This statement is reconstructed from memory and cannot be found in any of the court records that have been released.

3. This exchange was described to me by a ship's officer. It cannot be found in any available record of the Court of Inquiry.

Liberty, bristling with special-purpose antennae.

The assault was initiated by French-built high-performance Mirage jets armed with cannon and rockets. Later, slower Mystère jets (pictured here in photograph taken by McGonagle) followed up with napalm and more rockets.

INSET: Two men died in the forward gun tubs while trying to defend the ship.

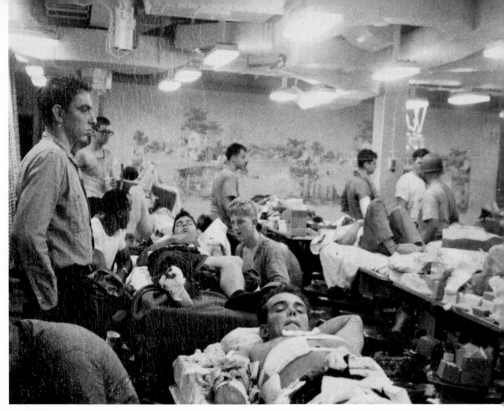

The crew's mess hall was used as an emergency hospital.

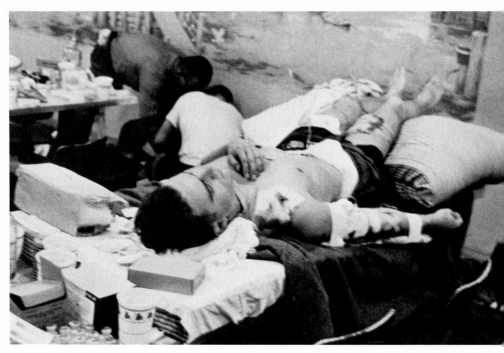

Mattresses were placed on tables and on the deck between tables. The ship's doctor and three medical corpsmen worked through the night to save dozens of seriously wounded men.

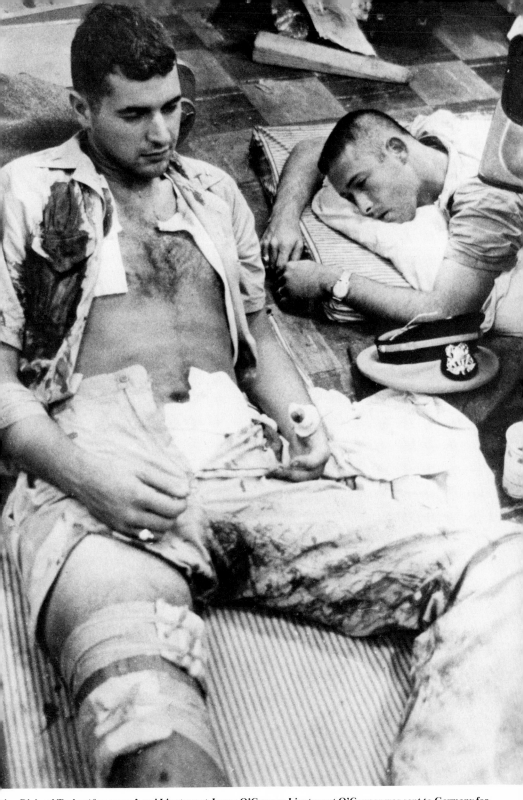

sign Richard Taylor (*foreground*) and Lieutenant James O'Connor. Lieutenant O'Connor was sent to Germany for
ergency surgery to remove a shrapnel-riddled kidney.

President Johnson called his advisors to an emergency meeting while the ship was still under attack, but White House intervention prevented any timely rescue attempt.

INSET: The superstructure was a solid mass of flame from direct napalm hits.

The torpedo tore a forty-foot hole in *Liberty*'s starboard side, killed twenty-five men, and caused a nine-degree list.

THE WHITE HOUSE
WASHINGTON

Thursday, June 8, 1967
10:15 a.m.

Mr. President:

The LIBERTY is listing badly to starboard.

W. W. Rostow

er the ship was disabled by aircraft cannon, rockets and napalm, torpedo boats were sent in for the kill.

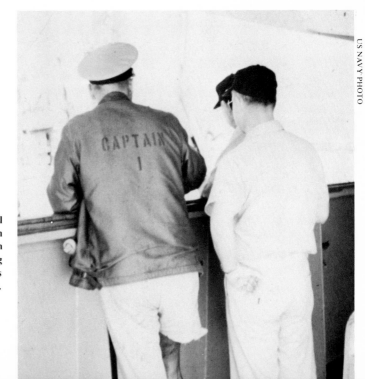

A Navy destroyer with medical assistance arrived seventeen hours after the attack. Captain McGonagle's trouser leg had been removed to treat his wound.

The full extent of the torpedo damage was revealed only after dry-docking at Malta.

INSET: **Rear Admiral Isaac Kidd** (*arrow*) joined the ship at sea to conduct a court of inquiry.

When bulkheads near the flooded compartment threatened to collapse, they were supported by a sturdy complex of timber and steel braces. Ensign John Scott, shown here, supervised the ship's damage control teams.

Lieutenant Painter helped calm hysterical crewmen after the torpedo explosion.

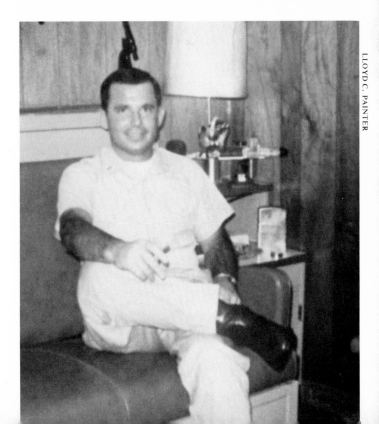

The crew worked for several days to remove bodies and clean up the torpedoed compartment.

Lieutenant George Golden, the engineer officer (*right*; shown here with Captain McGonagle), evacuated the engine room when warned of an approaching torpedo, and ran the engineering plant almost alone.

Left to right: Lieutenant Commander Philip Armstrong; Chief Petty Officer Harold Thompson; Chief Petty Officer Joseph Benkert; Chief Petty Officer Melvin Smith. A few days after this picture was taken, Armstrong and Smith were dead; all four men were cited for heroism or exceptional performance.

Despite a dangerous skull wound, Lieutenant (jg) David Lucas remained on the bridge during the worst of the battle. Here Captain McGonagle presents Lucas with a Silver Star medal for heroism. Both men were promoted after the attack.

A *Liberty* working party, resting from the grim task of recovering dead shipmates from the torpedoed compartment.

angle was 45 or 50 degrees, its elevation approximately 7,000 feet, and it was approximately five to six miles from the ship.

The airplane could not have been in the position McGonagle says, because McGonagle has described an impossible triangle; his report is in error by perhaps 300 percent. If the airplane *was* about 45 degrees above the horizon, as McGonagle says, then its altitude and its distance over the water from the ship must have been nearly identical. Other errors, not so easy to demonstrate but of similar magnitude, exist throughout his testimony.

The reader will recall that the first report of approaching aircraft was made by radar operators who detected high-performance aircraft at sixteen miles, bearing 082°. As the aircraft faded from the surface-search radar screen they were replaced by surface craft, again reported by radar operators at sixteen miles, bearing 082°. Lloyd Painter, as officer of the deck, also spotted the boats on radar and summoned the captain to see: "Captain, you gotta look at this! I never saw anything move so fast."

Then came the report from the radar operators that the boats were approaching at thirty-five knots. At that speed they would be along-side in about thirty minutes—time for the aircraft to disable *Liberty* before the torpedo boats arrived to finish her off.

The fact that the boats and the aircraft approached from the same direction at ideal intervals to deal a fatal one-two body blow smacks of a planned, coordinated attack—which is exactly what it was. But no such testimony was published by the Court of Inquiry.

———

McGonagle's testimony continues:

> Within a couple of minutes a loud explosion [came] from the port side of the ship. I immediately ordered the general alarm to be sounded, and this was done. . . . two 55-gallon gasoline drums . . . were burning furiously. [Moments later] the ship received an apparent bomb hit in the vicinity of the whaleboat stowed on the . . . starboard side, immediately aft of the bridge. Mr. Armstrong, Mr. O'Connor and others in the bridge area were thrown back into the bridge and other personnel in the pilot house were blown from their feet.

As I have described earlier, the initial attack, in which I was wounded as I stood on the ship's highest deck stupidly facing the approaching aircraft, hammered *Liberty* with at least two to three *dozen* rockets. The rockets arrived in staccato fashion, peppering the ship with rapid-sequence explosions, lifting the gunners bodily from the gun tubs, tossing them into the air, and only incidentally causing an explosion in the motor whaleboat. The gasoline explosion did not occur until the arrival of the *second* airplane, and by that time O'Connor was already wounded and so bloodied and helpless that some of the crew thought he was dead.

═══

The captain continues:

> It seemed to me that the attacks were made in a criss cross fashion over the ship, with each attack coming at approximately forty-five second to one minute intervals. . . . It is estimated that the total air attack was completed in approximately five to six minutes.

Those of us who were moving about the ship during the air attack know that no mortal could do so many things or be in so many places in five or six minutes; for example, Dr. Kiepfer and Corpsman Thomas VanCleave completed several surgical procedures during the air attack. Judging the duration of the attack from the work done, Kiepfer first guessed that the air attack lasted for an hour.

> In the latter moments of the air attack, it was noted that three high speed boats were approaching the ship from the northeast on a relative bearing of approximately 135 at a distance of 15 miles. . . . It is believed that the time of initial sighting of the torpedo boats was about 1420. The boats appeared to be in a wedge type formation with the center boat the lead point of the wedge. Estimated speed of the boats was about 27 to 30 knots.

Nowhere in the published testimony are we told that the boats were first detected by radar, approaching in a high-speed attack formation, moments *before* the first air strike.

> It appeared that they were approaching the ship in a torpedo launch attitude, and since I did not have direct communication with gun control or the gun mounts, I told [Seaman Apprentice Dale Larkins] to proceed to Mount 51 and take the boats under fire. . . .
> About this time I noticed that our Ensign had been shot away during the air attack and ordered [Signalman Russell David] to hoist a second

Ensign from the yardarm. During the air attack, our normal Ensign was flying. Before the torpedo attack, a holiday size ensign was hoisted. . . .

When the boats reached an approximate range of 2,000 yards, the center boat of the formation was signaling to us. . . . it appeared that they were flying an Israeli flag.

McGonagle *must* have been mistaken about sighting the Israeli flag at this point in the attack. For one thing, it would have been practically impossible to identify a tiny and wildly fluttering Star of David a mile away, particularly since any flags displayed by the torpedo boats would have streamed back, *away* from McGonagle and out of his line of sight.

I yelled to machine gun 51 . . . to hold fire [but] the man . . . fired a short burst at the boats before he was able to understand. . . . [Then] machine gun 53 began firing at the center boat. . . . At this time, they opened fire with their gun mounts and in a matter of seconds, one torpedo was noted crossing astern of the ship at about 25 yards. . . . without advance warning, the ship sustained a torpedo hit [and] took a 9 degree list to starboard. . . . The explosion caused the ship to come dead in the water. Steering control was lost. All power was lost. Immediately, I determined that the ship was in no danger of sinking and did not order any preparations to be made to abandon ship. It was my intention to ground the ship on shoal waters to the left of the ship's track to prevent its sinking if necessary.

Liberty men recall very clearly that the order *was* given to prepare to abandon ship. That order was passed by messenger, by sound-powered phone, and where it still worked, over the ship's general announcing system. In Main Engine Control, Lieutenant Golden received an order from the bridge to "disable the main engines and scuttle the ship." Elsewhere, orders came from the bridge to "demolish ship," and in the ship's log the entry was made, "1433—demolishion [sic] bill in affect [sic]."

======

McGonagle continues:

Immediately after the ship was struck by the torpedo, the torpedo boats stopped dead in the water and milled around astern of the ship at a range of approximately 500 to 800 yards. One of the boats signaled by flashing light, in English, "Do you require assistance?" We had no means to communicate with the boat by light but hoisted CODE LIMA INDIA [a flag-hoist signal meaning "I am not under command," not able to control movements of the ship]. The signal intended to convey the fact that the ship was maneuvering with difficulty and that they should keep clear.

In perhaps his only departure from 100 percent acceptance of McGonagle's testimony, Kidd did not support McGonagle's claim that the boats offered assistance "immediately," even though this timing tallied closely with a report from the government of Israel that assistance had been offered and refused at 1427; instead, Kidd concluded as a Top Secret "Finding of Fact" that the offer came from the boats "thirty minutes after attacking."[4] Even that finding is wrong, however. As we have seen, the flashing light and megaphone offer of assistance did not come until 1632, nearly *two hours after the torpedo explosion.* Much of the intervening time was spent machine-gunning our sailors as they attempted to extinguish the many still-raging fires; machine-gunning our life rafts, which had been put in the water in response to orders to prepare to abandon ship; and occasionally just drifting about with the engines apparently stopped, waiting for *Liberty* to sink.

McGonagle is an authentic hero of rare courage. He testified under tremendous strain; he was ill, weary, grief-stricken and apparently worried that he might be charged with some as-yet-unidentified offense. We don't know, perhaps we will never know, why his testimony is so wide of the mark. I belabor his testimony here not to diminish McGonagle—his stature is assured—but to demonstrate that much of what he said is *obviously* wrong and that his errors should have been clear (and *must* have been clear) to the Court of Inquiry.

Following the McGonagle interview, the court held rather limited interviews with twelve other *Liberty* officers and crewmen, finally reinterviewed McGonagle briefly to receive some records they had

4. Israel's claim to have offered help at 1427 corresponds exactly with McGonagle's initial message report that the torpedo attack occurred at that time. Actually, of course, the torpedo explosion came eight minutes later, and McGonagle, after correcting for clock error apparently caused by rocket explosions, eventually changed his report to read 1435. One suspects that Israel selected 1427 after reading McGonagle's initial report, which was broadcast in the clear on an uncovered radio circuit.

asked him to gather, and then adjourned on June 15 to return to London after two days of formal session aboard ship. Men who testified told me later that they felt deeply frustrated by the court's apparent lack of interest in details of the attack, its duration, intensity, the extent of preattack surveillance and the like. Most of the ship's officers, once they realized the shallowness of the questioning, dismissed the inquiry as "whitewash."

One officer whose testimony strayed repeatedly into areas not directly asked about was removed from the courtroom and privately reprimanded. "You are to answer the questions asked by the court and you are to say nothing else," he was told. "If testimony is desired in other areas, you will be asked about those areas." Another officer who left the narrow path that the questioning took was warned, "We don't want to hear about that."

What questions did the court ask? Little that might conflict with McGonagle's testimony. Nothing that might prove embarrassing to Israel. And testimony that *did* conflict with McGonagle or that tended to embarrass Israel was covered with a "Top Secret" label, if it was accepted by the court at all.

For instance, while McGonagle told the court that no order was given to prepare to abandon ship, Painter reported that such an order *was* given; Painter's testimony was ignored and no further questions were asked on that subject. After McGonagle described the air attack as having lasted five minutes, Painter and Thompson told the court that it lasted twenty to thirty minutes; their testimony was ignored and other crew members were not asked about the duration of the attack.

When the ship's radiomen reported the apparent jamming of *Liberty*'s radios, their testimony was classified "Top Secret" and was not followed up. Here was strong evidence that the attack was planned in advance and that our ship's identity was known to the attackers (for it is practically impossible to jam the radio circuits of a stranger), but this information was hushed up and no conclusions were drawn from it.

Several witnesses were asked about the flag. Scott testified that the flag was clearly displayed in the wind during his early morning watch and that he used it to help determine the wind direction; Lieutenant "Mac" Watson testified that he saw the flag flying during the noonhour reconnaissance and observed that it was extended in a breeze; Painter described the flag he saw in the morning when he came up to look at a reconnaissance airplane; Golden told the court that he saw the flag standing out in a breeze during the noon hour while reconnaissance aircraft flew over the ship; I filed an affidavit with the court in which I swore that the flag stood out all morning, clearly displayed in eight knots of wind; the ship's weather log recorded the precise wind reading each hour, proving positively that the relative wind was eight knots or more for most of the morning and was twelve knots shortly before the attack. And while the court was still in session, Kidd received a report that Israeli Defense Force aircraft had been heard reporting by radio to a ground station that they had made two or three identification passes over a ship that displayed an American flag—a ship which can only have been USS *Liberty*. All this evidence was ignored or classified "Top Secret," and was thus kept from public knowledge.

While several witnesses were anxious to establish for the record that napalm was used on *Liberty*, they found it difficult or impossible to testify about napalm. Ensign Lucas collected some jellied green goo from an unexploded napalm canister and presented it to the court in a medicine bottle. This the court accepted, although they seemed to Lucas to be oddly disinterested in it. The court *did* question Dr. Kiepfer about napalm burns among the survivors, but this exchange and the few other ambiguous references to napalm were classified "Top Secret" and thus kept from public knowledge.

Dr. Kiepfer, commissioned as a lieutenant after medical school, had been on active duty for less than nine months, and he was as unawed by brass as he was by the proceeding. "No one came to help us," he told the court. "We were promised help, but no help came," he said. "The Russians arrived before our own ships did," he told Admiral Kidd. "We asked for an escort before we ever came near the war zone, and we were turned down," he said.

The court bristled. This was not a line that the court intended to explore, and they told him so. "You *will* stick to the line of questioning, Doctor," Kidd snapped to end an exchange that is not to be found in the transcript. As with the others, Kiepfer was asked little that might conflict with the captain's testimony, and when he was finished he was told, as was each man who testified, "I am proud to be wearing the same uniform that you wear."

Other officers were asked about the state of readiness of the ship, the performance of the crew during the battle, the amount of training ordinarily conducted aboard *Liberty*, the attitude of the captain toward training. They were asked little more.

"Do you feel that Captain McGonagle permitted sufficient training in damage control procedures?" they were asked. "Did the crew respond expeditiously to drills?"[5]

———

Soon after the attack, Israel had offered a preliminary report of the circumstances. The message, telephoned to the embassy by Israel's Lieutenant Colonel Michael Bloch and copied verbatim by Commander Castle, read as follows:

1. Ship was sighted and recognized as a Naval ship 13 miles from coast.
2. Presence in a fighting area is against international custom.
3. The area is not a common passage for ships.
4. Egypt had declared the area closed to neutrals.
5. LIBERTY resembles the Egyptian supply ship EL QUSEIR.
6. Ship was not flying flag when sighted and moved at high speed westward toward the enemy coast.
7. Israeli Defense Force Navy had earlier reports of bombardment of El Arish from sea.[6]

Castle was already disenchanted with Israeli slowness of response to his queries, and was clearly not satisfied with this sketchy and evasive explanation. He pressed Bloch for a title for the report, and when Bloch could not supply one, urged him to call back. Soon Bloch called to provide "Further Information on Yesterday's Incident with the American Ship" as the official authorized title.

Castle promptly forwarded copies to the White House, State Department and other top government offices, and added his own observations:

ALUSNA [naval attaché] cannot understand how trained professional Naval Officers could be so inept to carry out yesterday's attack. Certainly

---

5. McGonagle was a true believer in drills and training. If anything, the men and some of the officers thought he was a nut on the subject. Before our arrival at Abidjan, for example, the crew spent many hours practicing emergency procedures to be taken in case the ship lost rudder control from the bridge—a typical McGonagle precaution in preparation for a difficult and narrow harbor. Then there were damage control drills, gunnery exercises, engineering exercises, lifeboat drills, man overboard drills. The men quickly became expert at every one of these drills while the suspicion grew that McGonagle was a bit daffy about training. The issue became clear on June 8. More than anything else, it was McGonagle's leadership and McGonagle's training that enabled the ship and most of the men to survive.

6. United States Defense Attaché Office, Tel Aviv, Secret message 091250Z June 1967.

IDF [Israeli Defense Force] Navy must be well drilled in identification of Egyptian ships. EL QUSEIR is less than half the size, is many years older, and lacks the elaborate antenna array and hull marking of LIBERTY. ALUSNA evaluates yesterday's erroneous attack resulted from trigger happy eagerness to glean some portion of the great victory being shared by IDF Army and Air Force and which Navy was not sharing.[7]

The Israeli government must have been desperate for a scapegoat to have singled out *El Quseir.* The entire Egyptian Navy consisted of a few converted Soviet and British destroyers, frigates and submarines, some minesweepers, several boats, two yachts and a single transport—*El Quseir.* An unlikely wartime threat, thirty-eight-year-old *El Quseir* was a coastal transport outfitted to pack up to four hundred men and forty horses into her 275-foot hull for short hauls. Very short hauls, one would hope. She was not a combat vessel, would have had a tough time unloading anything near El Arish, and was in such poor shape that she would soon be sold for scrap. Certainly she was an unlikely suspect for the fancied "shelling from the sea" of El Arish. No one could pretend that *Liberty* was mistaken for a destroyer, a submarine or the former royal yacht, so she would simply have to be mistaken for *El Quseir,* which was, after all, the only scapegoat around.[8]

Castle's report reached Kidd even before the court convened, and became part of Exhibit 10 of the Top Secret court record, along with a number of messages that Kidd had copied from the files of the Navy headquarters in London.

In the ensuing message traffic, our government reminded the government of Israel that *Liberty* had been fully identified by Israel at least six hours before the attack, and the Israeli government agreed. The information, Israel claimed, simply failed to reach the operating forces—and the officers in the war room who were aware of *Liberty*'s identification and location failed to connect *Liberty* with the

7. Ibid.

8. Israeli intelligence officers doubtless were aware that *El Quseir* was nowhere near El Arish. Early in 1976, John Scott (*Liberty*'s damage control officer) wrote to the embassy of the Arab Republic of Egypt on my behalf to ask the whereabouts of *El Quseir* on June 8, 1967. Several months later Major General Mohamed A. Abou Ghazala advised by letter and confirmed by telephone that *El Quseir* was in port in Alexandria throughout the Six Day War. Alexandria is about 250 miles from El Arish, or about twenty-four hours steaming for aging *El Quseir.* In an environment so hostile that even the Egyptian guided missile patrol boats were kept safely at their berths, no one could suppose that *El Quseir* would be sent near the Israeli coast.

ship that they attacked. The Israeli statement, then, that the ship was "sighted and recognized as a Naval ship" meant that it had been identified as a *United States* naval ship. And although Kidd was aware of this critical fact and held copies of many of the pertinent messages, the information was ignored and did not warrant comment among his ultimate findings.

On June 15 Kidd received a report from the American embassy of an interview with an Israeli naval officer who was aboard one of the attacking torpedo boats. The officer claimed that the torpedo boats had assumed *Liberty* to be an enemy and joined in the attack *because* they saw her under attack by Israeli warplanes. Interestingly, his story contradicts Israel's "official" excuse, which was to come out a few days later. In that excuse, Israel would claim that the aircraft attacked because they were called in *by the torpedo boats*. Neither Kidd nor anyone else in government ever commented publicly on these stories or their credibility.

Also known to Kidd was a threat made some months before by the Israeli Air Force chief of intelligence. When a U.S. Navy aircraft accidentally penetrated Israeli air space, the Israeli officer suggested that "next time [he] might have to attack the plane or ship." Although Israeli officers dismissed the remark as facetious, Americans did not find it amusing. The remark was discounted by the Court of Inquiry and no comment was made concerning it.

———

While Kidd's court was in session, the government of Israel ordered its own Court of Inquiry, assigning the task to Colonel Ram Ron, a former Israeli military attaché to Washington. When the report was completed, Commander Castle was summoned to the Israeli Foreign Liaison Office where Lieutenant Colonel Efrat, an aide to Israel Defense Force Chief of Staff Rabin, translated the main points from the Hebrew text and read them aloud. Castle copied verbatim from the oral presentation, here condensed and paraphrased:

• El Arish was erroneously reported to have been shelled from the sea. (The erroneous report, it turns out, came one full day before *Liberty* arrived on the scene.)
• Torpedo boats, belatedly sent to investigate the erroneous shelling report, erroneously reported *Liberty* to be moving at *thirty* knots (when it was actually making only five knots).

• Israeli gunnery doctrine (unwisely, Ron conceded) allows Israeli forces to open fire on unidentified ships moving faster than twenty knots near a bombarded shore.

• Since the foregoing errors marked *Liberty* as an "enemy" ship, the torpedo boat commander radioed ashore for an air strike on the ship.

• A dubious IDF naval operations section questioned the report that the ship was moving at thirty knots, whereupon the torpedo boat commander rechecked and erroneously verified *Liberty*'s speed as thirty knots.

• "Even the officers who knew of the identification of LIBERTY early the same morning did not connect LIBERTY with the unidentified ships said to be shelling El Arish," said Ron. "Even if the unidentified ship were thought to be LIBERTY, the fact that she was reported to be making 30 knots would have denied the identification since, when LIBERTY was identified in the morning, her max speed was determined to be 18 knots."

• Satisfied, the shore forces called the air strike.

• Upon completion of the air strike, Israeli torpedomen erroneously identified *Liberty* visually as Egyptian supply vessel *El Quseir* (whose top speed was known to be fourteen knots or less), noted that the ship appeared to be firing upon them, and commenced cannon and torpedo attack.

• "LIBERTY," said Ron, "made a grave additional mistake not less decisive than mistakes made by the Israeli Defense Force. . . . the American ship acted with lack of care by approaching excessively close to the shore in an area which was a scene of war and this at a time when it was well known that this area is not one where ships generally pass, this without advising the Israeli authorities of its presence and without identifying itself elaborately. Furthermore, it appears that the ship made an effort to hide its identity, first by flying a small flag which was difficult to identify from a distance; secondly by beginning to escape when discovered by our forces, and by failing to identify itself immediately by its own initiative by flashing light, and by refusing to do so even when asked by the MTBs. From all this [the investigating officer] conclude[s] that the ship LIBERTY tried to hide its presence in the area and its identity both before it was discovered and even after having been attacked by the Air Force and later by the Navy, and thus contributed decisively toward its identification as an enemy ship."

• Ron found: "It is concluded clearly and unimpeachably from the evidence and from comparison of war diaries that the attack on USS

LIBERTY was not in malice; there was no criminal negligence and the attack was made by innocent mistake."[9]

Efrat could not help noticing Castle's look of surprise and incredulity, and when he finished reading, asked Castle his "off-the-record" opinion of the findings. Although Castle did not answer, his forwarding message told the White House of the question and added:

> . . . ALUSNA pretended he had not heard the question and thanked the Colonel for his time. The burden of diplomacy bore heavily on ALUSNA whose evaluations are:
>
> A.   The standing order to attack any ship moving at more than 20 knots is incomprehensible.
> B.   . . . If the "thirty knot ship couldn't have been LIBERTY," it follows that it could not have been EL QUSEIR.
> C.   That a professional Naval Officer could look at LIBERTY and think her a thirty knot ship is difficult to accept.
> D.   Smoke which covered LIBERTY and made her difficult to identify was probably a result of the IDF Air Force attacks.

Colonel Ron's Court of Inquiry report is clearly unsatisfactory. It is evasive and seems carefully contrived not to explain what happened, but to shift the blame to McGonagle. The report *should* have been returned to Israel with a demand for a better explanation. The Israeli investigation, in the first place, should have been conducted by a flag officer. Indeed, the circumstances cry out for a flag officer. Colonel Ron was required to investigate the performance of forces commanded by officers considerably his senior—a situation virtually guaranteed to produce a finding of no fault. No one could have been surprised when this relatively junior *Army* officer concluded that the Israeli *Navy* had made several unprofessional (but noncriminal and nonnegligent) errors, and that everyone else involved in the attack was blameless. And more important, his story has a fatal flaw: the motor torpedo boat commander could not possibly have called in the air strike as claimed, because the boats were just entering radar range when the attack commenced and were many miles short of radar contact with *Liberty* when the air strike was called. The attack, then, must have been called and coordinated by forces ashore—*not* by the

9. United States Defense Attaché Office, Confidential message 181030Z June 1967.

torpedo boat commander—because the torpedomen were too far away to have detected the ship at all until the moment the air strike began.

Kidd received the Israeli report in time to include a copy in Exhibit 48 of his Top Secret transcript, but he failed to comment on it and the report apparently had no effect upon his findings. Perhaps he was influenced by a message from our Tel Aviv embassy: "The circumstances of the attack strip the Israeli Navy naked," said the embassy in a plaintive request to keep the report under wraps. More embarrassing than professed naval ineptness, Israel's official explanation of the attack simply could not stand close scrutiny, and it was not exposed to any. Government officials docilely agreed not to embarrass Israel by releasing Israel's report, and little was ever heard of it.[10]

======

In London, Rear Admiral Kidd and Admiral McCain worked together to edit the court report into its final form: the relatively complete *Record of Proceedings,* which included exhibits, photographs, messages, testimony, and much conflicting and contradic-

10. The essential facts of Israel's Court of Inquiry report first appeared in *Newsweek* on May 6, 1968, and in somewhat more detail in Goulding's book, *Confirm or Deny* (New York: Harper & Row, 1970). Attempts by ordinary citizens to obtain a copy of the report were fruitless until August 1976, when *Liberty*'s Dr. Kiepfer was suddenly handed a message synopsis by a patient who had obtained it under the Freedom of Information Act. Subsequent requests to obtain a copy through the Pentagon Freedom of Information Office were denied. An appeal of the denial on the grounds that the material had previously been released both to the press (Goulding and *Newsweek*) and to the public (Kiepfer's patient) was also denied. But even as the Pentagon denied the appeal, the Department of State—knowing not what the other hand was doing—declassified and released the message in its entirety; and at about the same time, the Navy Judge Advocate General released the American Court of Inquiry report (including the requested message) under the Freedom of Information Act, making the nine-pound package available to the public at $27 per copy.

The full text of the Israeli Court of Inquiry report, however, has yet to be released; the declassified version is the synopsis that was read to Commander Castle, who then telegraphed the text to the White House. According to a senior U.S. Navy officer whose duties gave him access to the full text, it provides another curious detail of Israel's reported failure to identify. In this story, Colonel Ron claims that although *Liberty* was identified and her track was plotted on a large chart in the war room, an off-going watch inadvertently erased the ship from the plot at the end of a shift. Consequently, when next sighted she was plotted as "unidentified." Just as the torpedoes were launched, so the story goes, an off-duty officer who happened to be in the war room recognized the error, and word was sent out to stop the attack, "but it was too late. The torpedo boat radioman cried, 'Hold fire! Hold fire!' just as the torpedoes were let go." Ron, in reporting this story, again overlooked the fact that the firing continued long after the torpedoes were launched.

tory information, and which was classified "Top Secret." Despite the many weaknesses, the transcript does present a fairly complete record of evidence that the court received, including much that conflicts with the findings. For instance, Israel's Court of Inquiry synopsis is there, even though the message arrived very late in the proceeding and was ignored. And most messages reviewed by the court appear in the file whether they support the court's position or tend to refute it.

On the other hand, a large volume of material—including original transparencies, bullet and rocket fragments, tape recordings, my sworn statement and other evidence that proved extraneous, bulky, awkward or sensitive—went into a large *separate* file, which was also classified "Top Secret." This file was ultimately delivered to a special storage vault in Wing Five of the Navy's Arlington Annex in Virginia, where it is safeguarded by the Navy Judge Advocate General. The court record contains no reference to this material, and its existence has never been admitted to the press or to other researchers.

On June 18, the completed report was approved by Admiral McCain, and for the next ten days Kidd worked with Phil Goulding's deputy, Richard Fryklund, to reduce the 707-page Top Secret transcript to a twenty-eight-page unclassified version.

The problem was enormous. Although the court produced several unsupportable or just plain wrong "Findings of Fact" that seemed designed to excuse the attack, a careful reading of the full report at least revealed the weakness of the findings. The much-abbreviated *Summary,* on the other hand, published only selected findings and part of McGonagle's testimony; none of the contrary evidence and none of the contradictory testimony can be found in the unclassified version. As a result, while the Top Secret report was mild enough, the *Summary of Proceedings* watered the court's product even more to cut the heart out of the few unwelcome and unpolitic findings that *were* made.

The opening paragraphs read as follows:

A Navy Court of Inquiry has determined that USS LIBERTY was in international waters, properly marked as to her identity and nationality, and in calm, clear weather when she suffered an unprovoked attack by Israeli aircraft and motor torpedo boats June 8 in the Eastern Mediterranean.

The Court produced evidence that the Israeli armed forces had ample opportunity to identify LIBERTY correctly. The Court had insufficient information before it to make a judgment on the reason for the decision by Israeli aircraft and motor torpedo boats to attack.

Paraphrasing the Top Secret report, the Pentagon said:

Available evidence combines to indicate that the attack was a case of mistaken identity. Flat, calm conditions and the slow five knot patrol speed of LIBERTY may have produced insufficient wind for streaming colors enough to be seen by pilots. The torpedo boat crews may have identified the colors for the first time when they got in close enough to see clearly through the smoke and flames. There are no indications that the attack was intended against a U.S. Ship.[11]

Admiral Kidd handled the conflicting preattack reconnaissance reports by acting as though McGonagle was the only reliable witness. My sworn statement was excised even from the Top Secret report; other testimony about surveillance was, for the most part, ignored and had little or no bearing upon the findings.

The unclassified version summarized findings on this subject to report "significant surveillance of the LIBERTY on three separate occasions from the air at various times prior to the attack," and went on to identify the significant flights as those that occurred at 0850, when "a single unidentified jet crossed her wake three to five miles astern"; at 1056, when "a flying boxcar crossed astern at a distance of three to five miles"; and at 1126, when "another aircraft circled ship."

Thus the court and the Pentagon characterized the surveillance as much more distant than most of it was, dismissed as insignificant the three orbits by two armed jets, ignored my unwelcome description of a direct masthead-level overflight, failed to acknowledge a report by John Scott of flying boxcar reconnaissance at sunrise and disregarded testimony from *Liberty* officers of additional reconnaissance flights during the noon hour.

Concerning Bloch's seven points telephoned to Castle on June 9,

---

11. It was nine years after the attack before I could prove my claim that the wind was strong enough to hold the flag aloft; in 1976 a former ship's officer delivered to me the original "Ship Weather Observation Sheet" for the day of the attack. The officer, frustrated with the court's unconcern for such things, took possession of the log after the court failed to do so. The log appears in Appendix H (pages 245–46), along with a table converting true wind (over the sea) to relative wind (over the ship).

the Pentagon (without mentioning Israel's excuse) paraphrased a legal opinion in the Top Secret report to say:

> The Court affirmed LIBERTY's right to be where she was. A neutral nation, the Court stated, has a legal right to dispatch a ship into international waters adjacent to an area of hostilities. So long as such neutral ship maintains the impartial attitude of neutrality, the Court pointed out, each belligerent has a duty to refrain from attacking her.[12]

Again without revealing the true source of the story, the Pentagon said:

> The Court also noted reports of rumors that the town of El Arish had been bombarded from the sea, but pointed out that neither LIBERTY, with four .50 caliber machine guns, nor EL QUSEIR, which is armed with two 3-pounders, could logically be suspected of having conducted a shore bombardment.

Concerning the erroneous identification that Israel presented as the crucial mistake, the Pentagon (still protecting the source of the *El Quseir* story) quoted directly from the Top Secret report to say:

> While EL QUSEIR bears a highly superficial resemblance to LIBERTY, she more closely resembles the majority of older tramp steamers operating in ocean shipping. EL QUSEIR is less than half the size and lacks the elaborate antenna array and distinctive hull markings of LIBERTY. The location of the superstructure island, a primary recognition feature of merchant type ships, is widely different. By this criteria as a justification for attack, any ship resembling EL QUSEIR was in jeopardy.

Describing the communication fiasco, which certainly contributed to the likelihood of attack, the Top Secret report said:

> . . . LIBERTY's 7 June Position Report which stated her final destination prompted concern in the [Pentagon] . . . and resulted in follow-on actions and directives to the ship . . . The ship is known not to have received at least five messages, each of which was . . . critical . . .

12. The full text of the legal opinion as it appears in the Top Secret *Record of Proceedings of the Court of Inquiry* is reproduced in Appendix I, pages 248–49.

The first sentence, of course, unknown to Kidd, is not entirely true. The JCS effort to recall the ship did not result from any sudden realization that she was near the war zone. *Liberty*'s position, after all, was well known to officials in the Pentagon and elsewhere. Rather, as we have seen, the recall order grew from a Defense Department "staff study," which recommended the immediate withdrawal of the ship and resulted in a last-minute Flash message requesting that the Joint Chiefs of Staff order *Liberty* promptly away from the coast.

On the same subject, the unclassified report quoted from Admiral McCain's endorsement to the Top Secret report, in which McCain said:

> Early on the 8th, the Joint Chiefs of Staff had issued orders for LIBERTY to move farther from the coast, even though such a move would partially degrade her mission. The messages were misrouted, delayed, and not received until after the attack. . . . since [McGonagle] was in international waters, his standard identification symbols were clearly visible, and foreign aircraft had inspected him three times that day, he had no reason to believe the ship was in danger of attack. . . . The Court reached no judgment on whether earlier arrival of the messages would have reduced the likelihood of the attack.

Despite statements from our embassy and evidence we have seen that *Liberty* was indeed identified by Israel during the morning, Kidd ignored the evidence. The Pentagon reported the court's negative findings on that score in this manner:

> Inasmuch as this was not an international investigation, no evidence was presented on whether any of these aircraft had identified LIBERTY or whether they had passed any information on LIBERTY to their own higher headquarters.

And in an introduction to the unclassified *Summary,* the Pentagon added:

> It was not the responsibility of the Court to rule on the culpability of the attackers, and no evidence was heard from the attacking nation. Witnesses suggested that the flag may have been difficult for the attackers to see, both because of the slow speed of the ship and because, after five or six separate air attacks by at least two planes each, smoke and flames may have helped obscure the view from the torpedo boats.

The addition of the phrase "attacks by at least two planes each," appearing as it does in both the Top Secret and unclassified versions, is apparently a last-minute attempt by Kidd to resolve conflicts in testimony. However, little was ever resolved. The unclassified report gives no hint of the conflicting and contradictory evidence, and the Top Secret version, which *does* suggest conflict (since it contains testimony of the officers and crew along with numerous messages and other evidence that was *not* released to the public), was destined to spend the next several years in special security containers reserved for Top Secret material and to be seen by only a very few senior officials. A Navy JAG (legal) Corps officer who finally achieved access to the document told me, after studying the 707 legal-size pages of testimony, photographs, evidence, legal opinions and findings: "The report is confusing. After you read the testimony, review the evidence, and then read the findings, your first impulse is to go back and see if you missed a couple hundred pages, because the evidence simply does not lead to the findings. Many of the findings are not supported by evidence at all. The message you get from the report is that Admiral Kidd had some orders that are not spelled out in his appointing letter."

While Admiral Kidd's Court of Inquiry was the only investigating panel to receive public notice, there were several such groups. As we have seen, Walter Deeley conducted an investigation for the Department of Defense, producing a large and colorful report. The Joint Chiefs of Staff detailed Major General Joseph R. Russ to head a fact-finding team; the JCS group apparently sent representatives to the Mediterranean for some on-the-spot investigating, particularly into the mishandling of communications, and produced a still-classified report that resists Freedom of Information Act inquiries. The Central Intelligence Agency completed a "staff summary" report on the attack. As we know, Foreign Intelligence Advisory Board Chairman Clark Clifford was detailed by President Johnson to head an immediate investigation into the matter for the President. All of these investigations seem to have been conducted in great haste. Volumes of information were collected and innumerable man-hours were spent, but much of the information was not pertinent and only Kidd's group collected any firsthand information from on board the ship. The others relied primarily upon McGonagle's testimony to the Court of Inquiry, or directed their inquiries into other aspects of the incident, such as communications. Each of the reports either concluded that the attack was probably conducted in error, or avoided making conclusions by lamely reporting that it could find no evidence that the attack was deliberate.

Perhaps the most penetrating official observation was made by Commander Castle in a wrap-up report to the White House: ". . . only the Israeli Defense Force knows with certainty the exact sequence of events that led to the tragic incident."

Chapter 11

"PRESS GUIDANCE"

... no information is to be classified solely because disclosure might result in criticism of the Department of Defense.

U.S. Navy Public Affairs Regulations, 1974

While the court was in session, Associated Press reporter Colin Frost spent his time hanging around the Maltese bars frequented by *Liberty* sailors. Frost had concluded early in the drama that all was not being told about the attack. He had made himself unpopular with the public affairs officers by asking hard questions—and he was not satisfied with the official answers. Now he drank beer with *Liberty* sailors and he listened. At first he learned little, as *Liberty* sailors were too well schooled in the danger of loose talk to fall prey to inquisitive reporters.

George Golden, however, was angry. Golden was *Liberty*'s acting commanding officer while McGonagle recuperated ashore. He had tried to tell the story of the attack to a court that had seemed not to want to hear, and he had listened to other officers and men complain of their dissatisfaction with the inquiry. Convinced that a true story would never be told through official channels, Golden drank with the reporter and told him what he had wanted to tell the court. Frost's story was on all the news wires before midnight and appeared prominently in most of the world's newspapers on Saturday morning.

VALLETTA, Malta, June 17 (AP)—Senior Crewmen of the U.S. Navy ship LIBERTY are convinced that Israel's air and torpedo attack on their ship, which cost 34 American lives, was deliberate, a responsible source said Friday in Valletta. They have testified to this effect to the Navy inquiry court now in secret session aboard the ship, which is undergoing emergency repair in a Malta drydock. Their belief was based on the fact that the Israelis had enough time to identify the ship and on the intensity of the attack.

Israel, in apologizing for the attack, said it was made in error. Experienced seamen to whom this correspondent has spoken do not accept this. The argument is that at this stage of the Mideast war, Israel had a supreme interest in covering up the true extent of her lightning successes for fear that the full knowledge of Egypt's plight would bring some form of Soviet intervention. The LIBERTY had both the crew and the gear to gauge the Israeli advance, and for that reason it had to go.

For four hours before the attack the ship had been under constant surveillance from Israeli planes circling overhead. "We were flying Old Glory, and it's absolutely impossible that they shouldn't know who we were," one survivor said. "This was a deliberate and planned attack, and the remarkable thing about it was the accuracy of their air fire."

Most fire was concentrated on the bridge where the ship's Executive Officer was killed. A bullet tore through the cabin of the Commanding Officer, Commander William McGonagle, piercing the plating just above his pillow. Had he been in the bunk, he would have been certainly killed. As it was, he was hit in the leg by shrapnel on the bridge.

Because of the secrecy imposed by the inquiry court, it is not possible at this stage to determine the precise number of jets involved. Indications, however, are that three did the actual damage. LIBERTY was already blazing from the jet attack when torpedo boats moved in. At least three torpedoes were fired in the classic pattern: one for the bow, one amidships and one for the stern.

How the ship made the six-day voyage to Malta mystified dockyard veterans who saw some of the worst-hit ships of World War II. Every movement of the ship sent water in its holds crashing against the bulkheads, which began to bulge and looked like they would collapse. Engineers shored them up with timber, like the props sometimes used to support old buildings.[1]

1. The New York *Times,* June 18, 1967, p. 20.

Golden told me later that Colin Frost did a fine job on that story. "He got everything I said straight and he quoted my exact words," he said. "I really hoped that the newspaper guys would realize from Frost's story that there was a cover-up going on and would keep probing, but I should have known better. It didn't do any good, and it just caused a lot of trouble."

Instead of exciting the press, the story aroused the Navy and aggravated the cover-up; in fact, the forces behind the cover-up were at work to counteract Golden's effort even before the story was printed. Alongside Frost's story when it appeared in the New York *Times* was a Reuter's News Service story:

VALLETTA, June 17 (Reuters)—Officers from the Liberty today rejected the idea that the attack was deliberate. One officer said that anybody who said the attack was deliberate was "out of his mind." He said that when the torpedo boat had realized her mistake she had flashed the message, "Terrible error. Can we help?"

An American Embassy spokesman here said: "We thoroughly accepted the Israeli apology and there is no question that the attack was not a mistake."[2]

To discourage any more unsupervised interviews, Admiral McCain's office in London fired off a Priority message to *Liberty:*

WHILE SOME MATERIAL IN STORY WAS RELEASED BY OFFICIAL SPOKESMAN, [portions] APPEAR TO BE BASED EITHER ON UNAUTHORIZED INTERVIEWS OR THE REPORTER'S CONJECTURE. SINCE HE EXPRESSED A STRONG BELIEF THAT THE ATTACK COULD NOT HAVE BEEN ACCIDENTAL [to public affairs officers] BEFORE LIBERTY ARRIVED IN MALTA, THE LATTER POSSIBILITY IS NOT UNLIKELY.

AT THE SAME TIME, THERE IS REASON TO BELIEVE HE ATTEMPTED TO CONVERSE ON THIS SUBJECT WITH LIBERTY CREWMEN ASHORE. BECAUSE OTHER REPORTERS MAY ATTEMPT TO FOLLOW UP, YOU MAY FEEL IT APPROPRIATE TO REPEAT PREVIOUS ADMONITION TO YOUR FINE CREW TO REFRAIN FROM SPEAKING ABOUT MATTERS UNDER INVESTIGATION UNTIL FINDINGS OF COURT OF INQUIRY HAVE BEEN ANNOUNCED.[3]

McCain's message also went to other officers in the chain of command, and to the American ambassador to Malta in Valletta, George

2. Ibid.
3. CINCUSNAVEUR Confidential message 181105Z June 1967.

J. Feldman. Ambassador Feldman berated Golden by telephone for the unauthorized news leak (still assumed to have originated with some undisciplined seaman), and then dispatched a Navy lieutenant to follow up in person. Admiral Martin sent a Navy captain.

A sixty-two-year-old Boston lawyer, Ambassador Feldman had filled increasingly important posts with both houses of Congress, in the State Department, and as a member of or counsel to committees of NATO and the United Nations. During recent political campaigns, he had held key positions in the Democratic National Committee, and in 1965 he was appointed to an ambassadorship by President Johnson. We can only speculate on what special instructions Mr. Feldman received from Washington, but we know that copies of McCain's message were telegraphed to Feldman and we know that Feldman saw his control of such leaks as a matter of duty. In any case, Ambassador Feldman's background gave him a fine appreciation for the diplomatic and political considerations in an international incident such as this one, and he set about seeing that things were indeed "kept in perspective."

Golden soon found himself harangued daily by Navy or embassy representatives who visited or phoned to complain bitterly of every news item that might have been provided by a *Liberty* sailor.

=====

On June 28 the news blackout was officially lifted, and *Liberty* crewmen were free to talk to the press for the first time. However, it soon became clear that this new "freedom" was fraught with so many restrictions as to be no freedom at all. Along with the supposed removal of the blackout came about two *dozen* messages providing "press guidance"—detailed instructions on how to deal with the press. Many of the messages were classified "Confidential," most of them came *after* June 28, and hardly any of them dealt with anything of a security nature. Almost the only sensitive issue involved was the length to which the government would go to assure that no one talked freely or privately with any reporter.

Liberty sailors were thus advised of their freedom to talk to reporters in the following language, read to them by their chiefs and division officers and posted on their bulletin boards:

> Interviews and statements to news media concerning the attack on LIB-
> ERTY 08 June are not to be given by individuals. If you are approached
> by someone wanting an interview or statement inform them that they

must contact the Public Affairs Officer at CINCLANTFLT who will make all arrangements. Also, inform the Commanding Officer or Executive Officer of the request made to you. The only information that ships company is allowed to discuss is that already made available to the press. Therefore, there is nothing new that we would be able to tell them in an interview.[4]

Division officers were given copies of the official report, and crewmen were advised to "borrow their Division Officer's copy and read the report," since "any statements or comments to others is confined to the exact wording in this report."

Few bothered to read it. Those who did shrugged in confusion, failing to recognize the incident as one which they had experienced. But the press was losing interest anyway. The attack was three weeks old when the news blanket was removed. The story was fading from newspaper and TV coverage and had already been forgotten by most Americans. And only about a hundred of *Liberty*'s 315-man crew remained aboard—the rest were either dead, hospitalized or transferred to new duty stations where they were unable to compare notes.

———

Chief Petty Officer Joseph A. Benkert, who had sat with me through the long night on June 8, was in Norfolk when the blackout was lifted, having left the ship in Malta. He was soon informed by his seniors that he could grant press interviews if he chose to, as long as he remembered to "stick to his own experiences and inform the public affairs officer in advance." Benkert did not want to be interviewed unless he was free to speak candidly and without restriction, so when he was contacted by reporter Clifford Hubbard of Norfolk's *Virginian-Pilot,* he politely declined. As it turned out, the choice was not his to make.

Soon he received a call from Commander David M. Cooney, the CINCLANTFLT public affairs officer, who advised him that he was expected to report promptly for a press briefing at CINCLANTFLT headquarters.

"I have decided not to be interviewed," he said.

"The arrangements have already been made, Chief. Please be on time."

4. This notice was published in "USS Liberty Plan of the Day" for Saturday, July 22, 1967. Similar language was used in "Plans of the Day" for June 30, July 1, and July 28.

For two hours Benkert was "briefed" for the upcoming thirty-minute interview. With Rear Admiral Renken present, but before the reporter arrived, Benkert was asked every conceivable question about the ship and the attack. And as he tried to answer, he was reminded that he could not discuss the ship's mission. He could not discuss Admiral Martin's promise to provide jet fighter protection or the failure of the fighters to arrive. Since he had not personally seen the reconnaissance airplanes, he could not discuss them; since he had not been on the bridge and timed the air attack, he could not discuss the duration of the air attack; since he had not personally seen a lab report on the napalm, he could not mention napalm. He could not discuss the machine-gunning of the life rafts. He could not report the preparations to abandon ship or any orders to scuttle or demolish the ship. He was not permitted to report that the flag was flying. He was forbidden to mention that the wind was blowing.

There was very little of substance that Joe Benkert *could* talk about. He was eating chili when the attack started, he said, and he went on to tell of racing to his battle station, of seeing the torpedo boats, of treating wounded—and he described the admiration we all felt for the commanding officer. Although it galled him, he carefully avoided any discussion of the many details his briefers had told him to withhold from the press.

There was much more he *wanted* to say, but Commander Cooney remained in the room, and so did Admiral Renken, and so did a captain who was on Renken's staff, and so did another Navy captain, and so did some officers that Benkert didn't recognize. And when the interview was over, Benkert was dismissed. The reporter stayed. Benkert was not privy to the conversation that followed, but he has wondered about it ever since, because the story that was printed seemed to Benkert to be even more bland and unrevealing than the interview.

"I don't know where they got the quotes for that story," Benkert told me later. "They didn't come from me. They didn't use what I said and they made up stuff I didn't say. At least ninety percent of that story is bullshit."

=====

While the court was still in session, *Liberty* had received interview requests from Ed McGrath of the Boston *Globe* and from NBC's Irving R. Levine, then in Rome. After a delay of more than two weeks, McGrath was eventually advised that no crewmen from Boston remained aboard, and his request quietly died; Levine was granted a one-hour interview with Admiral Kidd in Naples, and this delicate exchange was brought off by Kidd with characteristic aplomb.

Levine was shown the unclassified version of the Court of Inquiry report, and Kidd fielded all remaining questions to Levine's satisfaction. To Levine's request for an interview with McGonagle, Kidd replied that yes, McGonagle could be made available, but that the captain really did not seek publicity. Levine promised to recommend to the NBC home office that the camera crew not pursue the McGonagle interview.

Every major command east of the Lincoln Memorial was promptly advised of the Levine-Kidd meeting, and verbatim tape recordings of the conversation were dispatched to the Pentagon. With Levine went the last important press interest. No interview requests remained. Little matter. None was likely to have been productive anyway.[5]

In Israel, the authorities quickly capitalized upon the court's misleading report of the attack. From it they fabricated a largely fictional account designed to portray *Liberty* as a blundering, unmarked phantom who virtually *invited* the attack and thus was responsible for her own misfortune. This story was released to the press by one Micha Limor, purporting to have been a reservist on one of the torpedo boats.

TEL AVIV, July 6 (AP) By Micha Limor
The sun was already high in the sky when we received notification of an unidentified sailing vessel some 12 miles off the El Arish coast, suspected of being an enemy craft.

Sailors took their positions, engines were revved up, and in five minutes we were moving out in formation, torpedo boat after torpedo boat, toward the deep sea. We spotted the objective once on the radar screen. She was moving on a steady course, southeast at about 10 knots. We sailed toward the objective at an increased speed, looking at her through binoculars in an effort to identify the vessel.

Two of our planes flew over our heads a few minutes afterward. We saw them circle the ship several times, and then dive in to the attack. They spat two rockets into the gray ship, and plumes of smoke rose from her. Then the two jets headed away from the coast. About 2,000 yards from the ship, a strange spectacle met our eyes.

---

5. NAVSUPPACT NAPLES message 011240Z July 1967.

The high masts and the many weird antenna showed that this was a warship. The side of the vessel was blotted out by smoke, and apart from three numbers along her side, which meant nothing to us, we could not discern a thing.

We could see no flag on the mast, nor was anyone to be seen on the decks or bridge. For seamen, this can mean only two things: it was either a ghost ship or an enemy ship. To us—who do not believe in ghosts—it was clear that this was the enemy.

We spent several minutes trying to contact the ship and demanding identification by radio and heliograph. But she gave no answer. It was decided to pass by her in battle formation and demand identification by firing across her bow. So we moved past at a tremendous speed, firing across the empty bridge and bow. Suddenly a sailor appeared in view and started firing at us with a heavy machine gun from the bridge. We took the challenge and directed cannon against him. A moment later he fell, together with the machine gun.

Thus there was no doubt that we were faced by the enemy. The prolonged refusal to identify herself, the absence of any flag, the shooting at us, and above all the weird contraptions on the ship left us without any doubt. We wanted to make the ship surrender without sinking her. Once again we circled the vessel in battle formation, firing again and again. This had no effect. No one appeared. No one reacted. The shells caused little damage to the hull and the ship proceeded on its way. You could almost hear the men's teeth grinding aboard our boat. Nothing can annoy a torpedo boat crew more than being completely ignored. The order was given to prepare for torpedo attack.

We drew up along the left side of the boat and advanced at full battle speed. Just as in dozens of training exercises we reached the right angle and range—and let go. We thought only a miracle would save the ship. One of the torpedoes hit the boat amidships. There followed an enormous explosion and a huge water spout.

Fires broke out and the boat leaned sideways as if about to sink. We waited for survivors as is customary for seamen—whether friend or enemy. But no one appeared on deck. Suddenly something fell into the sea. One of our formation approached and picking it up from the waters found it to be a rubber lifeboat with the lettering "U.S. Navy."

That was the very first sign of identification. A moment later there arrived on the scene the helicopter that was to have picked up prisoners. He hovered over the boat and then signaled us: "They are raising the American flag."

It was crystal clear we had hit friends. Dozens of shells, rockets and torpedoes were needed to drag a sign of identity from them, said one of my seamen who, like the rest of his mates, was bitterly upset at the surprising turn of events.

He was right. The showing of the Stars and Stripes at the very first stage would have prevented all that happened subsequently.[6]

Limor's story can only have been released with official Israeli government sanction and censorship clearance; judging from the mistakes and the bias—Limor didn't even know which side of the ship was torpedoed (he writes that the torpedo boat "drew up along the left side of the boat" although it approached from the starboard quarter) and uses unnautical language that no sailor, not even a reservist, would use—it was probably written by an Israeli public affairs officer who never saw *Liberty* or the torpedo boats.

Had Limor circled the ship as he claims—indeed, had he even looked her over carefully—he would have seen *Liberty*'s name painted in huge letters across her stern; he would have seen the oversized American flag, which was hoisted on a yardarm as the boats were approaching, the original flag having been shot away by the airplanes; he would have seen Captain McGonagle, Ensign Lucas and others on the bridge; he would have seen several firefighters working to control napalm and gasoline fires—until his bullets perforated their fire hoses.

Limor describes "three numbers along her side, which meant nothing to us." These were apparently the ship's hull designator, GTR-5, painted in man-sized characters on the ship's bow. English is commonly known in Israel and would have been recognized by the torpedomen. They did, Limor tells us, readily read the U.S. Navy identification on our life raft (after they shot it loose with their machine guns); and in any case, every Israeli sailor must know that Egyptian ships record their hull numbers on their sides in cursive Arabic script.

While *Liberty* sailors shook their heads in despair over the story, few of us realized how closely Limor's tale was drawn from Admiral Kidd's "official" version of the attack. And those of us who wanted to rebut Limor were prevented by Pentagon "press guidance" from having any meaningful contact with the press.

6. "Israeli Sailor Describes Attack on USS Liberty," New York *Times,* July 7, 1967, p. 3 (here condensed).

Chapter 12

MALTA

The burden of diplomacy bore heavily . . .
Commander Ernest Carl Castle in message to the White House,
June 18, 1967

In Malta, while Captain McGonagle recuperated in his room at the Phoenicia Hotel, McHale's Navy regained its fighting spirit. When embassy officers were not grumbling about news leaks, they were complaining about fights. "You have the damnedest bunch of hooligans we have ever had in this port," Golden was told amid rude threats and orders to "shape up."

Liberty sailors were bloodied and bruised from encounters with other American sailors, and the other ships' men were equally mauled. Even some of the officers were scrapping. It seemed that every bar held at least one half-drunk bully who had to find out for himself whether *Liberty* sailors were as tough as the stories suggested.

Finally, Golden took drastic action. Civilian clothes were not authorized aboard ship for enlisted men in 1967, but this was a special case. He ordered every man to obtain and wear civilian clothing ashore. No longer easily identified with a *Liberty* ship's patch on the uniform, Golden hoped that the fighting would stop. And he promised to restrict fighters. It worked.

=====

Soon dozens of senior officers made the trip to Valletta. During the first few days it seemed to those on board that every admiral in the Atlantic Fleet must be eating the noon meal in *Liberty*'s wardroom. The wardroom mess, which usually accommodated only the ship's officers, now expanded to feed not twelve or sixteen, but typically thirty. And most of these were senior to McGonagle.

Commander Sixth Fleet came. Commander Service Squadron 8 came. His deputy came. Most of the deputy commanders-in-chief of the Atlantic Fleet came, as did several deputy commanders-in-chief of the U.S. Naval Forces, Europe. It was routine for *Liberty* to serve eight admirals for lunch, and several captains.

Dr. Kiepfer assumed the mess treasurer duty, replacing Steve Toth, who had died in the attack. And Dick soon discovered that Steve's gourmet tastes had exceeded his budget. He had stocked the wardroom mess with filet mignon and other expensive meats, with hundreds of tiny tins of exotic and expensive delicacies, caviar, candies, nuts and cheeses. The wardroom mess was a gourmet's delight, but soon the bill would have to be reckoned with, and it would run to nearly triple the usual monthly charge.

Kiepfer is a remarkable fellow, fully as remarkable in real life as he is in combat. A bridge master while still a teen-ager, Kiepfer plays at life the same way he plays bridge: by analyzing the game, searching for the best play, and occasionally executing a deft finesse or a stunning squeeze play. Studying the mountain of regulations that governed his mess treasurer job, he found that it was legal, and in fact a rather simple and not too controversial step, simply to charge the visitors *double* the Navy's usual messing charge. The wardroom mess soon became a moneymaking operation.

When it became clear that even the increased volume of business would fail to make a substantial dent in the oversupply of beef that Toth had brought aboard, Kiepfer sought a solution.

The American embassy, he learned, had difficulty obtaining good-quality American beef. Toth had carefully selected only the very best cuts of the most select prime beef and, because of the large quantity purchased, had paid only 79 cents per pound. The embassy, however, when it could get American beef at all, was forced to pay upwards of $1.79 per pound. They were more than pleased to accept several hundred pounds at $1.10 per pound.

The wardroom mess became solvent again for the first time since leaving Norfolk. In fact, the individual mess bills for the month of July were *minus* five dollars: each member of the mess, instead of paying for his meals, received a five-dollar payment for having eaten. And because each transaction was fully and properly reported to the Bureau of Naval Personnel, Kiepfer maintained a lively correspondence with the Bureau for more than three years as Washington tried to fathom what was going on.

Golden began to receive reports of individual heroism during the attack. These he carefully investigated, interviewing witnesses personally and directing that write-ups be made in appropriate cases for submission to higher authority.[1]

Posthumous awards were recommended for five men: the Navy Cross for Philip Armstrong and Francis Brown, and Silver Star medals for Stephen Toth, Alexander Thompson and David Skolak. Thirty-eight awards were recommended for survivors, and these ranged from the Navy Commendation Medal to the Silver Star. Carpenter, Golden, Kiepfer, Larkins, Lockwood, Lucas, Scott and others were recommended by Admiral Martin for Silver Stars, and McGonagle was recommended by Admiral McCain for the nation's highest military award, the Medal of Honor.

Skolak, who died in a forward gun mount while trying to fire at the marauding jets, was for some time a candidate for the Medal of Honor. Reports persisted that Skolak was fearless, that he exposed himself to fire while retrieving wounded, that he exposed himself to great danger in order to man the machine gun and that he persisted in fighting long after he was badly wounded. Unfortunately, the best witness to Skolak's performance was Thompson, and Thompson died as Skolak had, in the gun mount. Had Skolak died on the bridge, it might have been different; there would have been witnesses. As it turned out, there were simply not enough witnesses to provide the

---

1. One brazen fellow nominated himself for an award for heroism. He wrote a stirring letter for McGonagle's signature describing his imagined exploit, drafted a proposed citation to accompany the award, bribed a confederate to verify the phony story, and delivered the illicit package to Lieutenant Golden—who saw through the scheme immediately. The pitiful chap is still despised by the many *Liberty* men and officers who know the story.

very strong substantiation required for a Navy Cross or a Medal of Honor, so Skolak's family received a Silver Star.

Someone nominated Lieutenant Painter for a Bronze Star for his performance as leader of the repair party responsible for the after part of the ship. Painter ran himself to exhaustion for most of the afternoon, exposed himself to machine-gun fire repeatedly as he checked battle damage in exposed areas, braved rocket fire as he helped carry wounded, and finally managed to restore order when men reacted with hysteria to the second torpedo attack warning.

A citation was prepared and forwarded to the captain. But an officer, long a foe of Painter's, brought a tale that Painter had unnecessarily exposed wounded men to danger by evacuating them to the main deck while the ship was still under fire from the torpedo boats. McGonagle listened to the story and ordered the nomination withdrawn. Too bad. Had Ensign Scott been asked, he would have testified that Painter was responding to the "prepare to abandon ship" order that Scott had personally relayed from the bridge.

———

Early in *Liberty*'s stay in Malta, Dr. Kiepfer learned that *Liberty* had carried two large cases of nylon stockings for the benefit of embassy employees who could be expected to shop in the ship's store. The stockings could not be returned, and now they were to be disposed of as surplus. Quick to grasp an opportunity, Kiepfer entered a bid —the *only* bid as it turned out—and soon came into possession of six gross (864 pairs) of top-quality nylon stockings in assorted sizes and colors for a bargain price of less than 6 cents per pair.

Nylon hose opened doors for Kiepfer and the *Liberty* wardroom that mere cash failed to open. An apparently impenetrable door was the one to the nearby Royal Garrison Yacht Club, owned and operated by the British Royal Navy. Because naval officers of other NATO nations visited Malta, the club extended honorary guest privileges to visiting NATO officers. In this manner *Liberty* officers enjoyed the use of the Royal Garrison Yacht Club.

British yacht clubs, however, are unlike their American counterparts, and American naval officers rank as second-class citizens in such clubs anyway. So it came to pass that although *Liberty* officers were nominally granted membership privileges, the privileges were rarely available when *Liberty* officers wanted them. Boats were seldom around when *Liberty* officers wanted to use them. Reservations could be made, but boats were usually already reserved for the times

Liberty officers requested. On those few occasions that a boat *was* available, it was usually in an inaccessible part of the boathouse, blocked in by other immovable boats, lacked mast, rudder or sail, or was otherwise unusable. And if somehow the missing parts were located and the immovable boats were moved, there was no available help or instruction in the use of the boat davit required to move the thing into the water.

Kiepfer attacked the problem in a characteristically Kiepfer manner: head-on.

"Mr. Hamilton-Jones,"[2] he said to an employee of the club, "I have acquired a quantity of nylon hose. I'm not married. I have no real use for the hose. I can't sell them, as it would not be proper for me to profit personally from the hose. I wonder if you know how I might dispose of them."

Mr. Hamilton-Jones promised to consider the problem, but had no ready solution.

"Perhaps," suggested Kiepfer, "perhaps you could take some to your wife. If I brought, say, ten pairs, do you think your wife would accept them?"

Mr. Hamilton-Jones supposed that she might.

The following day Dr. Kiepfer arrived, carrying a neat package of ten pairs of the finest-quality nylon hose in the exact size and shade worn by Mrs. Hamilton-Jones.

By coincidence, Mr. Hamilton-Jones just happened to have a boat available. In fact, the boat was in the water and rigged with sail. What's more, that boat was not otherwise spoken for and would be at the disposal of Dr. Kiepfer and his friends for the duration of their stay in Malta.

Liberty officers sailed regularly from then on, usually finding the boat rigged and waiting.

———

Rear Admiral Alphonse McPhot[3] was the commander of a Sixth Fleet task force. McPhot visited *Liberty* early in her repair period and he, too, enjoyed sailing. Admirals, though, don't personally handle such mundane matters as the reservation of boats. Such things are the duty of the flag lieutenant, and Rear Admiral McPhot had a very capable young flag lieutenant.

2. Not his real name.
3. Not his real name.

But McPhot, who could cause lesser admirals to tremble and senior officers to weep, was unable to obtain the use of a boat. On several occasions the flag lieutenant called the Royal Garrison Yacht Club to request a boat, but a boat was never available. The flag lieutenant grew desperate. After all, it was his job to satisfy such cravings as McPhot felt for small-boat sailing. He visited Mr. Hamilton-Jones, explained his great need, and hoped that a boat would materialize. It did not.

Rear Admiral McPhot sat at Kiepfer's table in the wardroom, and during lunch mentioned to Kiepfer his disappointment at being unable to obtain a boat from the Royal Garrison Yacht Club. Kiepfer listened with the keen interest with which naval officers soon learn to attend admirals.

"Admiral, I'll look into it first thing after lunch."

Immediately after lunch Dr. Richard Kiepfer telephoned Mr. Hamilton-Jones and asked whether it would be possible to reserve a small sailboat for McPhot's use.

It was possible. When did McPhot wish to sail? The boat would be ready.

So Rear Admiral McPhot called upon Mr. Hamilton-Jones to find a boat rigged and waiting.

"I certainly do appreciate this," he said. "I'll be here only a few days and this is the first boat you have had available."

"Oh, I say," said Mr. Hamilton-Jones, "well, I didn't know you were a friend of the doctor's."

=====

Nylon hose soon proved as negotiable as cash. With them, Kiepfer arranged not only for sailboats, but for all manner of otherwise unavailable services. Food, drink and hotel accommodations were obtained. Sightseeing tours were arranged. One morning a sedan, complete with driver, reported to the ship for duty; the car remained on duty for almost a month. With nylons, Kiepfer earned a place among cumshaw experts and boondogglers of antiquity: for one hundred pairs he leased a four-bedroom villa, complete with maid. The place soon became off-duty headquarters for the ship's officers and a conversation piece for the neighbors as it enlivened the otherwise dull neighborhood with seemingly perpetual parties.

Chapter 13

MEDICINE

Luck in the long run is given only to the efficient.

Helmuth Von Moltke, 1800–1891

A dozen of us were slated to move from Naples Naval Hospital to the United States via Frankfurt Army Hospital. Doctors protected my leg for the trip with a spica body cast, which encased my body from armpits to toes with plaster of Paris. Then, to complete the package, the nurses taped a carnation to my foot, and next to the carnation they fashioned a shipping tag, which read, "If lost, drop in any mailbox. Return to Delores, U.S. Naval Hospital, FPO New York 09521."

A week later I arrived at Portsmouth Naval Hospital near Norfolk. Dave Lewis went to Bethesda Naval Hospital near Washington; George Wilson went to Great Lakes Naval Hospital near his home in Chicago. Joe Lentini and Dick Carlson made the trip to Portsmouth with me; Jeff Carpenter and Don Herold came on a later flight. The others were widely dispersed to hospitals near their homes.

Liberty was still in Malta, but most of the technicians and most of the wounded had been sent home ahead of the ship. Among the officers, Armstrong, Toth and Pierce were dead. O'Connor was hospitalized at Landstuhl, Germany, recovering from the removal of his kidney; Dave Lewis was being treated for his hearing loss; of the ten officers still aboard, all but Scott and O'Malley had received wounds. Dick Taylor, the supply officer, had been sent as far as Naples, where he had managed to talk the doctors into letting him return to the ship; so now he was back aboard.

As the first ship's officer to return to Norfolk, I was visited by most of the *Liberty* crewmen who were in town. During the attack, hardly anyone was aware of what was happening beyond his own little sphere. Now I began to receive reports from throughout the ship. Thomas Smith told me of dropping life rafts overboard in response to the "prepare to abandon ship" order, and of seeing the rafts sunk by machine-gun fire. Lloyd Painter and others told me the same story when they arrived. Jeff Carpenter told me of his experiences on the bridge and of seeing his fire hoses punctured by machine-gun fire from the torpedo boats. Joe Lentini told me of finding himself underwater in a flooded compartment. Doug Ritenburg told me of swimming through oily water in a flooded research compartment. These stories I collected like pearls, unsure as yet what I might do with them, but certain that they needed to be preserved.

I was soon contacted by a television reporter who wanted to interview me on camera for the evening news—and any candid report at this point would have created a sensation. The Navy had no objection to the interview, I was told, as long as I contacted the public affairs officer in advance so that I could be "briefed." But I didn't want to repeat Benkert's experience. I didn't return the reporter's call.

═══════

The dead arrived home about the same time I did, and these were promptly buried. Jim Pierce and Philip Armstrong were buried at Arlington National Cemetery. Captain Joseph C. Toth held a burial plot at Annapolis, and this he relinquished to his son, Steve. He came to see me a few days later. I had first met Captain Toth during dinner aboard ship in April, and he had displayed the aggressive, suntanned, energetic good health typical of a Navy captain. Now, barely two months later, he had changed. He was thinner, haggard-looking. He looked smaller. Suddenly he was a weary old man.

"What happened out there, Jim?"

"It's a long story, Captain. Where do you want me to start?"

"Tell me why that captain didn't get his ship out of there. You could see smoke on the beach. You knew it was dangerous. Why didn't he leave? I blame him. It was his fault. He should not have been there at all."

Captain Toth was seething with anger. This graying, still distinguished-looking man spoke with tears in his eyes. His hands trembled as he told me of his anger and frustration over the loss of his only son. He had been to Washington, he told me, to see his congressman, demanding a full and complete investigation. He received sympathy, but no help and no answers. He called on senior officers in the Pentagon, and again he found no answers. He wanted to know who was responsible, why the ship was sent in so close to shore, why she was not protected, why help did not come.

Captain Toth was personally acquainted with Vice Admiral Martin, the commander of the Sixth Fleet, so he wrote to Admiral Martin asking the same questions he asked of everyone else. He showed me the reply. Admiral Martin wrote a very kind, sympathetic letter of condolence on flag officer stationery, which he signed informally with his first name, but he offered no new information. His letter simply brushed off the attack as an unfortunate accident. This was the official story: it was an accident. So sorry about Steve.

Captain Toth soon became a bitter and disillusioned man. He had worked to make his son a naval officer. He had helped Steve get an appointment to the Naval Academy, had encouraged him, watched him grow and mature. Now Steve was dead. He was sure that someone in the Navy was at fault, and he could not uncover the truth. He knew he was being fed gobbledygook and he didn't know what to do about it. The old captain remained angry and, being angry, he aged at a remarkable rate. Within a year he was dead.

———

While *Liberty* was in Malta, the question of "hostile fire pay" for the *Liberty* crew arose. This became a thorny matter for the money managers. Vietnam was the only combat zone recognized by the Pentagon. Hence, by bureaucratic reasoning, one could not receive the customary extra stipend of about $45 per month awarded to those who risked hostile gunfire unless one was in Vietnam.

When this policy was questioned through the *Liberty* chain of command, the Pentagon was forced to make a decision. Rumor had it that Secretary McNamara personally participated in the judgment. Those who were shot at and hit, it was decided, were obviously subject to hostile fire and would receive appropriate pay for that month; those who were not hit would not receive hostile fire pay; those who were wounded and as a result of those wounds were hospitalized would receive hostile fire pay for up to four months of the period of hospitalization.

This decision would have been Solomon's undoing. It created ill will and resentment among the eighty-eight men who were lucky enough not to have been hit, and it saved the Navy perhaps $4,000 in hostile fire pay. The men knew that in Vietnam one received hostile fire pay for simply being in the country. It was not necessary to be shot at, or even to be in a dangerous area. And if a man *was* hit, he continued to draw hostile fire pay for the entire period of hospitalization; it did not stop arbitrarily after four months.

Ironically, the short-sighted decision ultimately increased the cost of the attack. Men felt they had been cheated of a payment that had been earned. Consequently, they were less than usually inhibited about taking $45 worth of ship's equipment with them upon transfer, or filing a claim for $65 combat damage to a radio that had cost $10, or forgetting to return a set of golf clubs.

Theft, which had never been a serious problem on *Liberty,* suddenly became a problem. Before the effects of the dead officers were packed and inventoried, one man systematically looted their staterooms, helping himself to cameras, tape recorders and even a supply of Alka-Seltzer. Sentries and quarterdeck watch-standers were instructed to inspect *every* package carried off the ship; and when the thefts continued, the sentries themselves were threatened with prosecution for laxity. The captain's 8mm movie camera disappeared. The bridge camera vanished. New typewriters, still in the manufacturer's cartons, disappeared. A man caught stealing from a shipmate was fined $120 and restricted to the ship for two weeks. But the thefts seemed to reflect anger and frustration more than anything else, and they continued.

Several men qualified for hostile fire pay by discovering and reporting wounds that they had not previously felt compelled to report. Their names were then added to the list of those wounded in action, and they were subsequently awarded the Purple Heart for wounds received in action; eventually, they were also compensated by Israel for minor shrapnel wounds, generally to the tune of $200 or $300.

It was during this period, also, that the Pentagon, at the behest of the State Department, started gathering information that would be used to prosecute a claim for damages against Israel.

A Navy lawyer took a medical statement from me during my second month in the hospital. It was impossible to guess what might be the lingering effects of my injuries, how long I would be hospitalized, or what all this might do to my military career. I was disturbed that the government was apparently prepared to act upon what I considered to be incomplete information. I didn't realize that I was lucky to be left in peace.

Survivors transferred to San Juan were less fortunate. In an incredible abuse of authority, military officers held two young *Liberty* sailors against their will in a locked and heavily guarded psychiatric ward of the base hospital. For days these men were drugged and questioned about their recollections of the attack by a "therapist" who admitted to being untrained in either psychiatry or psychology; at one point they avoided electroshock therapy only by bolting from the room and demanding to see the commanding officer. And before being released, they were forced to promise, in writing, never to discuss the *Liberty* attack *or* the hospital episode.

Chapter 14

NORFOLK AND HOME

Not alone is the strength of the Fleet measured by the number of its fighting units, but by its efficiency, by its ability to proceed promptly where it is needed and to engage and overcome an enemy.

Admiral Richard Wainwright, U.S.N., 1911

Repairs to the ship were completed on the fourteenth of July, dock trials were conducted on the fifteenth, and the ship got underway for Norfolk early the next morning. Probably the Maltese were glad to see her go. Certainly the work of the police, the shore patrol, the embassy staff, and the shipyard guards and gatekeepers would be simpler with the ship gone.

A young unmarried officer was nearly left behind as he and a friend slept late in Kiepfer's villa. The pilot was aboard. The lines were singled up and ready to be cast off. The crew was mustered and accounted for. But the young officer was absent.

Departure could not be delayed, but a certain amount of stalling was possible. Kiepfer trained binoculars on the shipyard's main gate while others fumbled with equipment. Cables were attached to the gangway, ready to lift it away. Suddenly, when the ship could delay no longer, a cry came from the bridge: "Hold it! Here comes a cab."

The taxi's passenger door was open even before the car stopped. The passenger stuffed a large bill into the driver's hand and rushed —looking sheepish, unshaven and sleepy in rumpled civilian clothing —across the gangway. The deck department officer gave the thumb-up signal to the crane operator, and the gangway was hoisted.

Liberty was underway.

She had been repaired, more or less, but she was not ready for sea in any real sense. Her holes had been covered—at least, steel plates had been welded over them to keep out light, air and water, but these were more "patch" than "repair." Major work had been done on the torpedo hole, as otherwise the ship could not have sailed. She was without radar and her keel was twisted. If one stood on the bridge at the ship's centerline, it was clear that the starboard portions of the main deck were several inches higher than the corresponding parts on the port side. The entire ship was twisted from the force of the torpedo explosion. This could be seen even more clearly from about halfway up the ship's mast; it was here that it was first detected by maintenance men who had gone aloft to clean and repair radio antennas.

Because she was not fully seaworthy, she was accompanied again by fleet tug *Papago*. *Papago* would provide assistance with radar, communications and navigation, and with this help it was hoped that *Liberty* could negotiate the Atlantic without incident.

As it turned out, USS *Papago* nearly accomplished what Israel had failed to do. It was night as *Liberty* reached the Strait of Gibraltar. This heavily traveled gateway to the Mediterranean sees more than its share of collisions in the best of times; *Liberty* made the transit at night, without radar, and in thick fog.

Papago led the way. *Liberty* followed a few hundred yards in her wake. The ships moved together at low speed, *Papago* scanning her radar for approaching ships and guiding *Liberty* through the obstacle course with terse radio commands.

The officers on *Liberty*'s bridge were blind. While foghorns of other ships could be heard in the distance, these came from everywhere, and their distances and directions seemed to change so quickly that it was impossible to know how many ships were near.

Papago identified ships on her radar scope as "Contact A," "Contact B" and so on, and radioed this information to a man on *Liberty*'s bridge who kept a running plot of each ship's track—information that was not always satisfying to the officer of the deck when he heard foghorns where no ships had been reported. Lookouts on the forecastle extended the conning officer's sight and hearing for perhaps a hundred feet, and everyone knew the ship could not be stopped in less than half a mile. Once again, *Liberty* was in serious danger.

Captain McGonagle sat in his chair on the bridge. Occasionally he lifted the heavy Navy-issue Bausch and Lomb binoculars to his eyes to search for other ships. This was more habit than help, as he could see only a gray haze. Above the murmur of the ship's engines he could hear many foghorns, and he could not be certain of their location. When he could tolerate the risk no longer, he turned suddenly to his conning officer, and without explanation said, "Sound General Quarters."

"Sound General Quarters," the conning officer repeated promptly as he relayed the order to the quartermaster.

"General Quarters, sir?" asked the startled quartermaster, certain he had misunderstood.

"Affirmative. Sound General Quarters," confirmed the conning officer.

"Sound General Quarters, aye, sir," the quartermaster responded as his palm pushed the lever activating the alarm.

Clang, clang, clang, clang, sounded the alarm. Men moved from their bunks, startled into wakefulness, pulling on trousers, slipping into shoes without socks.

"What the hell's goin' on?"

"Must be the goddamned Israelis come back to finish us off."

In less than five minutes the *Liberty* crewmen were awake, dressed and at battle stations. McGonagle used the general announcing system to explain that the ship was operating without radar in dangerous conditions in a heavy fog, and that he had sounded the General Quarters alarm as the quickest and surest way to get everyone awake and on their feet. Everyone but Kiepfer. Unflustered, he stayed in bed. There would be time enough to get up when he heard the crash.

Now at General Quarters, the ship continued slowly through the Strait while the fog, if anything, grew thicker. The crew fidgeted restlessly or dozed at battle stations while McGonagle and the officers on the bridge strained to keep track of ships reported by *Papago* and stared anxiously into the thick blanket that hung around the ship.

Once, a message from *Papago* ordered *Liberty* to turn right. The officer of the deck turned, then exchanged several urgent messages with *Papago*, *Liberty* questioning the course given, *Papago* insisting that the course was a safe one. Finally, McGonagle trusted his instinct over *Papago*'s advice and ordered the conning officer to turn away. Just in time. A few minutes later he would have run aground in the Strait. Once again McGonagle had saved his ship from destruction.

Days later, in the open sea, it became necessary to transfer some material between the two ships, and for this purpose a high line transfer was arranged. *Liberty,* her best helmsman at the wheel, steered her straightest possible course while *Papago* came close alongside. The material was then hauled over on lines handled by seamen.

But something went wrong.

Suddenly *Papago* veered toward *Liberty* in a move that everyone on deck knew would cause a collision. They had not counted on McGonagle. Almost in one move McGonagle sounded the collision alarm, ordered *Papago* to stop her engines and turned *Liberty* toward *Papago.* By turning toward her, *Liberty*'s stern swung away from her and the ships separated safely. And McGonagle grew even more in the eyes of his crew.

From that moment rumor spread that *Papago* was really an Israeli gunboat in disguise. At any time she could be expected to hoist the Star of David (or the Jolly Roger) and blow *Liberty* out of the water.

======

On July 29, *Liberty* arrived at Little Creek Naval Station, near Norfolk, with helicopters overhead and a few hundred people on the ground. Although few events seem to move more slowly than the arrival of a ship, *Liberty* eventually found her place alongside the pier and the crane crews finally positioned the gangway.

First aboard were the local brass, followed by Miss Norfolk and Miss Hospitality, who were followed by television cameramen, who were followed by radio and newspaper reporters, who, finally, were followed by Mrs. McGonagle and the wives and family of the *Liberty* crewmen. The reunions were emotional, made more so by the presence of some of the newly widowed wives, who were called to the ship by habit and duty.

McGonagle endured another painful news conference, this one under television lights in the still-scarred wardroom. Again he mouthed the official fabrication that it was all an unfortunate mistake. Then it was over. *Liberty* was home.

During the next few weeks, I was visited at the hospital by nearly all of the ship's officers. While Captain McGonagle said little, the other officers were unanimous in their anger at the Israelis and in their conviction that the attack was deliberate.

Among the most angry and vocal was Lieutenant Maurice Bennett. Maury Bennett had been invited to accompany McGonagle to Washington for an interview with the Chief of Naval Operations, Admiral David L. McDonald. He was looking forward to this opportunity to meet the Navy's most senior officer and to discuss the attack with him. For myself, I was eager to hear Maury's report of the encounter. Perhaps Admiral McDonald would help clear up some of the mystery surrounding the attack. To our surprise, Maury returned from Washington silent and subdued.

"What happened, Maury?"

"We met with Admiral McDonald and Senator Fulbright."

"And?"

"That's all. It was an accident. There's nothing more to say."

"Bullshit! We both know better than that, Maury. It was deliberate goddamned murder. Did you get brainwashed up there?"

"That's all I can say. It was an accident."

Maury left the distinct impression that he had been told not to discuss the meeting, and he would not allow himself to be drawn out. In fact, seven years would pass before he would discuss what had *really* happened in that meeting.

Forgotten in the confusion of the attack and its aftermath was the story, early in the trip, that a spy had been placed aboard to investigate illegal use of alcohol among officers and crew. Because I reported to the ship for duty only a few days before sailing, many of the officers and most of the crew suspected that I was the spy; no one suspected the ship's doctor, who came aboard about the same time I did and who merrily participated in all the ship's shenanigans.

Shortly after *Liberty* returned to Norfolk, Dr. Kiepfer was summoned to the office of Rear Admiral Henry Algernon Renken. Kiepfer had hoped that Rear Admiral Renken would somehow forget the assignment Renken had given him. Kiepfer had not wanted the job then and he did not want to see the Admiral now, but the visit was unavoidable.

"Well, what did you find out?" Renken asked after exchanging pleasantries.

"Fine ship. Fine crew. Those men really came through like professionals. You can be proud of them."

"I am, Doctor, I am," said the admiral. "But what I want to know about now are the liquor violations."

"Yes, sir. This is not an easy report to make. I made some close friends on that ship. Under the circumstances the report is a little easier to make, as I don't suppose a lot will be made of it. Yes. Your information was correct. Nearly every officer drank. And most of the chiefs. And much of the crew."

Kiepfer knew he was not reporting anything that the admiral did not already know; he made the report, and to protect his shipmates he avoided using names. He hated the job and was pleased when the conversation shifted to other subjects.

As Kiepfer was leaving, the admiral returned to the subject of alcohol.

"The British have liquor aboard ship."

"Sir?"

"Dry wardrooms are almost a tradition in our Navy. But no ship could perform any better than *Liberty* did, liquor violations or not. Maybe we should put liquor back on *all* our ships."

=====

Meanwhile, time passed slowly at Portsmouth Naval Hospital. My body cast had been removed. Now I was scheduled to spend six to eight months in leg traction—an interminable period on my back fighting boredom and bedsores. Soon, however, a friend from the cruiser *Newport News* offered to help. Commander Dick Grant, a Navy pilot, was an accomplished stage hypnotist, and he suggested that hypnotism might speed my recovery. While I was under hypnosis, he told me that my spirits would remain high despite the long confinement, that my muscle tone would remain good despite the inactivity, and that my leg fracture would heal rapidly; and he taught me to reinforce the suggestions with self-hypnosis. Although neither of us was convinced that hypnosis could do these things, we thought it would be fun to try.

It may have worked. I never felt depressed, my muscles remained firm and, most amazing of all, my leg healed so quickly that I was removed from traction fully two months ahead of schedule. "In a week or ten days, when you are strong enough to handle crutches, we'll let you go home," my doctor said as he gave me the news.

Hypnosis had convinced me that I could walk immediately, without lessons or physical therapy, and I spent the rest of the day trying to convince a skeptical hospital staff. Finally, an exasperated physical therapist arrived with a husky male nurse. "Now, catch him when he falls," she said. But I didn't fall. I fairly waltzed around the room, almost as though I had never been hurt.

"I'll be damned," said the nurse.

"Amazing," said the therapist.

"You know," said a hospital corpsman two months later, "we had a lieutenant here a few weeks ago who got right out of bed after four months and walked on crutches with no therapy at all."

"Is that so?"

"You know," said a fellow patient some time later, "you are a living legend in that physical therapy department."

"No kidding?"

On January 23, 1968, much of the *Liberty* attack scenario was played out again when North Korean naval forces captured the environmental research (intelligence) ship USS *Pueblo*[1] and her eighty-three-man crew in international waters off the Korean coast near Wonsan after a bloody, one-sided fight. I remember my feeling of angry frustration as I compared the two attacks: *Pueblo,* like *Liberty,* was lightly armed, unescorted, unprotected and ill prepared to protect herself against an armed enemy; *Pueblo,* like *Liberty,* failed to receive fighter protection or any other armed support; *Pueblo,* like *Liberty,* could not be protected because the nearest aircraft were equipped only for a nuclear mission and because conventionally armed aircraft were too far away and lacked refueling tankers. The story is told by William Beecher in the New York *Times* of January 24, 1968:

1. *Jane's Fighting Ships* lists three "Environmental Research" ships: USS *Banner* (AGER-1), USS *Pueblo* (AGER-2) and USS *Palm Beach* (AGER-3). These are former Army supply ships of about 180 feet, usually assigned a crew of six officers and about seventy-five enlisted men. *Jane's* reports that the ships have been converted for passive intelligence operations, are fitted for electronic intelligence, and carry sonar equipment for submarine noise identification and hydrographic work.

Washington, Jan. 24—The closest jet fighter-bombers to the intelligence ship Pueblo were rigged solely for a nuclear mission, ranking Pentagon sources said today. Thus, they added, the planes could not have been readied in time to aid the beleaguered ship yesterday after she called for help. This was offered as a principal reason North Korean gunboats were able to seize the Pueblo and force her into Wonsan harbor without opposition.

Contributing causes, some officials conceded, were a lack of ready American fighter planes with nonnuclear payloads. There were 12 Phantom F-4 jet fighters in South Korea at the time, officials said. Half of them were on alert for possible call to use nuclear weapons. The remaining planes were on standby. All of the aircraft were equipped with bomb racks and other equipment applicable only to the nuclear mission. It would have taken at least two to three hours for the nuclear bomb racks and associated devices to be replaced with conventional bomb racks, gun pods and air-to-air pylons.

The three squadrons of Phantoms in Japan were too far away and did not have aerial refueling tankers available, officials said. Similarly, the Enterprise, with its 90 planes, was about 600 miles away, steaming toward Vietnam.

The capture of USS *Pueblo* would never have been seriously considered if our government had not demonstrated through the *Liberty* fiasco that we were not prepared to protect our intelligence vessels.

While the American public supposed that Sixth Fleet aircraft had responded "within moments" to the ship's cry for help—for that is what the public was told—the Soviet Union was not deluded. The Soviet Union carefully monitored the entire affair through their network of SIGINT (intelligence) vessels, which included a SIGINT trawler *within the American formation.* No one knew better than the Soviets that our pilots were hamstrung; the Soviet operators must have watched with amazement as the powerful Sixth Fleet bungled the rescue.

Having observed the fleet's inability to protect *Liberty,* the Soviets were aware that an American intelligence vessel was ripe for harvest. Soon the North Korean government became the agent for the plucking of USS *Pueblo,* an act that was probably the most productive intelligence coup of this century.

━━━

In February 1968, just a few days after the *Pueblo* capture, USNS *Sergeant Joseph P. Muller,* [2] a civilian-operated U.S. Naval Ship, was

2. See Reference 1, Chapter 4, page 36, for a discussion of *Muller.*

on special operations (intelligence) duty off Cuba when her engines failed and the ship drifted helplessly toward Cuban national waters.

Communications, which had failed both *Liberty* and *Pueblo,* worked smoothly. At the first sign of serious danger, *Muller*'s Teletype circuits were patched directly through to the Joint Chiefs of Staff in the Pentagon, where the situation was directly monitored and controlled by the country's most senior military officers. For weeks, *Muller* had been escorted full-time by a fully armed destroyer that remained just five miles farther out to sea than *Muller.* Now the destroyer came in closer and passed a towline to the old civilian freighter to pull her back to safer, deeper water. The line snapped.

Fighters were scrambled from a U.S. air base in Florida. *Muller* crewmen were comforted to see the aircraft near them, ready to provide protection if necessary. Another line was passed to *Muller* and this, too, parted. During the next hour, several lines and various methods of rigging them were tried, and one after another the lines parted as *Muller* continued to drift toward the beach.

The men knew that Castro was eager to capture their ship and crew. *Muller* was an unwelcome symbol of freedom on the Cuban horizon. Almost weekly she would retrieve men, women and even whole families who had escaped from the Cuban mainland. They came in boats, on rafts, floating on inner tubes; even some strong swimmers came. Castro was sufficiently concerned that he dispatched a group of Cuban agents, who were promptly rescued and who then proceeded to ask obvious leading questions. So *Muller* men knew that they would be a great prize for Castro; and as they continued to drift toward shore they were reassured by the presence of an armed destroyer alongside and armed fighters overhead. They knew that if Castro took them, they would not come cheap.

Just as the ship was about to cross into Cuban waters, a towline held and she was quickly towed to safety. A young *Muller* sailor described the experience in a letter home, and his parents were sufficiently impressed that they told a Chicago newspaper about it; but the wire services failed to pick up the story, and it remains little known except to those who were involved.

The Navy, meanwhile, concluded that such extraordinary measures to protect special-duty ships were not worth the cost, and soon took all such ships out of service.

In February, I was released from the hospital on limited duty and was assigned to temporary duty in Norfolk, then to school in Pensacola. While movers worked in our Norfolk townhouse, packing for the move to Florida, the mailman brought a note from McGonagle. He had been promoted to captain in the year since the attack, and was now to be further honored. The note, dated June 5, 1968, read:

> Dear Jim, The President of the United States of America has awarded me the nation's highest award, the Congressional Medal of Honor. You are cordially invited to attend the presentation, by the Secretary of the Navy, at 11:30 A.M., 11 June 1968, at the Washington Navy Yard, Washington, D.C. Sincerely, William L. McGonagle, Captain, U.S. Navy

My reactions were several. Why was the invitation mailed only six days before the ceremony? This was hardly adequate notice for a trip requiring overnight accommodations in Washington, baby sitters, transportation and other arrangements.

Why was the presentation to be made by the Secretary of the Navy? And why in the Navy Yard? Medals of Honor are ordinarily presented in the White House by the President with great fanfare and elaborate ceremony. McGonagle's medal should have been awarded with no less pomp.

A naval officer concerned with medals and awards told me the story: "The government is pretty jumpy about Israel," he said. "The State Department even asked the Israeli ambassador if his government had any objection to McGonagle getting the medal. 'Certainly not!' Israel said. But to avoid any possible offense, McGonagle's citation does not mention Israel at all, and the award ceremony kept the lowest possible profile."

Medal of Honor winners and their guests are traditionally treated by the United States to a luxurious dinner at a first-class restaurant. Captain and Mrs. McGonagle were put up at the Shoreham Hotel, and it was decided to have the award dinner at the hotel restaurant. In keeping with the spirit of the affair, however, someone failed to notify the restaurant.

Guests arriving at the appointed hour asked the maitre d' for the McGonagle party. McGonagle? Could it be another name? Another night? The hotel staff moved quickly to avert a disaster. When the McGonagles arrived, they found their guests just being seated at hastily set tables, and never suspected that anything had gone wrong.

The next morning Navy Secretary Paul Ignatius presented McGonagle's medal in a modest ceremony perhaps two miles from the White House. It was done with a minimum of fanfare and almost no publicity at all. It was done while the President was in the White House. And it was done within hours of a White House ceremony in which the President awarded medals to a pair of Vietnam heroes.

Such public recognition was not for McGonagle. The Washington *Post* did not cover the story; the *Evening News* pictured a weeping McGonagle on page sixteen over a brief caption.

McGonagle went on to assume command of a newly constructed ammunition ship, USS *Kilauea*. On June 28, 1968, USS *Liberty* was decommissioned at a brief ceremony at Portsmouth, Virginia. Two years later she was sold for scrap to the Boston Metals Company of Baltimore for $101,666.66.

Chapter 15

ISRAEL PAYS DAMAGES

Ships . . . must be followed by the protection of their country throughout the voyage.

Admiral Alfred Thayer Mahan, U.S. Navy,
The Influence of Sea Power Upon History (1890)

A few days after the war, the government of France reneged on a contract for delivery to Israel of fifty Mirage fighters.[1] The United States, in turn, began negotiations with Israel for delivery of fifty Phantom F-4 fighters.[2]

Liberty sailors, meanwhile, aware that concurrent negotiations were underway to obtain Israeli compensation for *Liberty* deaths and injuries, and guessing that each was a bargaining card for the other, followed the news reports with interest. We were convinced that the question of Israeli damage payments would be resolved only after the jet-fighter contract was firm.

Some sources report that Israel tried to avoid liability for the attack by asserting, among other things, that it resulted from

1. The New York *Times,* November 4, 1967, p. 10.
2. The New York *Times,* December 19, 1967, p. 4.

McGonagle's negligent presence near a war-torn coast, and that it would not have occurred but for our own failure (due to communication problems) to order the ship out of the area. Nevertheless, death claims submitted soon after the attack were paid in full in June 1968, when our government received a check for $3,323,500 in behalf of families of thirty-four men killed in the attack.[3] That money represented 100 percent payment of claims averaging about $100,000, although the individual amounts varied widely according to the numbers and ages of dependents. Meanwhile, personal-injury claims were prepared for the *wounded,* and these took somewhat longer.

For the next several months a tug of war took place as scattered newspaper articles reported the pending sale of aircraft to Israel[4] and opposing factions defended their prejudices. Letters to the editor of the New York *Times* in January 1969 urged the government to cancel the sale because of Israeli attacks upon Lebanon;[5] and later that same month a congressman urged President Nixon to hasten delivery of the airplanes.[6] In February, President Nasser of Egypt suggested that delivery of the airplanes should be made contingent on Israel's withdrawal from Arab territories;[7] but a few days later Nasser's government announced that it would not hold the Nixon administration responsible for the sale.[8]

All appeared in readiness for delivery when, late in February 1969, individual *Liberty* survivors received word from the Department of State of the exact amounts to be claimed. In each case, officials of the Veterans Administration had reviewed the medical records to determine the extent of injury and, if disabled, the percentage of disability. The government decided that just compensation for total disability was $350,000. Therefore, $35,000 was to be claimed for men 10 percent disabled, $70,000 for those 20 percent disabled, and so forth. Although the government supported very large claims for the few severely disabled men, most *Liberty* claims were for less than $1,000, and many were from $200 to $400 for minor burns and shrapnel wounds.[9]

3. Department of State press release, May 13, 1969.
4. The New York *Times,* December 28, 1969, p. 1.
5. The New York *Times,* January 3, 1969, p. 26.
6. The New York *Times,* January 27, 1969, p. 14.
7. The New York *Times,* February 3, 1969, p. 1.
8. The New York *Times,* February 13, 1969, p. 4.
9. State Department representatives explained the formula to *Liberty* officers in 1968 while claims were still being processed. In 1975, I asked the Department of State for access under

Finally, on March 19, newspapers reported that 120 Israeli pilots were being trained by the United States Air Force to fly the soon-to-be-delivered airplanes.[10] Compensation for *Liberty* wounded could not be far behind.

On March 28, diplomatic notes were delivered to the government of Israel demanding payment for personal injuries—a separate note for each individual. Tersely worded on single sheets of paper, each note began, "The Embassy of the United States sends Greetings to the Government of Israel," and went on to mention the date and place of the attack, the name of the individual for whom compensation was demanded, and the amount of money considered appropriate. The notes were signed for the "Embassy of the United States of America," and dated the same day delivered.

Actually, the amounts asked were not seriously in contention, as informal agreement was reached before the letters were delivered. Israel hired a crack team of American lawyers to defend her interests, and these lawyers examined the medical records to verify that the claims were reasonable. They were reasonable, the lawyers reported, and should be paid in full.

The government of Israel maneuvered to protect its legal position. And, again, stories persist that Israel attempted to disclaim legal responsibility for the attack, but on April 28, 1969, $3,566,457 was received from the government of Israel in payment of injury claims. The money represented 100 percent payment of 164 claims totaling $3,452,275 on behalf of injured crewmen, $92,437 for expense incurred by the United States in providing medical treatment to the injured men, and $21,745 for reimbursement for personal property damaged or destroyed in the attack.[11] Checks were mailed to claimants on May 15. Seven men found no solace in money and filed no claim.

In August 1969, Israel received her first consignment of F-4 Phantom fighters.[12] State Department officials with whom I have discussed these events deny that there was any connection.

---

the Freedom of Information Act to records of those meetings pertaining to my own claim. I was told that there is no recollection that such meetings were held and, if they were, no records were kept of the proceedings. That such a system was used, however, tends to be borne out by the claims paid, which were generally divisible by $17,500 (5 percent increments of disability) in the larger awards, and by $3,500 (1 percent increments) in the smaller awards.

10. The New York *Times,* March 19, 1969, p. 7.
11. Department of State press release, May 13, 1969.
12. The New York *Times,* September 7, 1969, p. 9.

Meanwhile, the United States asked for only a token payment for the loss of the ship. After spending $20 million for refitting and $10 million more for "technical research equipment," the United States asked only $7,644,146 for the ship's loss—apparently based upon the current value of a typical ship of *Liberty*'s type and age. And Israel quickly promised to pay. Then, as the affair slipped from public memory, the government of Israel became less concerned with justice and more concerned with economics. The bill remains unpaid as this book goes to press in 1979.

Chapter 16

REFLECTIONS
ON THE COVER-UP

Most official accounts of past wars are deceptively well
written, and seem to omit many important matters—in
particular, anything which might indicate that any of our
commanders ever made the slightest mistake. They are
therefore useless as a source of instruction.

Montgomery of Alamein,
Memoirs, xxxiii (1958)

Two years after the attack I received a letter from former United
States Information Agency writer Eugene G. Windchy, who was
writing a book on peacetime naval incidents. Windchy had interviewed Kiepfer and McGonagle by telephone. Now he had some
questions for me.

I was not yet ready to talk freely with newsmen about the attack,
but Windchy's letter seemed harmless. He asked only whether the
ship's name was painted on her stern (of course it was) and why we
were apparently unable to identify the aircraft we saw before the
attack (we *had* identified some of them). I saw no harm in answering,
so I prepared a brief reply.

Even before I could clear my reply with my commanding officer,
an urgent message arrived from Washington warning of Windchy's
inquiries and demanding immediate reports of any contacts made by
him. Following the Navy chain of command, I asked my department

head to inform my commanding officer. In a few minutes the intercom on my desk barked: "The captain wants to see you in his office
right away. Better hurry! He's fuming."

The commanding officer, I soon discovered, was angry that I had
not informed him immediately of Windchy's request, and he seemed
genuinely alarmed. His reaction reached far beyond the requirement
of the message from Washington, and I wondered why. When I told
him of my conviction that the attack was deliberate and that the
truth was being covered up, he endured the recitation with a blank
expression and asked not a single question. His only concern was to
assure that I did not answer Windchy's letter.

So ended Windchy's inquiry. Months later Windchy told me
by telephone that *none* of his letters was answered. He never knew
why.[1]

Meanwhile, others began asking questions also. Joe Benkert, now in
Washington and still smarting from the press interview in Norfolk,
began to question survivors and others who might shed some light
on the affair, and to compile a file on the attack.

Benkert remembered the several rolls of pictures he had taken
with the captain's Polaroid camera during the latter moments of the
torpedo-boat assault. Some of these might have proved that the boats
continued to fire long after the attack was supposedly over; but
McGonagle told him to give the pictures to Admiral Kidd, and
Benkert never saw them again. Benkert also remembered that two
rolls of 35mm film were shot by the ship's photographer, Chuck
Rowley, before the attack. Some of the pictures should have shown
how close the reconnaissance aircraft came. He gave those to Admiral Kidd also, and when they came back they were unprintable.

He set about trying to learn what he could about the several
peculiar things he had seen. However, he was not sufficiently discreet, and word of his inquiries reached his seniors. Soon he was
summoned to the office of his department head, a Navy captain, who
wanted to know what he was doing and why.

"Well, uh, I'm just collecting information for a scrapbook. Nothing classified. Just for my own information."

---

1. Windchy's work resulted in his 1971 Doubleday book, *Tonkin Gulf,* concerning Vietnam's 1964 attack on USS *Maddox,* which preceded the "Tonkin Gulf resolution." The book
contained several references to the *Liberty* attack.

"A scrapbook? You don't need a scrapbook. You'll be much better off if you forget the whole thing. Just knock it off and forget about it."

"But Captain, I—"

"Forget it, Chief. That's an order."

Thus the cover-up was perpetuated by honest men whose concern, no doubt, was to follow orders and protect the national security, not knowingly to foster a cover-up.

Important clues to the mechanics of much of the cover-up can be found in Phil Goulding's book, *Confirm or Deny.* Goulding describes the *Liberty* incident as seen from his office in the Pentagon: the sketchy information, the inquisitive press, the speculation, the time constraints. Among other things, he is troubled by White House reaction to fragments in the press and by his own distrust of the ability of the press to deal fairly with incomplete information.

"After a rash of misleading and speculative stories appeared early in the week after the attack," Goulding wrote, "I recommended to McNamara that we clamp a lid on all *Liberty* news until a Navy Court of Inquiry meeting in Valletta, Malta, finished its investigation. He agreed, asking the Navy to handle its inquiry as rapidly as it could so that we could give the people an unclassified version of its findings."[2]

Although probably not Goulding's intent, it was here that the cover-up went into high gear. Five hours after that message was released, Admiral McCain's London headquarters sent a high-precedence message demanding immediate reports and transcripts of all news interviews conducted.[3] Meanwhile, Kidd and McGonagle warned the *Liberty* crew to say nothing to anyone. Soon Ambassador Feldman entered the scene, applying further pressure. Commander Cooney flew to Naples to help keep the lid on. Public affairs officers visited the ship.

These men were not charging off on their own; they were responding to an order—the message from the Secretary of Defense, which Goulding had recommended and which he had drafted. Each man had received the order that no further comment would be made at

2. Goulding, *Confirm or Deny* (New York: Harper & Row, 1970), p. 129; the clampdown order was issued in SECDEF message 141747Z June 1967.
3. CINCUSNAVEUR message 142145Z June 1967.

this time, and each man relayed and enforced the order within his own area of responsibility.

On June 28, when the official report was released and the news blackout was officially lifted, the message from Goulding's office advising of that fact contained this unfortunate wording:

> . . . IF MEMBERS OF THE CREW NOW DESIRE TO GIVE INTERVIEWS AND RESPOND TO PRESS QUERIES ABOUT THE ATTACK ITSELF THEY ARE AUTHORIZED TO DO SO. OTHER SUBSTANTIVE QUERIES ABOUT THE ATTACK WILL BE HANDLED BY OASD(PA) [Goulding's office in the Pentagon]; *NARRATIVE AND TESTIMONY REFERRED TO ABOVE ARE THE ONLY PORTION OF COURT OF INQUIRY THAT HAVE BEEN DECLASSIFIED.* NORMAL SECURITY PROCEDURES ARE OTHERWISE APPLICABLE [emphasis added]."[4]

One wonders whether Phil Goulding, a newspaperman, intended to release a message that said, in effect, that the blackout was still on and would remain on, and that nothing at all could be said unless the Court of Inquiry had already said it. That is how the message was understood, and that is how it was interpreted as a direct order to the *Liberty* crew and to others who might be interviewed.

—————

Describing the press reaction to the court's report, Goulding wrote: "A great many other questions were asked by the press after publication of the Court of Inquiry findings, and there was considerable dissatisfaction with the findings. . . . the editorial writers, not having taken the time or trouble to find out what the Court of Inquiry was authorized to do, left the implication that the Navy and the Department of Defense were engaged in a giant conspiracy to deceive the American people."

No wonder. The court failed to address the questions that the press and the people wanted answered. If the court could not report the truth about the attack, then someone else in the government should have. But no one did. Instead, witnesses were silenced, the government pretended that nothing untoward was going on, and the questions remained unanswered. In short, a cover-up.

There *were* a number of perfectly legitimate security issues that

---

4. SECDEF message 282051Z June 1967.

had to be reckoned with: the mission and capabilities of the ship; the reaction time of the fleet; the deployment and control of nuclear weapons; the deployment of submarines. All of these things are sensitive and could provide useful information for a potential enemy. However, the cover-up went far beyond that.

Close questioning of McGonagle would have revealed the flaws in his account. Instead, as we have seen, everything he told the court was accepted as fact, and with only minor exceptions everything that conflicted with McGonagle's testimony either was classified "Top Secret" or was kept out of the official record.

While it is entirely possible that McGonagle testified as he did because he was *ordered* to testify that way, it is equally possible that his memory was faulty—as incredible a memory lapse as that may seem. From brief conversations I have had with McGonagle, I am convinced that there truly are large gaps in his recollections, that he has honestly forgotten much that happened on June 8. For instance, he seems to have no recollection at all of the initial rocket attack, and starts his story, as we have seen, with the gasoline drum explosion caused by the *second* airplane. Such pointless oversight seems more a trick of memory than a deliberate attempt at cover-up.

Memory gaps are common among *Liberty* survivors. For instance, Dave Lewis, who once told me in detail of seeing Chief Smith swept away to his death and of watching the bulkhead dissolve as the room filled with water, can no longer remember anything that happened during that period. George Wilson cannot recall putting a tourniquet on my leg. Frank McInturff cannot remember who helped him carry stretchers. Dave Lucas has forgotten much that happened during the attack and, as we have seen, is confused about the sequence of events he *does* recall. Yeoman Brownfield, even though he was on the bridge for much of the air attack, told a reporter that he can recall only *three* strafing runs. And although I prepared a statement for the court, I forgot that fact and some related details until reminded years later by a *Liberty* officer.

It is no wonder, then, considering the pressure he was under, that McGonagle's memory seems less than perfect. Among the records available to help him, probably the most important—certainly the most detailed record of the ship's operational situation—was the quartermaster's notebook. However, since McGonagle's review of the quartermaster's notebook did little to improve his testimony, it is likely that the notebook failed to provide a complete record. (If so, much of the responsibility for this failure is my own, as officer of the deck during the morning.) We know that McGonagle *did* consult the notebook, because he listed it with the court as a source of his information.

It is impossible now to check the accuracy or completeness of the notebook, because the most pertinent pages were *not* entered into evidence by the court, and the original notebook, if not destroyed, is buried in some inaccessible archive; the transcript contains quartermaster's notebook pages covering the afternoon (after 1300) only, whereas pages covering the period of heavy reconnaissance during the morning are conspicuously absent.

Unless someone deliberately doctored evidence, which seems unlikely (the habit of the court was to *ignore* evidence, not to doctor it), we must assume that the notebook failed to reflect all of the reconnaissance activity. McGonagle, then—troubled, sick and relying upon his own sometimes faulty memory and probably incomplete logs—may well have told the story to the best of his ability.

===

Admiral Kidd, for his part, was under pressure of a different sort. He had only a few days and limited resources to produce a public report on a controversial international incident. At the same time, he was required to protect classified information. And despite his warrant to look into "all of the pertinent facts and circumstances leading to and connected with the armed attack," he was nevertheless, as Goulding reminds us, limited in the scope of his inquiry. His purpose was to determine whether anyone *in the Navy* was at fault. He was not authorized to rule on, or apparently even to accept testimony bearing on, the culpability of the attackers. It was a difficult task. When witnesses did not agree, he had to make a decision. He could not entertain and resolve every conflict. So he accepted the commanding officer's testimony and gave short shrift to any witness who disagreed.

Isaac Kidd is a marvelously brilliant and thorough man. I once watched him at work, and I was awed by his genius. One would expect him to see through and to resolve at least some of the more obvious discrepancies in the testimony he received. But to compound his problems, Kidd was ill. The high temperature he had when he came aboard eventually reached 104 degrees, and the bronchial infection probably turned into pneumonia. He should have been in a hospital. Yet he stayed on his feet and continued to work sixteen and eighteen hours a day for nearly two weeks until the report was completed and a cleared summarized version was delivered to the press. With his seniors urging him to hurry and with the press and Congress clamoring for his report, Admiral Kidd apparently lacked the time, the energy, the heart or the authority to challenge a weary, grieving and heroic McGonagle.

=====

President Johnson must have known from the submarine photography that the attack consumed much more than five minutes and that it was probably deliberate. (According to *Liberty*'s Lieutenant Bennett, he *did* know. After years of silence on this subject, Bennett told me that in 1967 Senator William Fulbright informed Captain McGonagle and Chief of Naval Operations Admiral David L. McDonald in Bennett's presence that the President knew the attack was deliberate and had ordered the information covered up "for political reasons.")[5] The President *must* have known that McGonagle's description of the attack was inaccurate. He must have known that nuclear-armed aircraft were launched, and he would have been humiliated by public knowledge of failure to defend the ship. But even the President didn't have the full story; so when he elected to keep quiet about his knowledge of the attack, he was simply withholding another piece of the puzzle. Ordinarily, the press might have put the pieces together; however, the press was effectively hamstrung by the steady stream of "press guidance" messages that issued from the Pentagon.

Aside from the purely political motive of covering up the story to protect Israel, or the more direct purpose of avoiding public protest over our government's failure to protect the ship, there are indications that our government may have had yet another reason for covering up the circumstances of the attack.

The story first came to me from a Navy master chief petty officer who was working with the Central Intelligence Agency on a sensitive

5. On January 21, 1974, while buying coffee from a machine in a Navy building in Washington, D.C., Bennett ended almost seven years of silence on this subject to tell me, "The government knows the truth. Knew it all the time. Senator Fulbright told us that Johnson ordered a cover-up to protect Israel and to avoid causing a ruckus." Although Bennett confirmed that conversation on several later occasions, Captain McGonagle denies that he was present and Senator Fulbright has told me that he has no recollection of such a meeting. As this edition goes to press the apparent discrepancy remains unresolved.

project. The master chief had lost friends in the attack and happened to mention that fact during a meeting at CIA headquarters. Several people were in the room at the time and the subject soon changed. Later, one of the CIA employees returned to the topic in private conversation, seemingly anxious to inform the chief that the attack was no real surprise to the CIA. "Sending *Liberty* to Gaza was a calculated risk from the beginning," the man said. "Israel had told us long before the war to keep our intelligence ships away from her coast. *Liberty* was sent anyway because we just didn't think they were serious. We thought they might send a note of protest or, at most, harass the ship somehow. We didn't think they would really try to sink her." Although the man knew nothing of the circumstances of the attack itself, he insisted that our government was well aware that *Liberty*'s presence would be unwelcome in Israel.

At about the same time I learned of that conversation I received a report that there *was* a note of protest. "There was plenty of warning," a former Israeli government official told another friend. "Israel warned the United States to get that ship out of there. The United States just didn't react." Again, although the speaker knew nothing of the details of the attack, he insisted that the Israeli government had protested the ship's presence just a few hours before the attack.

Both of these stories are unconfirmed and secondhand; I cannot vouch for their accuracy, and I am not acquainted with either source. However, the two anonymous tales do tend to reinforce one another, they support much of what we *do* know about the attack and, if true, they explain the eleventh-hour frenzy to recall *Liberty,* and they provide a motive for the cover-up that followed.

American failure either to protect or to move the ship after a protest and implied threat would certainly compound our government's responsibility for whatever followed. When the failure resulted in attack and great loss of life, our government would not be inclined to lay out all the circumstances for public discussion.

During the several years since the attack, press interest in the story has never died and cover-up efforts have only rarely relaxed. *Liberty* crewmen living near Washington are approached regularly by reporters; yet, despite the attempts, few accounts have gone beyond the government's own version of the affair, and most reports that have gotten further have been based on speculation and imagination. The reporting effort has been thwarted by the vigilance of the Pentagon, by the reticence of the crew and, apparently, by suspicious publishers —who wisely see a political motive behind much of the writing.

Some survivors might consent to be interviewed if they were free to speak candidly, but they are not. For example, in 1975 *Liberty* officers were asked by the Chief of Naval Information (a post now held by *Rear Admiral* David Cooney, the former CINCLANTFLT public affairs officer) whether we would consent to be interviewed by a newsman.

Had the policy changed? I telephoned Cooney's office to ask what restrictions would attach to an interview.

"Nothing has changed," I was told. "Whatever restrictions were in effect in 1967 will still apply today." I asked whether we would be free to discuss preattack reconnaissance, duration of the attack, the fact that napalm was used, the fact that our flag was flying or that our life rafts were machine-gunned in the water. No, those things could not be discussed.

"How do you really feel about the interview?" I asked.

"We aren't encouraging cooperation," Cooney's man said, "although you are perfectly free to talk to the reporter if you want to. We will just want to know what questions he is going to ask and what answers you intend to give, and my boss"—Cooney again?—"will want to be present to see that it all stays on track."

Nothing had changed. Any interview would be a sham and would be restricted to previously published information. I declined the invitation. So did all my fellow officers.

=====

Despite the frustrations, press and public interest remain strong more than twelve years after the attack. However, even in 1979, *Liberty* interviews were frustrated by the government and *Liberty* inquiries were sometimes pigeon-holed indefinitely by government departments in violation of federal law.[6] Clearly, the USS *Liberty* cover-up is alive and well.

6. The Freedom of Information Act of 1974 (81 Stat. 54; 5 U.S.C. 552) governs the release of public information and requires each government agency to respond within ten days to a request for release of records. In unusual circumstances, that ten-day period may be extended for not more than an additional ten days. Despite those requirements, as this is written, three of the author's requests are still pending after delays of seven, seventeen, and nineteen months and despite repeated appeals to the agencies and to members of Congress. Apparently, court action will be needed to pry more information from the government.

Epilogue

WHY DID ISRAEL ATTACK?

We can chart our future clearly and wisely only when we know the path which has led to the present.

Adlai Stevenson,
Speech, Richmond, Virginia, September 20, 1962

On May 24, 1967, as *Liberty* left Abidjan ultimately to patrol the Gaza Strip, President Lyndon Johnson met in the White House with Israel's Foreign Minister Abba Eban. The purpose of Eban's visit was to advise the President of an impending all-out attack against Israel by the United Arab Republic and to determine what support Israel might expect from the United States.

Johnson's response must have been disappointing. He stressed that it would be necessary to work through the United Nations before the United States became directly involved, and added, "If it should become apparent that the U.N. is ineffective, then Israel and her friends, including the United States, who are willing to stand up and be counted, can give specific indication of what they can do."

Eban, displaying papers from a briefcase, reminded Johnson of American commitments to Israel and of Johnson's own strongly pro-Israel statements. "I am fully aware of what three past Presidents have said," Johnson said bluntly, "but that is not worth five cents if the people and the Congress do not support the President."

Mr. Johnson wanted Mr. Eban to understand, and to inform his government, that the United States would not support Israel if Israel initiated hostilities. The President chose his words carefully as he said, "The central point, Mr. Minister, is that your nation not be the one to bear responsibility for any outbreak of war." Then he added, very slowly and positively, "Israel will not be alone unless it decides to go alone." When Eban remained silent, Johnson repeated the statement: *"Israel will not be alone unless it decides to go alone."*

Mr. Eban returned to Israel, obviously impressed with the President's message. On May 28 the Israeli Cabinet decided to postpone military action, and on May 30 Prime Minister Eshkol sent Mr. Johnson a message confirming his understanding of the conversation with Eban. That conversation, he said, had "an important influence upon our decision to await developments for a further limited period."[1]

Six days later Israel attacked the Arab countries. Arab forces were slaughtered in huge numbers while largely Soviet-supplied equipment was destroyed and captured with embarrassing ease by overwhelmingly superior Israeli forces. The Israelis slashed their way across the Sinai. They opened the Gulf of Aqaba. They captured the old city of Jerusalem from Jordan.

Jordan agreed to a cease-fire. With most Arab forces in full retreat, the United States and the United Nations pressured Israel to back off. But even now the Israelis prepared to invade Syria.

Syrian artillerymen had shelled Israeli settlements from the Syrian Heights for nineteen years. And for nineteen years Syrian forces had strengthened their positions until they extended along thirty-five miles of mountain ridge from the Sea of Galilee to the foot of Mount Hermon. The bunkers were built of thick, reinforced concrete to withstand Israeli 500- and 1,000-pound bombs, and were designed with overhanging lips to resist the flow of napalm. The defenses were more than ten miles deep, consisting of row upon row of emplacements, cannons, tanks, tank traps, rocket launchers and antiaircraft guns.

Israeli forces were assembled for the attack as *Liberty* approached. It was to be a major assault under the worst tactical conditions

1. Lyndon Baines Johnson, *The Vantage Point—Perspectives of the Presidency 1963–1969* (New York: Holt, Rinehart & Winston, 1971).

against a well-entrenched enemy who commanded all the high ground. The Syrian deployment consisted of five infantry brigades, each with a battalion of modern Russian tanks; and behind the infantry was a freshly reinforced striking force of four more armored and mechanized brigades.

Brigadier General Elazar planned to pound the positions from the air, then carve a road up the side of the hill with bulldozers. Finally, he would send the tanks, tracked vehicles and infantry up the newly made road.

Syrians had been bombarding the lowlands steadily since the second day of the war, and Elazar's troops were eager to strike back. The Israeli general chose a ridge on the northern end of the border, fifteen hundred feet above the plain, for the initial breakthrough into Syria. This was one of the steepest points; thus it was one of the least heavily defended. Elazar assembled his troops and waited. At last, after several delays, he received his orders: the invasion was to begin Thursday morning, the eighth of June.

But less than three hours before the scheduled assault and less than two hundred miles away, USS *Liberty* arrived near El Arish. She slowed to five knots and ambled along the coast in good position to intercept radio messages from throughout the war zone, including much of the traffic from the invasion site.

A well-equipped electronic intelligence-collection platform positioned as *Liberty* was could have learned a great deal about the tactics, procedures, morale, discipline, order-of-battle and military objectives of both sides. And the lessons learned would have helped to build a data base of radio frequencies, call signs, unit identities and other information that would have helped to interpret and forecast other battles to be fought at other times and places.

Indeed, any good intelligence officer must have concluded that *Liberty* was an intelligence ship—and Israeli intelligence officers are among the best in the world. Any doubt about the ship's mission would have been resolved by the photographs taken during the morning (more special-purpose antennas than a guided-missile frigate) and by her behavior (a high-speed transit of the Mediterranean followed by a snail's pace crawl along the war-torn coasts).

But shortly after *Liberty*'s arrival—even as Israeli troops prepared to move toward their objective—General Elazar received new orders: the invasion was to be delayed for twenty-four hours.

Randolph and Winston Churchill tell us that the final postponement "would seem to have been [General Moshe] Dayan's decision," and they go on to speculate about the reasons.[2] The additional day, say the Churchills, was needed for the Israeli Air Force to "soften up" the Syrian positions, and for troops who had been switched from other fronts to rest. Also, say the Churchills, a successful Thursday attack would have encouraged Syria to accept the United Nations' call for a cease-fire—and Israel did not want to allow Syria that easy way out.

The Churchills do not tell us why those reasons became evident only as *Liberty* arrived on the scene or what influence the sudden appearance of a notorious American "spy ship" must have had on the invasion plans—nor do they tell us what might have compelled General Dayan suddenly to step in. But it seems more than coincidental that last-minute orders to delay the invasion came so soon after the arrival of USS *Liberty.*

———

The Israeli government was acutely aware of President Johnson's warning: the American President had told Foreign Minister Eban that he would support Israel *only* in self-defense, not in attacks against her neighbors. It was important, then, for Israel to be seen as an innocent victim fighting to ward off hoards of wild-eyed Arabs. Not surprisingly, Israel claimed that nearly everything she did was in self-defense. The preemptive strikes of the fifth of June were in self-defense. The capture of El Arish, the naval and paratroop assault on Sharm el-Sheikh, the sweep through Sinai, and the armed penetration of Jordan were all in self-defense. Now, with the war virtually over and with the world crying for peace, could Israel put troops in Syria without being seen as an aggressor?

Probably not.

Not with USS *Liberty* so close to shore and presumably listening. *Liberty* would have to go.

So—by remarkable coincidence, if not by design—General Elazar was forced to delay the invasion until *Liberty* was dispatched. Instead of attacking Syria, Israel's air, sea and shore-coordination forces worked together to attack a United States ship. Only then, with *Liberty* safely out of the picture, was Elazar turned loose. At 1130 Friday morning, June 9, as *Liberty* limped toward Malta, the first Israeli bulldozers climbed the mountain above Kefar Szold. A

2. Randolph S. Churchill and Winston S. Churchill, *The Six Day War* (Boston: Houghton Mifflin, 1967).

few hours later General Elazar took possession of the ridge to achieve a major objective of the war.

The invasion of Syria just a few hours after the attack on *Liberty* came as a surprise to most of the world. There seemed to be no connection between the two events, and writers who claimed to see a connection had no facts to back up their speculative stories. They had no facts because the facts were kept from them.

=====

In the months following the *Liberty* attack, the Central Intelligence Agency received a number of reports in support of the view that it was deliberate.

First to arrive was a message from Turkey dated June 23, 1967, reporting that the Turkish General Staff was convinced that the attack was deliberate. The report gives no indication what led to the conviction, but it is interesting that a foreign government with no stake in the affair had apparently come to such a disconcerting conclusion.[3]

A month later a message to the CIA reported a conversation with a confidential Israeli source who strongly implied that the attack was no error. The message read in part:

> He said that "you've got to remember that in this campaign there is neither time nor room for mistakes," which was intended as an obtuse reference that Israel's forces knew what flag the LIBERTY was flying and exactly what the vessel was doing off the coast. [The source] implied that the ship's identity was known at least six hours before the attack but that Israeli headquarters was not sure as to how many people might have access to the information the LIBERTY was intercepting. He also implied that there was no certainty or control as to where the information was going and again reiterated that Israeli forces did not make mistakes in their campaign. He was emphatic in stating to me that they knew what kind of ship USS LIBERTY was and what it was doing offshore.[4]

This report gains credibility when we recall that Israel *did* identify the ship six hours before the attack. Hence, the informant does indeed have access to inside information.

On November 9, 1967, a confidential source reported clearly and

---

3. CIA intelligence information cable, "Turkish General Staff Opinion Regarding the Israeli Attack on the USS LIBERTY."

4. CIA information report, "Comment on Known Identity of USS LIBERTY," July 27, 1967.

unequivocally that General Moshe Dayan ordered the attack. The message read:

> [The source] commented on the sinking [*sic*] of the US Communications ship *Liberty*. They said that Dayan personally ordered the attack on the ship and that one of his generals adamantly opposed the action and said, "This is pure murder." One of the admirals who was present also disapproved the action, and it was he who ordered it stopped and not Dayan.[5]

The messages, released under the Freedom of Information Act after heavy deletions by CIA censors, created a momentary stir when they appeared in the New York *Times* as a "public service message" by an Arab group under the heading "Are We Welcoming the Murderer of Our Sons?" The notice was timed to embarrass Dayan, appearing as it did simultaneously with his arrival in New York on September 19, 1977, but the hysterical tone probably cooled the press. Except for one mild question by a Washington-based radio reporter, Dayan was not asked about the attack, and the CIA promptly cleared him of any wrongdoing with a news release that called the reports "raw and unevaluated intelligence." "Israel," said the CIA, "did not learn the Liberty was an American ship until after the attack."

As we well know, Israel *did* know that the ship was American and admitted to our government that they knew the ship was American; Israel claims only that the *attacking forces* failed to get the word. In view of the less-than-candid CIA statement, I asked the CIA for a copy of a staff summary cited in the news release. When the summary finally arrived, an accompanying letter directed my attention to paragraph seven, which, said the CIA, would set forth the grounds upon which the agency's opinion was based. The report, however, fails to set forth any grounds at all and barely expresses an opinion. The pertinent section reads: "Thus it was not until [1512 *Liberty* time] that the Israelis became convinced that the *Liberty* was American."[6]

We are shown only the conclusion; nowhere are we made privy to information that leads to or supports the conclusion. The ten lines

5. CIA information report, "Attack on USS *Liberty* Ordered by Dayan."
6. CIA intelligence memorandum SC No. 01415/67, "The Israeli Attack on the USS Liberty," June 13, 1967.

preceding it are deleted from the summary by the CIA censor. But 1512 is the time at which the torpedo boats fired upon the life rafts, picked the bullet-riddled rafts out of the water, and departed; and that is the time that Israeli troop-carrying helicopters arrived and hovered near the ship's bridge not fifty yards from the oversized American flag that flew from the yardarm; and that is the time the last shot was fired. Presumably, the CIA accepts some of these circumstances as evidence that the ship was (or *must* have been) identified—if, in fact, it had not been identified long before.

=====

The CIA summary, prepared from early reports while *Liberty* was still en route to Malta, contains many errors and adds little to what has been published in the press. In an effort to learn more, *Liberty*'s Lieutenant Bennett (now Commander Bennett), assigned to the National Security Agency near Washington, prepared an official letter from the National Security Agency to the Central Intelligence Agency requesting access to all CIA files on the attack. Unlike a private request, this was entirely within government channels; Bennett was adequately cleared and had a reasonable excuse to see the material.

Soon Bennett was telephoned by a lieutenant commander aide to Admiral Stansfield Turner, the CIA director. "Why do you want to see the file?" he asked. Bennett explained. "Will you guarantee the security of the material?" Bennett guaranteed. Several days later the officer phoned again. "You must promise not to copy any of these files, and you must assure us that you are not writing anything for publication." Bennett promised.

It looked very much like Bennett would finally get the complete file—the uncensored, official story of what really happened to USS *Liberty*. Then the lieutenant commander called a third time. "There is nothing to send," he said. "Everything in our file has already been released under the Freedom of Information Act."

If that was true, it is highly unlikely that Bennett's request would have taken so long to answer or that it would ever have reached the CIA director's office. No matter. Admiral Turner's office had spoken, and it was unlikely that anything further would be learned from the Central Intelligence Agency.

=====

Much of the *Liberty* story is still a puzzle; for each question answered, another looms in its place. We know that the true story of the attack was covered up; but was it covered up by habit, fear and blind overreaction, or did a responsible American official deliberately withhold the truth? Was the cover-up ordered by the President of the United States? If so, did the President know the truth, or was he simply being cautious in the face of inconclusive evidence? Did senior officials in our government really believe that this carefully coordinated air/sea/commando/intelligence effort could have been a mistake? Was the attack ordered by a crazed Israeli officer, or was it a deliberate, calculated act of the Israeli government? Did General Dayan order the attack? We know that the ship was inadequately protected. Has any senior officer been required to answer to that? We know that Israel's excuse for attacking the ship cannot possibly be true. Why has our government not demanded a better explanation?

These questions cry out for answers. Some of the answers seem obvious while others have defied investigators for more than ten years. Perhaps the time has come for a committee of Congress to explore the remaining questions in order to tell the American people why thirty-four men died and why the truth has been hidden for so long.

Author's Note

A few days after the *Liberty* attack, Jim O'Connor's wife, Sandy, called upon a Jewish neighbor and found the woman almost in tears. "Oh, Sandy," the neighbor said, "I'm so sorry. I wanted to come see you, but I've been too ashamed."

Sandy was surprised and saddened to learn that her friend identified so closely with Israel that she felt guilty for Israel's crime. "Jews didn't attack *Liberty,*" Sandy explained. "An Israeli officer gave the order, and *he* is the one who should be ashamed."

I expressed a similar view in a letter written from the hospital. "Although someone who happens to be Jewish is criminally responsible for what happened to our ship," I wrote, "we must not blame Jews generally or even Israelis generally. Probably some field commander made the decision. We should blame him. Maybe even the Israeli top leadership made the decision. If so, we should blame them. But no one should blame every Jew or every Israeli. Jews died on that ship too."

I have written a book that exposes negligence, cover-up and misconduct. Reaction to my book (if, indeed, there is a reaction) will probably divide along political lines, and many readers will believe that the book was politically motivated. That is unfortunate.

I have told this story because it cries out to be told and because I believe that I am uniquely qualified to tell it. My presence on the bridge, my continued contact with key witnesses, and my access to large numbers of declassified government documents have given me a special understanding of the events surrounding the attack.

Many of the previously published stories on this subject have been weakened by inability to obtain reliable information. Some stories have been based on guesswork and faulty research. Many stories have lent the ship an aura of intrigue that she does not deserve. For example, reporters—no doubt fascinated by the prominent TRSSCOMM antenna—have breathlessly described a "Big Ear" on *Liberty*'s main deck, which supposedly intercepted radio messages "a hundred miles away." This is nonsense. One writer described a mysterious civilian in unmarked Army fatigues who was supposedly in charge. There was no such person; Lieutenant Commander David Edwin Lewis, United States Navy, was in charge of the Research Operations Department and wore the regulation U.S. Navy uniform. We have been told of "disturbing information" delivered to McGonagle a few hours before the attack, presumably warning of some Israeli plan for war. There was no such information. We have been told of "SOD units"; *Liberty* had nothing called an SOD unit. We have been told of "Pinnacle messages"; *Liberty* sent nothing called a Pinnacle message. One writer confidently informed his readers that *Liberty* didn't sink because she was specially equipped with huge steel plates that lowered automatically to seal the torpedo hole. And one particularly inventive "reporter" described frantic messages between McGonagle and the nuclear submarine USS *Andrew Jackson,* passed during the heat of battle by your author, James Ennes; however, your author did not relay any such messages, and USS *Liberty* did not communicate directly with any submarine while I was aboard.

An imaginative statement by one reporter would be picked up, embellished, and reported anew by other reporters. For instance, the hundred-mile "Big Ear" described in early *Liberty* reporting became a five-hundred-mile "Big Ear" in later stories. Actually, of course, the ship had no "Big Ear" at all, and no sonar capability and no underwater listening devices and no jamming equipment—all of which have been ascribed to her.

Having seen the speculative, erroneous reporting and the mistakes, half-truths, misleading statements and omissions in government accounts, I have made a special effort to verify and document my findings. Wherever possible, I have reported the sources of material facts. When controversial information came to me from an individual who could be embarrassed or damaged by being named, I have attempted to indicate the position and reliability of the source without using his name. In many cases, informants are still on active duty in the Navy. For their protection as well as my own, I have avoided telling active-duty military persons that my questions might lead to a book. To name such informants now would be quite unfair.

In some cases, information that came to me could not be documented in any of the official records that I was allowed to see. The presence of a submarine near USS *Liberty* is one example: no record of such a submarine can be found in the records that have been released—probably because details of submarine operations are very closely held and are almost never released. In such cases I have described the source of the information in general terms by footnote so that the reader may judge for himself.

I have been particularly frustrated in my efforts to find messages or other documents to prove my contention that nuclear-armed aircraft were sent to our defense and were prematurely recalled. Although the story persists and details from various sources all fit together logically, nowhere in the message logs or in the official scenarios that I have seen is there a suggestion that ready aircraft were sent. This is not surprising, since messages pertaining to atomic weapons are processed and filed separately from other messages. Because I trust the sources of this story, because it fits neatly into the known scenario, and because it helps to explain why *Liberty* was still without help more than three hours after first asking for it, I have reported the incident as fact—which I believe it is. Since available records do not reflect the flight and because the government may well deny that such a flight was made, I have described in a footnote the evidence that led me to the conclusion.

In a like manner, I have attempted to advise the reader, as much as possible, of the evidence that supports other key details of the story. Much evidence came from the formerly Top Secret Court of Inquiry report, which the Navy declassified and released in July 1976; other documentation came from declassified State Department files and from material released by the Lyndon Johnson Library in Austin. In addition, I received a steady flow of information from former *Liberty* crewmen, some of whom saved copies of nearly every document that passed through their hands following the attack. And a 12,000-word account I wrote in the hospital proved helpful later as a memory jogger. Finally, seven years of military duty in Washington, D.C., brought me into frequent contact with persons knowledgeable about the ship, and also helped to maintain contact with former shipmates.

I have had strong support from former shipmates, most of whom are eager to have this story told. For their sake, and for the thirty-four men who did not return, and for the several who will never fully recover, and for the innumerable wives, parents and children who suffered quietly at home, I have tried very hard to uncover and to report fairly and objectively the full, unvarnished story of what USS *Liberty* was all about and what happened to her.

With luck, this book may remove another stone from the wall that too often screens the government from the American people; with luck, this book may help make the next cover-up a bit more difficult to pull off.

LIBERTY'S TRACK

SEQUENCE OF EVENTS

JUNE 7, 1967

1. ———Israeli troops assemble at Lake Tiberias (Sea of Galilee) to prepare for invasion of Syria, scheduled to commence 1130 June 8.

JUNE 8, 1967

2. 0600 USS *Liberty*, 170 miles from invasion site, is reconnoitered by flying boxcar.

3. 0900 USS *Liberty*, 160 miles from invasion site, is reconnoitered by jet.

4. 1000 USS *Liberty* is reconnoitered by two armed jets, which report by radio to their headquarters that ship is flying the American flag.

5. ——— Israel orders twenty-four-hour delay in Syrian invasion.

6. 1030 USS *Liberty* is overflown at near-masthead level by flying boxcar.

7. 1100 USS *Liberty* is reconnoitered by flying boxcar.

8. 1130 USS *Liberty* is reconnoitered by flying boxcar.

9. 1200 Three Israeli torpedo boats leave Ashdo[c] on high-speed run to *Liberty*.

10. 1215 USS *Liberty* is reconnoitered by flying boxcar.

11. 1245 USS *Liberty* is reconnoitered by flying boxcar.

12. 1400 Israeli jets commence attack on *Liberty*.

13. 1409 USS *Saratoga* acknowledges *Liberty's* cry for help.

14. 1435 Torpedo explosion floods Research Ope[r]ations Department spaces, killing twenty-fiv[e]

15. ——— Torpedo boats circle ship, firing upon ship's firefighters.

16. 1515 Torpedo boats fire upon *Liberty* life raf[ts] then depart.

17. 1632 Torpedo boats return to *Liberty*; offer assistance.

JUNE 9, 1967

18. 1130 Israel invades Syria.

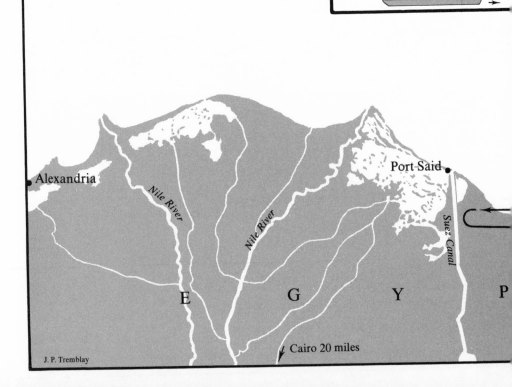

Alexandria

Port Said

Nile River

Nile River

Suez Canal

E   G   Y   P

Cairo 20 miles

J. P. Tremblay

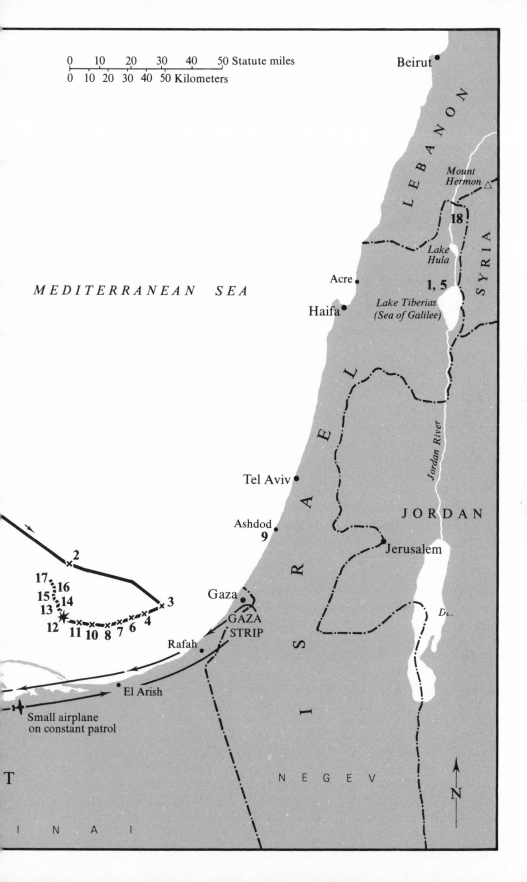

0 10 20 30 40 50 Statute miles

0 10 20 30 40 50 Kilometers

MEDITERRANEAN   SEA

Beirut

L E B A N O N

Mount Hermon △

18

Lake Hula

Acre

1, 5

Haifa

Lake Tiberias (Sea of Galilee)

S Y R I A

Jordan River

Tel Aviv

J O R D A N

Ashdod

9

Jerusalem

2

×

17   16

15   14

13

12   11 10 8 7 6 4

× × × × ×

3

Gaza

GAZA STRIP

Rafah

El Arish

Small airplane on constant patrol

I S R A E L

De

T

N E G E V

N

S I N A I

Appendixes

Appendix A

We have discussed in the preceding text five messages—all mishandled, delayed or lost—any one of which might have saved the ship had it been received by *Liberty*. On the following pages we will describe each message in more detail. All five messages are in standard military format and include the following elements:

Precedence. This is a speed-of-handling indicator assigned by the origina-tor. *Routine* is used for routine administrative messages; *Priority* is for messages that require preferential handling; *Immediate* is for urgent operational matters; *Flash* is the highest precedence and is reserved for enemy contact reports and other reports of extreme urgency.

Date-and-time-group. Each message is assigned a six-digit identifying number called a date-and-time-group (DTG). DTG 072230Z JUN 67, for example, identifies a message filed with the communication center at 2230 Greenwich mean time on June 7, 1967.

Originator. The originating command is identified by the letters *FM*.

Action and information addressees. Addressees identified in the heading by the letters *TO* are normally expected to take specific action; addressees identified by the letters *INFO* receive the message only for information. Because any one message may be addressed to numerous commands and may therefore be sent in several directions at the same time, we will refer to various "copies" of a particular message (USCINCEUR's copy, *Liberty*'s copy, and so on).

THE FIRST MESSAGE

PRIORITY
072230Z JUN 67
FM JCS
TO USCINCEUR
INFO CNO
CINCLANT
CINCLANTFLT
CINCUSNAVEUR
COMSIXTHFLT
USS LIBERTY
[and others]

CONFIDENTIAL JCS 7337 J-3 SENDS
SUBJ: USS LIBERTY (U)
REF: JCS 6724/0115457Z JUN 67
1. IN VIEW PRESENT SITUATION EAST MED, OPERATING AREA SPECIFIED
REF FOR GUIDANCE ONLY AND MAY BE VARIED AS LOCAL CONDITIONS
DICTATE. CHANGE CPA UAR TO 20 NM, ISRAEL 15 NM.
GP-4

Message Handling Chronology

07/2241Z   (08/0041 *Liberty* time) Message is delivered to the Army Communication Center serving the Joint Chiefs of Staff in the Pentagon.

08/1200Z   *Liberty* attacked. At this point the message is still awaiting processing in the JCS Pentagon Comm Center.

08/1255Z   USCINCEUR copy leaves Pentagon.

08/1315Z   *Liberty* copy leaves Pentagon, incorrectly routed via NAVCOMMSTA PHILIPPINES (Naval Communications Station, Philippines).

———   NAVCOMMSTA PHILIPPINES receives and reroutes message.

08/2135Z   NAVCOMMSTA ASMARA (Ethiopia) transmits message on fleet broadcast for now-disabled *Liberty*.

Telephone Call

07/2350Z   (08/0150 *Liberty* time) A JCS duty officer directs the CINCUS-
NAVEUR duty officer by telephone to move *Liberty* one hundred miles from the U.A.R. and Israeli coasts and promises
that a confirming message will follow. Instead of taking immediate action, the CINCUSNAVEUR duty officer drafts a message
to COMSIXTHFLT but holds it pending receipt of the confirming
message.

THE SECOND MESSAGE

IMMEDIATE
080110Z JUN 67 ZFF3
FM JCS
TO USCINCEUR
INFO CNO
CINCLANT
CINCLANTFLT
CINCUSNAVEUR
COMSIXTHFLT
USS LIBERTY
[and others]

T O P   S E C R E T   JCS 7347 J3 SENDS
SUBJ: USS LIBERTY (U)
REFS: A. JCS 7337/072230Z JUN 67
      B. COMSIXTHFLT 071503Z JUN 67 (NOTAL)
      I. (U) CANCEL REF A.
      2. (TS) REQ LIBERTY COMPLY NEW OP AREA DEFINED LAST SENTENCE PARA 2 REF B, UNTIL FURTHER NOTICE, I.E., NOT CLOSER THAN 100 NM TO ISRAEL, SYRIA, EGYPT AND 25 NM TO CYPRUS.
GP-3
BT

Message Handling Chronology

08/0112Z   (08/0312 *Liberty* time) Message delivered to JCS Comm Center.

08/0211Z   USCINCEUR copy leaves Pentagon.

08/0212Z   USCINCEUR receives message.

08/0312Z   CINCUSNAVEUR receives message.

08/0350Z   *Liberty* copy leaves Pentagon, misdirected to NAVCOMMSTA PHILIPPINES.

08/0440Z   *Liberty* copy leaves NAVCOMMSTA PHILIPPINES, correctly rerouted to *Liberty* via Army Comm Center Pentagon and NAVCOMMSTA MOROCCO.

————   Army Comm Center Pentagon misdirects *Liberty* copy to National Security Agency, Fort Meade, Maryland, where it is filed in error without action.

08/0630Z   COMSIXTHFLT receives message.

08/1200Z   *Liberty* attacked.

Telephone Call

08/0325Z (08/0525 *Liberty* time) USCINCEUR duty officer telephones
CINCUSNAVEUR duty officer to direct him to take action on JCS
080110Z JUN 67. The telephone conversation is later confirmed
by USCINCEUR 080625Z JUN 67.

Teletype Conference

08/0445Z (08/0645 *Liberty* time) CINCUSNAVEUR duty officer contacts
COMSIXTHFLT duty officer by point-to-point Teletype, and in
a telephonelike exchange, directs COMSIXTHFLT to take JCS
080110Z JUN 67 for action—to take action, that is, to move
Liberty one hundred miles from the coast. CINCUSNAVEUR
subsequently confirms the Teletype conference with an official
message, CINCUSNAVEUR 080455Z JUN 67.

THE THIRD MESSAGE

IMMEDIATE
080455Z
FM CINCUSNAVEUR
TO COMSIXTHFLT

UNCLAS EFTO
A. JCS 080110Z JUN 67
1. TAKE FORAC

The purpose of this message is to confirm the original order given to COMSIXTHFLT by point-to-point Teletype at 08/0445Z. Through an apparent oversight it is not addressed to *Liberty*. Had *Liberty* received a copy of this message, the ship would certainly have requested a copy of the reference.

Message Handling Chronology

08/0455Z (08/0655 *Liberty* time) Message is delivered to Comm Center.
08/0518Z COMSIXTHFLT receives copy.

THE FOURTH MESSAGE

IMMEDIATE
080625Z JUN 67
FM USCINCEUR
TO CINCUSNAVEUR
INFO JCS
CINCLANT
CINCLANTFLT
COMSIXTHFLT
USS LIBERTY
[and others]

C O N F I D E N T I A L ECJC/JRC 09045 USNAVEUR FOR N-32 AND N-31, JCS FOR JRC. SUBJ: USS LIBERTY (U).
REF A. FONECON LTC RUSSELL THIS HQ, AND CDR JORGENSON, DUTY OFFICER, NAVEUR, 080325Z JUN 67.
 B. JCS 7347, 080110Z JUN 67.
 (C) THIS CONFIRMS REF A TO TAKE REF B FORAC.
GP-3
BT

Message Handling Chronology

08/0625Z   Approximate time message is delivered to USCINCEUR Comm Center.
08/0711Z   USCINCEUR Comm Center sends message by two routes to ensure delivery.
————   Message lost by Army Comm Station, Pirmasens, Germany.
08/0735Z   CINCUSNAVEUR and COMSIXTHFLT receive copies via alternate route.
08/1050Z   A garbled version of message is broadcast to *Liberty* via NAV-COMMSTA ASMARA. Message is unintelligible. In any case it is meaningless, as *Liberty* has not received the reference.
08/1200Z   *Liberty* is attacked.
08/1646Z   Ungarbled version is broadcast to *Liberty* via NAVCOMMSTA ASMARA.

THE FIFTH MESSAGE

IMMEDIATE
080917Z JUN 67
FM COMSIXTHFLT
TO USS LIBERTY
INFO JCS
USCINCEUR
CNO
CINCLANT
CINCLANTFLT
CINCUSNAVEUR
[and others]

S E C R E T
USS LIBERTY OPERATIONS
A. JCS 011545Z JUN 67 (NOTAL)
B. JCS 080110Z JUN 67 (NOTAL)
C. COMSIXTHFLT 062349Z JUN 67
I. PARA I REF C IS MODIFIED BY REF B. PROCEED IMMED TO OPERATE
WITHIN A 25 MILE RADIUS OF POSIT 33-40N 32-30E UNTIL FURTHER NO-
TICE. DO NOT APPROACH COAST OF UAR, ISRAEL, SYRIA OR LEBANON
CLOSER THAN ONE HUNDRED MILES, AND CYPRUS NO CLOSER THAN
TWENTY-FIVE MILES.
2. NO TASK ORGANIZATION ASSIGNED TO LIBERTY.
3. ACKNOWLEDGE.
GP-3
BT

Message Handling Chronology

08/0917Z   (08/1117 *Liberty* time) Message delivered to COMSIXTHFLT
Comm Center.
08/1035Z   Transmitted to shore station for relay to *Liberty.*
08/1058Z   Received by NAVCOMMSTA MOROCCO.
08/1108Z   CINCUSNAVEUR receives copy.
08/1200Z   Army Comm Station ASMARA receives *Liberty* copy for relay
to NAVCOMMSTA ASMARA.
08/1200Z   (08/1400 *Liberty* time) Attack commences.
08/1215Z   Army Comm Station ASMARA misdirects *Liberty* copy to NAV-
COMMSTA GREECE.
08/1506Z   NAVCOMMSTA GREECE reroutes *Liberty* copy to *Liberty* via
Army Comm Station ASMARA.
08/1510Z   NAVCOMMSTA ASMARA receives *Liberty* copy for relay.
08/1525Z   NAVCOMMSTA ASMARA sends *Liberty* copy via fleet broadcast.

AND EVEN A SIXTH MESSAGE

IMMEDIATE
FM JCS
TO USS LIBERTY
INFO USCINCEUR
CNO
CINCLANTFLT
CINCUSNAVEUR
COMSIXTHFLT
[and others]

This Top Secret message, bypassing all intermediate commanders in *Liberty*'s chain of command, directed the ship to terminate her assignment and proceed immediately to sea. The House Armed Services Investigating Subcommittee was not told of this message. It spent the morning of June 8 being passed from ship to ship and from communication station to communication station in search of a circuit to *Liberty* that was cleared for Top Secret traffic. Finding no such circuit, the message went undelivered. Months later, special arrangements were made for Technical Research Ships to copy a special Top Secret broadcast to ensure delivery of urgent run-for-your-life messages, but by then, of course, the horse was dead. The medicine was not needed.

Appendix B

USS LIBERTY'S CALL FOR HELP
AND CINCUSNAVEUR'S CONFUSED RESPONSE

IMMEDIATE
081235Z JUN 67
FM USS SARATOGA
TO CINCUSNAVEUR
INFO CTG 60.1
CTG 60.2
COMSIXTHFLT

UNCLAS
FOLLOWING RECEIVED FROM ROCKSTAR
I AM UNDER ATTACK. MY POSIT 31-23N 33-25E. I HAVE BEEN HIT.
REQUEST IMMEDIATE ASSISTANCE.

USS *Saratoga* acknowledged receipt of *Liberty*'s first call for help at 08/1209Z, about ten minutes after the first shot was fired. Such reports are relayed immediately to COMSIXTHFLT and other local commanders on point-to-point operational radio circuits. At 08/1235Z, USS *Saratoga* sent a confirming message report via the military shore-based Teletype relay system. That message, reproduced above, was received by CINCUSNAVEUR headquarters in London at 1255Z. "Rockstar" is *Liberty*'s voice radio call sign.

The message below, CINCUSNAVEUR's belated reaction, illustrates the confusion that prevailed as CINCUSNAVEUR wasted valuable time attempting to verify that *Liberty* was really under attack.

FLASH
081340Z JUN 67
FROM CINCUSNAVEUR
TO USS LIBERTY
INFO NAVCOMMSTA MOROCCO
NAVCOMMSTA GREECE
NAVCOMMSTA SPAIN

UNCLAS

1. ESTABLISH IMMEDIATE COMMUNICATIONS WITH ANY MED AREA COMMSTA.
2. NAVCOMMSTA MOROCCO TAKE ALL AVAILABLE ACTIONS TO ESTABLISH COMM WITH USS LIBERTY. REPORT WHEN ESTABLISHED.
3. FOR USS LIBERTY: REQUEST CONFIRM REPORT OF ATTACK.

Appendix C

OPERATIONAL IMMEDIATE
081305Z
FROM COMSIXTHFLT
TO USS LIBERTY

UNCLAS
YOUR FLASH TRAFFIC RECEIVED. SENDING AIRCRAFT TO COVER YOU.
SURFACE UNITS ON THE WAY. KEEP SITREPS COMING.

Here, one hour and five minutes after commencement of the attack, was
COMSIXTHFLT's report of help on the way. *Liberty*'s life rafts were machine-
gunned at 1315Z.

Appendix D

As I have noted, reports persist that at least two flights of rescue aircraft were sent to *Liberty*'s defense. According to these reports, the first flight of four nuclear-armed F-4B Phantom jet fighter bombers was hastily and angrily recalled personally by Secretary of Defense McNamara and Chief of Naval Operations McDonald. The second flight, armed with conventional weapons, was sent somewhat later and was recalled upon receiving notice from Tel Aviv that Israel had admitted attacking the ship and had apologized.

The first report of separate flights came to me from a chief petty officer in the carrier *America*, who described the departure, without fanfare, of four "ready" aircraft that he knew to be equipped with nuclear weapons. A destroyer officer, whose ship was alongside the carrier for refueling, told me of receiving a message by sound-powered telephone from *America*'s bridge: "Don't panic. We're getting ready to launch the ready Cat!" Sometime later the ship was called to General Quarters and *additional* aircraft were launched. The long wait before sounding General Quarters was described by an officer who watched part of the drama from *America*'s bridge: "It took forever. They had to change rocket pods on the airplanes and had to bring bombs and rockets up from belowdecks." A radio operator described hearing Secretary McNamara, by radiotelephone, angrily order Vice Admiral Martin to recall the aircraft. It was clear to those listening, the operator told me, that McNamara's concern was that the aircraft were nuclear-armed.

The operator was not the first to report the hasty recall of those airplanes. Barely a month after the attack, tiny *Counterattack,* a New York–based newsletter, reported McNamara's personal intervention and McDonald's follow-up order. "Naval Operations," said *Counterattack*, "acting in response to high authority, ordered Admiral William I. Martin, commanding the Sixth Fleet, to recall the planes forming in the air for attack. In seconds, Admiral David L. McDonald, the Chief of Naval Operations, was on the radio telephone repeating and emphasizing the order." *Counterattack* concluded, "The American Navy was prevented, in a new era of military compliance, from going to the rescue of one of its own crews."

When I questioned a *Liberty* officer, he readily confirmed the dispatch and recall of nuclear-armed jets—although not, to his knowledge, from the carrier. "Oh, the Court of Inquiry talked about that," he said. "We knew nuclear-armed jets were sent. We were told that they came from Libya and that they were recalled by order of the White House."

Nasser confidant Mohamed Hassanein Heikal (*The Cairo Documents* [New York: Doubleday, 1973]) provides a supporting report. Heikal tells us that Johnson sent a hot-line message to Nasser via Kosygin, advising that "two American fighters had been obliged to pass over Egyptian positions on their way to help the American communications ship *Liberty* . . ." No Egyptian positions were between the Sixth Fleet and *Liberty*; any American aircraft passing over Egyptian positions could only have come from American bases in Libya. Thus it appears that Sixth Fleet aircraft were not the only aircraft sent to defend *Liberty,* nor perhaps the only aircraft to bring nuclear weapons.

According to former CIA staff member Patrick J. McGarvey (*CIA: The Myth and the Madness* [New York: Saturday Review Press, 1973]), still another flight was considered. McGarvey tells us that the Joint Chiefs of Staff proposed a "quick, retaliatory air strike on the Israeli naval base which launched the attack."

Given the tendency to bury embarrassing details, and given the not-surprising shrinkage of files over the years, it is nearly impossible now to sort out all of the details of *Liberty*'s aborted "rescue." The following is the sequence of events as reconstructed from court records, naval messages, White House logs, and CIA files (all times are USS *Liberty* time):

1400   Attack commences.

1409   Carrier USS *Saratoga,* operating near Crete with USS *America* and COMSIXTHFLT, acknowledges *Liberty* request for help. (Although at 1435 *Saratoga* sent a Teletype message reporting the attack to CINCUSNAVEUR in London—with an information copy to COMSIXTHFLT—this message would not have been COMSIXTHFLT's first notification of the attack. *Saratoga* maintained a number of operational and tactical radio circuits for relay of urgent tactical messages to the fleet commander.)

————   COMSIXTHFLT advises, HELP IS ON THE WAY, while *Liberty* is still under air attack. (From personal recollections only.)

1435   Torpedo explosion. *Liberty* goes off the air until 1600. *Saratoga* relays attack report to CINCUSNAVEUR.

1450   COMSIXTHFLT orders carriers *America* and *Saratoga* to send aircraft to defend *Liberty.*

1500   (approx) Commanding officer, Naval Communication Station, Morocco, notifies his Washington headquarters by telephone that *Liberty* is under attack.

1505   COMSIXTHFLT sends message to *Liberty,* SENDING AIRCRAFT TO COVER YOU. *Liberty* is off the air and does not receive message.

1510 CINCUSNAVEUR headquarters in London receives telephone report from Morocco that ship is under attack.

1511 USCINCEUR notifies the National Military Command Center in Washington that *Liberty* is under attack; this is the first *official* notice to reach Washington.

1516 CTF 60 orders *Saratoga* and *America* to send eight aircraft to defend *Liberty*. (Sixty-seven minutes have now passed since *Liberty*'s first request for help. An hour has passed since *Liberty* was first told, HELP IS ON THE WAY. Twenty-five minutes have passed since COMSIXTHFLT ordered *Saratoga* and *America* to send help. Probably Phantom jets are already en route.)

1520 COMSIXTHFLT advises CINCUSNAVEUR that twelve aircraft will be launched at approximately 1545 to arrive near *Liberty* about 1715.

1539 COMSIXTHFLT authorizes use of force to protect *Liberty*.

1545 Scheduled launch of rescue aircraft.

1549 Rostow informs President Johnson of *Liberty* attack.

1555 *Liberty* regains transmitter, has no receiver.

1600 *Liberty* radioman Joe Ward transmits: "Flash, flash, flash. . . . We are under attack by aircraft and high-speed surface craft."

1610 COMSIXTHFLT is on the air with *Liberty*. COMSIXTHFLT operator acknowledges receipt of *Liberty* message. *Liberty* requests immediate assistance, reports flooding, nine-degree list, four dead, fifty wounded.

1614 Defense attaché office, Tel Aviv, reports that Israel has admitted and apologized for erroneous attack on *Liberty*.

1616 JCS authorizes use of force to protect *Liberty* from further attack.

1630–1637 McNamara is on telephone at Pentagon, collecting background information for news release on *Liberty* mission, manning, last port.

1639 COMSIXTHFLT reports that he has recalled all Sixth Fleet aircraft in view of the Israeli message report of erroneous attack.

1645 COMSIXTHFLT on radiotelephone tells *Liberty*, "Assistance is on the way."

1700 President Johnson receives notice of Israeli apology and simultaneously sends hot-line message to Premier Kosygin, advising that aircraft are en route to investigate.

1700–1720 *Liberty* out of communications due to power failure.

1706 President Johnson arrives in White House Situation Room to preside over emergency meeting called to deal with *Liberty* attack.

1715 CINCUSNAVEUR sends wrap-up message to JCS, CNO and others, advising that all aircraft have been recalled.

1717 Cover-up commences: CINCUSNAVEUR message relays deputy secretary of defense order that all news releases on attack will be made in Washington.

1730   Pentagon releases first news report of attack.

1745   White House meeting adjourns.

1820   President Johnson sends second hot-line message concerning *Liberty* to Premier Kosygin.

1849   COMSIXTHFLT final situation report informs CINCUSNAVEUR that all Sixth Fleet aircraft have been recalled and accounted for.

1915   McGonagle sends his wrap-up message report of the attack.

2136   Johnson sends third and final *Liberty* message to Premier Kosygin on hot line.

While this scenario is inconclusive as evidence that two flights of rescue aircraft were sent, it clearly indicates that all was not well in the Sixth Fleet. After promising to send air protection within ten minutes of need, the record shows that the Sixth Fleet required more than three hours to send conventionally armed aircraft. The Navy has never explained (nor even admitted) this long delay, nor is there any explanation why the aircraft that *were* finally launched were expected to take ninety minutes to make the 400-mile trip. The A-4 Skyhawk is capable of more than 600 miles per hour; the F-4 Phantom can fly more than 900 miles per hour; only the A-1 Skyraider (318mph top speed) could be expected to require ninety minutes, but these piston-driven World War Two relics were no match for the jets attacking *Liberty* and should not have been sent. Carrier-based aircraft could not have fulfilled COMSIXTHFLT's promise of jet assistance in ten minutes, but they should have been able to make the trip within *thirty* minutes. At worst, carrier aircraft should have arrived in time to catch the motor torpedo boats in the act of machine-gunning *Liberty*'s life rafts. Promptly sent, they *might* have arrived in time to prevent the torpedo attack.

Why did the jet aircraft fail to arrive? If my sources are to be believed, help was promptly dispatched but was recalled on Secretary McNamara's order.

Lending credence to this view is a naval message in which COMSIXTHFLT authorized his pilots to use force at 1539, some thirty-five minutes *before* the use of force was authorized by the Pentagon. If JCS authority was required, one would expect COMSIXTHFLT to await JCS authority before authorizing his pilots to attack. But he did not wait. Apparently, the first flight lacked JCS approval and was hastily recalled when McNamara learned that COMSIXTHFLT had sent help on his own authority; the JCS message was to authorize the *second* flight to use force.

One of the President's first acts upon learning of the Israeli apology was to advise Premier Kosygin by hot-line message that our aircraft were en route—and he felt such urgency that he kept his advisers waiting while he drafted the message. Had McNamara ordered *all* aircraft recalled, the President would not have been compelled to notify Kosygin that they were en route. There would have been no aircraft to report. But since McNamara had recalled only the dangerous ready aircraft, the President was *now* concerned about the approach of the conventionally armed *second* flight. In other words, had there been only one flight, Johnson would not have been concerned; McNamara recalled *that* flight of aircraft before he left the Pentagon to attend the emergency White House meeting.

Finally, as we have seen, the radio operator at Morocco tells us that shortly after the attack he was visited by an agent of the Naval Investigative Service, who sought to record on tape all his recollections of the attack and of the communications surrounding it. This is a most extraordinary measure that the Navy takes only when authorities fear that sensitive information has been compromised. Delayed dispatch of rescue aircraft or hasty recall of "ready" aircraft would have been embarrassing and thus was probably considered "sensitive." Only the most unusual circumstances could have brought McNamara and McDonald personally to the radiotelephone, and no ordinary fiasco could warrant the vast cover-up that we have seen. I believe that the dispatch of "ready" aircraft, their hasty recall, and the failure of the fleet to respond promptly with conventionally armed aircraft are among the reasons that the story of the attack has been covered up.

After agonizing over the possibilities, I must accept the reports that there were two flights—one recalled hastily and prematurely by Secretary McNamara when he learned that nuclear weapons were aboard, and the second recalled by COMSIXTHFLT when he learned that Isreal had attacked "in error." No other sequence of events explains the elements that we know to be true, such as the complete failure of the United States Navy to send help to an American ship within easy range.

Appendix E

UNITED STATES EMBASSY TEL AVIV REPORT
OF ERRONEOUS ATTACK BY ISRAEL

FLASH
081414Z
FROM USE TEL AVIV ISRAEL
TO WHITE HOUSE
CNO
DEPT STATE
COMSIXTHFLT
CINCUSNAVEUR
JCS
[and others]
CONFIDENTIAL 0825 JUN 67.
ALUSNA CALLED TO [foreign liaison office] TO RECEIVE REPORT. ISRAELI
AIRCRAFT AND MTB'S ERRONEOUSLY ATTACKED U.S. SHIP AT 08/1200Z,
POSITION 31-25N 33-33E. MAYBE NAVY SHIP. IDF HELICOPTERS IN RESCUE
OPERATIONS. NO OTHER INFO. ISRAELIS SEND ABJECT APOLOGIES AND
REQUEST INFO ON OTHER US SHIPS NEAR WAR ZONE COASTS.
GP-3

This message was sent two hours and fourteen minutes after the commencement of the attack. At the moment, *Liberty* was not being fired upon and
there were no Israeli forces near her. Eighteen minutes after this message
was originated, torpedo boats returned to *Liberty* for the first time in a
friendly manner.

Appendix F

Appendix G

LIBERTY'S FIRST REPORT OF DETAILS OF THE ATTACK

This first report of details of the attack was dictated by McGonagle to Lieutenant Bennett as the captain lay on the port wing of the bridge in an exhausted and severely weakened condition.

UNCLAS

IMMEDIATE

081715Z JUNE 1967
FROM USS LIBERTY
TO NAVCOMMSTA GREECE

UNCLAS
SITREP FOLLOWS—AIR ATTACK

1. AT TIME 081205Z, COURSE 283T SPEED 5 KTS, POSITION 31–35.5N 33-29E, SHIP ATTACKED WITH UNIDENTIFIED JET FIGHTERS BELIEVED ISRAELI. APPROX SIX STRAFING RUNS MADE ON SHIP. AT TIME 081225Z THREE TORPEDO BOATS, ONE IDENTIFIED AS ISRAELI, APPROACHED STARBOARD QUARTER AT HIGH SPEED. HULL NUMBER 206-17. AT APPROX 081427Z TOOK TORPEDO BOAT UNDER FIRE AT 2000 YARDS. BOATS LAUNCHED TORPEDO ATTACK AND STRAFING RUN. ONE TORPEDO PASSED APPROX 75 YARDS ASTERN. ONE MINUTE LATER TOOK TORPEDO HIT STARBOARD SIDE. SHIP HAS TEN DEGREE STARBOARD LIST. WATERTIGHT BOUNDARY ESTABLISHED. AM HOLDING. AFTER ATTACK TORPEDO BOATS CLEARED TO EAST ABOUT FIVE MILES. CLEARING AREA AT TEN KNOTS.
2. PHOTOS OF AIRCRAFT AND BOATS TAKEN. AFTER ATTACK COMPLETED, TWO ISRAELI HELOS ORBITED SHIP AT 500 YARDS. TIME 081255Z. ISRAELI INSIGNIA CLEARLY VISIBLE. PHOTOS TAKEN. SEVERAL PROJECTILES RECOVERED FROM TOPSIDE AREA. NUMBER DEAD ESTIMATED TEN, SEVERELY WOUNDED 15, TOTAL WOUNDED 75, NUMBER MISSING UNDE-TERMINED.
3. SHIP UNABLE TO CARRY OUT MISSION. WILL REPORT PERSONNEL CASU-ALTIES ASAP.
4. EXTENSIVE SUPERFICIAL TOPSIDE DAMAGE. LOWER DECKS FORWARD DESTROYED.
5. COMMUNICATIONS CAPABILITY LIMITED. WILL PROVIDE FILM AND PROJECTILES AS DIRECTED. SHIP WILL REQUIRE DRYDOCK AND EXTEN-SIVE REPAIRS.

Appendix H

The "Ship Weather Observation Sheet" reproduced on page 247 reflects in Greenwich mean time the *actual* speed and direction of the wind *over the water* as recorded by a *Liberty* quartermaster on June 8, 1967. To obtain this information, a quartermaster first determines the *relative* speed (as experienced on board the moving vessel) with a shipboard instrument, then adjusts the figures to compensate for the ship's movement and thus to determine the actual wind speed and direction.

By working backwards from the actual wind reading thus calculated, it is possible once again to determine the relative wind. This is the amount and direction of wind over the ship's decks that blew upon the American flag on the ship's mast. Those calculations produce the following relative wind readings:

Time (GMT)	Ship's Time	Ship's Course/Speed	Actual Wind Direction/Speed	Relative Wind Direction/Speed	Wind Direction Relative to Ship's Heading
0300Z	0500	123T/10Knots	316T / 8Knots	085T / 3Knots	322R
0400Z	0600	190T/10K	334T / 9K	250T / 6K	060R (blowing
0500Z	0700	123T/10K	313T / 10K	040T / 2K	277R tubes)
0600Z	0800	130T/10K	320T / 8K	090T / 3K	320R
0700Z	0900	255T/10K	310T / 4K	280T / 8K	025R
0800Z	1000	255T/5K	315T / 5K	285T / 9K	030R
0900Z	1100	255T/5K	357T		
1000Z	1200	283T/5K	290T / 4K	285T / 9K	002R
1100Z	1300	283T/5K	265T / 7K	275T / 12K	350R
1200Z	1400	(attack commenced)			

The quartermaster failed to record the wind speed at 0900Z/1100, and the wind direction that he did record appears to be in error (a 42-degree wind shift to the right, followed an hour later by a 67-degree shift to the left, appears unlikely). Also, the 0700Z/0900 entry has been corrected here for an obvious error in which the quartermaster recorded the reciprocal of the actual wind direction. However, the faulty entries notwithstanding, the log proves that for most of the morning the wind over *Liberty*'s deck was sufficient to hold the flag aloft.

Knight's Modern Seamanship, a standard seaman's reference work, describes the following wind effects:

1–3 knots is "light air," and produces a sea surface with ripples that have the appearance of a scale, but without foam crests; wind does not move wind vanes, but wind direction can be seen by smoke drift.

4–6 knots is a "light breeze," and produces small wavelets, still short but more pronounced; crests have a glassy appearance, but do not break; wind is felt on face; leaves rustle ashore.

7–10 knots is a "gentle breeze," and produces large wavelets with crests that begin to break, and foam that is of glassy appearance; scattered white "horses" may be seen; leaves and small twigs are in constant motion ashore; wind *will extend a light flag.*

11–16 knots is a "moderate breeze," with small waves becoming longer and with fairly frequent white "horses"; this is a good working breeze for a fishing smack, causing considerable heeling; ashore, small branches are moved and dust and loose paper are raised.

SHIP WEATHER OBSERVATION SHEET

OPNAV FORM 3144-1 (9-64)
0107 714 4100

DEPARTMENT OF THE NAVY

SHIP WEATHER OBSERVATION SHEET

USS _Liberty AGTR-5_   DATE (GMT) _Thursday 8, June_ 19 _67_

AT/PASSAGE FROM _Rota, Spain_   TO _OP6-AREA_

TABLE I

TIME (GMT)	WINDS □ IF ESTIMATED Direction (True)	Force (Knots)	VISI-BIL-ITY (Miles)	WEATHER (Symbols)	BAROMETER (Inches)	TEMPERATURE Dry Bulb	Wet Bulb	CLOUDS Amount (Tenths)	Height	Type	SEA WATER TEMP (Degrees and tenths)	SEA WAVES Direction (True)	Period (Seconds)	Height (Feet)	SWELL WAVES Direction (True)	Period (Seconds)	Height (Feet)
00	315	7	10	CLR	29.70	—	—	—	—	—	72	—	—	—	—	—	—
01	310	5	10	CLR	29.89	—	—	—	—	—	72	—	—	—	—	—	—
02	287	6	10	CLR	29.89	—	—	—	—	—	72	CALM			CALM		
03	316	9	10	CLR	29.90	—	—	—	—	—	72	CALM			CALM		
04	334	9	10	CLR	29.91	—	—	—	—	—	72	CALM			CALM		
05	313	10	10	CLR	29.91	—	—	—	—	—	72	CALM			CALM		
06	320	8	10	CLR	29.91	—	—	•	—	—	73	CALM			CALM		
07	130	4	10	CLR	29.93	—	—	—	—	—	74	"			"		
08	315	5	10	CLR	29.93	—	—	—	—	—	74	"			"		
09	357				29.93	—	—	—	—	—	74	"			6		
10	280	7	10	CLR	29.93	—	—	—	—	—	74	6			6		
11	265	7	10	CLR	29.90	—	—	—	—	—	74	CALM			CALM		
12																	
13																	
14																	
15																	
16																	
17																	
18																	
19																	
20																	
21																	
22																	
23																	

1200Z
1300Z

TABLE II
SYNOPTIC OBSERVATIONS

FIRST GROUP OF MESSAGE	Day of Week (1-7) (GMT)	Oc-tant (0-3)	POSITION OF SHIP Latitude (Degrees and tenths)	Longitude (Degrees and tenths)	TIME (GMT) (Coded)	Total Cloud Am (Coded)	WIND Direction (True) (00-36)	Speed (True) (Knots)	Visi-bil-ity (90-99)	WEATHER Present (00-99)	Past (0-9)	PRESSURE Barometer Corrected (Mb)	AIR TEMP (°C)	CLOUDS Amount of Low Cloud (0-9)	Type of Low Cloud (0-9)	Height of Low Cloud (0-9)	Type of C_M	Type of C_H	Dir of Ship (0-9)	Course of Ship (0-9)	Speed of Ship (0-9)	3-HOUR PRESSURE TENDENCY Characteristic (0-8)	Amount of Change (Mb and tenths)	SIGNIFICANT CLOUD Indicator	Amount (Eights)	Type	Height
1	2	3	4	5	6	7	8	9	10	11	12	13	14	15	16	17	18	19	20	21	22	23	24	25	26	27
	Y	Q	$L_a L_a L_a$	$L_o L_o L_o L_o$	GG	N	dd	ff	VV	ww	W	PPP	TT	N_h	C_L	h	C_M	C_H	D_s	V_s	a	PP	8	N_s	C	$h_s h_s$
SHIP					00																		8			
SHIP					06																		8			
SHIP					12																		8			
SHIP					18																		8			

Indicator	AIR-SEA DIFF. (Coded)	DEW POINT (°C)	SEA WAVES Indicator	Direction (Coded)	Period (Coded)	Height (Coded)	SWELL WAVES Indicator	Direction (Coded)	Period (Coded)	Height (Coded)	ICE ACCRETION Indicator	Source	Thickness	Rate	SEA ICE Indicator	Kind	Effect	Bearing	Distance	Orientation	DO NOT TRANSMIT Dry Bulb (Degrees and tenths)	Wet Bulb (Degrees and tenths)
28	29	30	31	32	33	34	35	36	37	38	39	40	41	42	43	44	45	46	47	48	A_1	
0	$T_s T_s$	$T_d T_d$	1	$d_w d_w$	$P_w H_w$		1	$d_w d_w$	P_w	H_w	2	I_s	$E_s E_s R_s$		ICE	C_i	K	D_i	r	+	Celsius	
0			1		1		1				2				ICE							
0			1		1		1				2				ICE							
0			1		1		1				2				ICE							
0			1		1		1				2				ICE							

EXAMINED

Appendix I

Comments on the seven points provided by IDF FLO, LCOL MICHAEL BLOCH, as "Further Information on Yesterday's Incident with the American Ship."

Point 1—Ship was sighted and recognized as a naval ship 13 miles from coast.

Comment—from 0849 on 8 June LIBERTY was steaming in international waters on a track generally parallel to the coast of the UAR. At one point the ship was, in fact, 13.6 miles from the coast.

Point 2—The presence (of a neutral-nation naval ship) in a fighting area is against international custom.

Comment—The duties of a neutral under international law do not include a duty to ensure that its ships or personnel leave or refrain from entering an area of hostilities or an area adjacent to an area of hostilities. Nationals of a neutral country who may happen to be in belligerent territory nevertheless retain their right to protection by their neutral home state; and a belligerent must grant to neutral diplomatic envoys—including those accredited to the enemy—the right to quit the territory unmolested. A neutral nation, in this respect alone, thus has a legitimate reason and a legal right to dispatch a ship into international waters adjacent to an area of hostilities, in fulfillment of its obligation to protect its nationals and to evacuate those who desire evacuation. It was in fulfillment of such a mission that USS LIBERTY was engaged. Far from being contrary to international custom, the presence of neutral ships on just such missions as LIBERTY's is a common, if not a universal, incident of situations involving the outbreak of hostilities. So long as such a neutral ship maintains the impartial attitude of neutrality, each belligerent has a duty to refrain from attacking her. Action by such a neutral ship to repulse an unlawful belligerent attack by force, where the neutral has not first attacked the belligerent, does not constitute "hostilities" against the belligerent and does not constitute an abandonment or a violation of neutrality.

Point 3—The area (where LIBERTY was steaming when attacked) is not a common passage for ships.

Comment—Given the conceded proposition that a ship of a neutral is steaming in international waters, the question of whether or not such waters are "common passage" is totally irrelevent to its right to be there.

Point 4—Egypt (an opposing belligerent) had declared the area (where LIBERTY was steaming when attacked) closed to neutrals.

Comment—Closing certain adjacent waters, including those otherwise considered to be high seas, has some precedent in history as a belligerent practice, notably in World Wars I and II when most of the belligerents, including the United States, declared "war zones," "military areas," and "defensive sea areas" and either attempted to close such areas completely and [*sic*] to severely circumscribe passage through them as a neutral. The consistent position of the United States has been to reserve generally all of its rights in the premises, including the right not only to question the validity of such "war zones" but to present demands and claims in relation to any American interests which may be unlawfully affected, directly or indirectly, by virtue of their enforcement. As a general proposition, closing or attempting to restrict any portion of the high seas has not been recognized in international law as a belligerent right.

Point 5—LIBERTY resembles the Egyptian supply ship EL QUSEIR.

Comment—While EL QUSEIR bears a highly superficial resemblance to LIBERTY, she more closely resembles the majority of older tramp steamers operating in ocean shipping. EL QUSEIR is less than half the size and lacks the elaborate antenna array and distinctive hull markings of LIBERTY. The location of the superstructure island, a primary recognition feature of merchant type ships, is widely different. By this criteria as a justification for attack, any ship resembling EL QUSEIR was in jeopardy.

Point 6—Ship was not flying flag when sighted. She moved at high speed westward toward enemy coast.

Comment—LIBERTY flew a size 9 (approximately five feet by eight feet) U.S. ensign from her foremast throughout the morning of 8 June and until it was shot down by the Israeli air attack. At least 5 minutes prior to the torpedo attack a size 7 ensign (approximately seven feet by thirteen feet) was hoisted at the main yardarm. At 0849 LIBERTY changed course from 130°T to 253°T. At 0905 LIBERTY reduced speed to 5 knots and continued to steam at that speed until after the initial air attack. At 1132 LIBERTY altered course to 283°T and continued on this course until after the ship was attacked.

Point 7—IDF Navy had earlier reports of bombardment of El Arish from sea.

Comment—It is inconceivable that either the IDF Navy or Air Force would associate LIBERTY, with her 4-50 caliber [*sic*] machine guns or EL QUSEIR, armed with two 3 pounders, with a shore bombardment.

Appendix J

OFFICIAL BIOGRAPHY
OF COMMANDER WILLIAM L. MCGONAGLE,
UNITED STATES NAVY, 1968

Commander William L. McGonagle was born in Wichita, Kansas, on November 19, 1925. He enlisted in the Navy in January 1944, and upon completion of the NROTC program at the University of Southern California in June 1947, was commissioned an Ensign in the United States Navy.

After a three year tour of duty aboard the USS *Frank Knox* (DDR-742) where he served as First Lieutenant, Gunnery Officer, ASW Officer, Engineering Officer, and Communications Officer, Commander McGonagle was ordered to the USS *Kite* (AMS–22). Aboard the *Kite* he served as Gunnery Officer, Engineering Officer, and Executive Officer. During his tour the *Kite* was awarded the Presidential Unit Citation, the Korean Service Medal with six battle stars and the United Nations Ribbon for service during the Korean Conflict.

In January 1952, Commander McGonagle was assigned to the U.S. Naval Advance Base, Bremerhaven, Germany, where he was Officer-in-Charge of 18 German built and manned minesweepers engaged in clearance and check sweeping for mines planted during WWII in the Baltic and North Seas.

Upon promotion to Lieutenant in 1953, Commander McGonagle was ordered to the U.S. Naval Communications Station, Philadelphia, where he served as Personnel Officer and Administrative Assistant. Upon completion of this tour in January 1955, Commander McGonagle reported to the USS *Rochester* (CA-124) as First Lieutenant. He served in this billet for two years before receiving orders to assume command of the USS *Mataco* (ATF-86).

From January 1959 to June 1961 Commander McGonagle was an instructor in Naval Weapons, Operations and Tactics and Naval Leadership for the NROTC at the University of Idaho.

From July 1961 to July 1963 Commander McGonagle served as Commanding Officer of the USS *Reclaimer* (ARS-42). Commander McGonagle served on the staff of COMSERVPAC as Current Operations Officer immediately prior to assuming command of the USS *Liberty* (AGTR-5) on April 25, 1966. Commander McGonagle, upon being relieved on October 2, 1967, reported to the USS *Kilauea* (AE-26) as prospective Commanding Officer.

Commander McGonagle is married to the former Miss Jean Stoneham of Glendale, California.

Appendix K

The following message was sent by *Liberty*'s escort upon arrival in Malta:

FROM: COMMANDER DESTROYER SQUADRON TWELVE
TO: COMMANDER TASK FORCE SIXTY

DUE TO THE OUTSTANDING PROFESSIONAL KNOWLEDGE AND UN-
DAUNTED SPIRIT OF HER VALIANT COMMANDING OFFICER, OFFICERS,
AND CREW, AND STILL CARRYING MANY WHO GAVE UP THEIR LIVES FOR
THEIR COUNTRY, USS LIBERTY SAFELY REACHED PORT AFTER STEAMING
ONE THOUSAND MILES WITH CRITICAL DAMAGE THAT WOULD HAVE
SENT MOST SHIPS OF HER TYPE TO THE BOTTOM.

=====

From: Commander Service Squadron EIGHT
To: Commanding Officer, USS LIBERTY (AGTR-5)

1. In battle efficiency competition for fiscal year 1967, USS LIBERTY (AGTR-5) was adjudged the outstanding ship in her competitive group.
2. The spirit, interest and the great effort exerted by each ship in the group made the competition this year particularly keen and most difficult. Your achievement reflects an outstanding shipboard training program, a high degree of leadership and exceptional professionalism.
3. Commander Service Squadron EIGHT commends the Commanding Officer, the officers and men of USS LIBERTY for the high standards achieved in your pursuit that led to winning the coveted Battle Efficiency Award. WELL DONE.

/s/ Captain BUNTING, USN

=====

ROUTINE
291725Z JULY 1967
FROM: COMSERVRON EIGHT
TO: USS LIBERTY
INFO: COMSERVLANT

UNCLAS

I. SQUADRON STAFF AND ALL UNITS OF SERVRON EIGHT JOIN ME IN WELCOMING YOU HOME.

2. YOU HAVE PROVEN YOURSELF TRUE PROFESSIONALS IN EVERY SENSE OF THE WORD. WE ARE PROUD TO SERVE IN THE SAME SQUADRON WITH YOU. CAPTAIN BUNTING SENDS.

====

From: Commander SIXTH Fleet
To: USS LIBERTY (AGTR-5)

As you prepare to depart for CONUS, I commend to every man who sails in SIXTH Fleet the fact that USS LIBERTY has become a legend in her own time. My personal monitoring of transmissions during the attack and observations made aboard subsequently induce the highest in praise for a great ship, a gallant Commanding Officer, and a superb crew. We have shared your grief for those who lost their lives, we remind ourselves that you were classic examples of unswerving devotion to duty. For CDR MCGONAGLE and men of LIBERTY: WELL DONE. SIXTH Fleet is proud to have claimed you.

/s/ Vice Admiral MARTIN, USN

====

PRIORITY
282132Z JULY 1967
FROM: CINCLANTFLT
TO: USS LIBERTY
INFO: COMSERVLANT / COMSERVRON EIGHT / COMSECONDFLT / CINCUS-
NAVEUR / COMSIXTHFLT

UNCLAS

WELCOME HOME TO LIBERTY
1. THE COMMANDER IN CHIEF EXTENDS TO THE OFFICERS AND MEN OF THE LIBERTY A WARM WELCOME AND A HEARTY CONGRATULATIONS FOR A JOB WELL DONE. THE PRIDE THAT WE ALL FEEL IN SUCH EXEMPLARY PERFORMANCE OF DUTY UNDER MOST DIFFICULT CIRCUMSTANCES IS MIXED WITH SADNESS AT THE LOSS OF MANY OF YOUR SHIPMATES. IT WILL BE IN THE MINDS OF ALL OF US AS WE WELCOME YOU BACK TO YOUR HOMEPORT THAT YOU HAVE SUFFERED GREAT LOSSES. THIS IS NOT TO SAY THAT THE CREDIT FOR HEROIC AND EFFECTIVE WORK WILL BE DIMINISHED OR THAT THE ENTHUSIASM FOR THOSE RETURNING WILL BE RESTRAINED. BUT THIS RETURN DOES HAVE POIGNANCY IN THAT SOME SHIPMATES AND LOVES ONES ARE NOT COMING BACK.
ADMIRAL HOLMES.

====

From: Commander in Chief, U.S. Naval Forces, Europe
To: USS LIBERTY (AGTR-5)

On your departure from United States Naval Forces, Europe, I wish God Speed to the valiant Commanding Officer, Officers, and Bluejackets of LIBERTY. Your exemplary courage and outstanding performance under the most stringent combat conditions are an inspiration to every Navy man.

/s/ Admiral John S. McCain, Jr., USN

====

PRIORITY
161033Z JUNE 1967
FROM: CINCUSNAVEUR
TO: USS LIBERTY

UNCLAS

TO COMMANDER W. L. MCGONAGLE, USN, COMMANDING

1. THE TRAGEDY IS BEYOND RECALL. WHAT SOLACE THERE MAY BE, HOWEVER SMALL, LIES IN THE MAGNIFICENT PERFORMANCE OF THE OFFICERS AND MEN OF LIBERTY IN AN ACTION OF HISTORIC STATURE IN THE FACE OF AN UNPROVOKED ATTACK. UNDER MOST DIFFICULT AND TRYING CIRCUMSTANCES NOT ONLY DID THE SHIP DEFEND ITSELF VALIANTLY, BUT THROUGH SUPERB SEAMANSHIP ON THE PART OF ALL HANDS, THE SHIP WAS BROUGHT SAFELY INTO PORT.
2. YOU, YOUR OFFICERS AND MEN ANSWERED THE CALL TO DUTY WITH UNQUESTIONED VALOUR. THE PERFORMANCE OF ALL HANDS STANDS OUT AS AN EXAMPLE IN HISTORY OF THAT TYPE OF COURAGE WHICH MARKS AMERICAN MANHOOD AS THE FINEST IN THE WORLD.
3. I AM PROUD TO BE ASSOCIATED WITH YOU.

ADMIRAL JOHN S. MC CAIN, USN.

====

From: United States Commander in Chief, Europe
To: USS LIBERTY (AGTR-5)

Having had the opportunity to review completely the action involving your command 8–14 June, I desire to express my deep admiration for the outstanding performance of the officers and crew of LIBERTY. The manner in which your crew performed while under attack and in returning your damaged ship to port is a lasting tribute to their training and your leadership and a great example to all who follow a career at sea. It is clearly evident that the exercise of your personal leadership in spite of wounds and shock, was the major factor in keeping LIBERTY afloat and operating until assistance arrived.

We have been proud to have LIBERTY in the European command. The performance of LIBERTY personnel has been in keeping with the highest traditions of the United States Armed Forces.

/s/ General Lyman L. Limnitzer, USA

====

PRIORITY
152106Z JUNE 1967
FROM: CHIEF OF NAVAL OPERATIONS
TO: USS LIBERTY

UNCLAS

THE SORROW THAT MUST BE YOURS AS A RESULT OF THE TRAGIC DEATHS AND INJURIES OF YOUR MANY SHIPMATES CANNOT BE ASSUAGED BY ANY ACTIONS TAKEN NOW. YOU CAN, HOWEVER, FIND SOLACE IN WHAT MUST HAVE BEEN ONE OF THE FINEST PERFORMANCES OF ANY SHIP IN REACTION TO AN UNPROVOKED ATTACK. SAVING YOUR SHIP AND SAILING HER SAFELY TO PORT IS IN ITSELF A FINE TRIBUTE TO YOU AND YOUR VALIANT CREW. A PROUD NAVY SALUTES YOUR GALLANT SHIP FOR ITS UNPARALLELED PERFORMANCE.

====

Dear Commander McGonagle,

As you are aware from message traffic, the last of your men have left this ship for duty or further hospital treatment. I am pleased to be able to report that they all are making very satisfactory recoveries, even the most seriously injured, although some of them will be hospitalized for some time. They are an outstanding group of men and it was a pleasure to treat them. Their quiet fortitude and patience was evident from the outset and was a great asset throughout their stay aboard AMERICA. They quickly won the admiration of our men and many friendships rapidly formed. All shared in the pleasure of their recovery and wished them well as they left. You and the Navy have every reason to be proud of your men as they are a fine example of fortitude in a time of adversity, in the best Navy tradition.

CDR John Gorden and LCDR Pete Flynn both spent many hours in the operating room and in intensive care in the wards. They and the corpsmen of AMERICA gave everything they had to insure a complete recovery in each case. It was a pleasure to see them work and to see the great interest they took in each man.

We all hope you and your crew are rested and that LIBERTY is being repaired expeditiously. We wish you a pleasant voyage home.

Sincerely,
D. D. Engen

The President of the United States takes pleasure in presenting the PRESIDENTIAL UNIT CITATION to

USS LIBERTY (AGTR-5)

for service as set forth in the following

CITATION:

For exceptionally meritorious and heroic achievement on 8 June 1967 during an armed attack by foreign aircraft and motor torpedo boats while sailing on an assigned mission in international waters in the Eastern Mediterranean. Very shortly after noon, LIBERTY was attacked without warning by foreign jet fighter aircraft and motor torpedo boats, and suffered major topside damage from strafing aircraft, serious damage amidships from a direct torpedo hit, and heavy casualties to the crew. The ship's radar, most of the external communications capability, all of the life rafts, and most of the ship's boats were lost due to the severity of the damage inflicted, the resulting fires, and exploding gasoline stored topside. Although two-thirds of the crew were killed or wounded, those surviving displayed outstanding professionalism, undaunted spirit, and extraordinary heroism in their efforts to save their ship. Following the directions of their Commanding Officer, they contained and extinguished the various fires caused by the attacks, and fought to control the flooding caused by the torpedo hit. Medical teams cared for the seriously wounded, expeditiously performing a task both great and difficult. Taking a vital part in the wide variety of actions necessary to save their ship and their shipmates, all surviving crew members were instrumental in returning LIBERTY one thousand miles safely to port. Their exceptional courage, perseverance, and devotion to duty reflect the highest credit upon themselves and the United States Naval Service.

Appendix L

COMMANDER'S MESSAGE TO SIXTH FLEET

ROUTINE

172?54Z JUNE 1967
FROM: COMMANDER SIXTH FLEET
TO: SIXTH FLEET

UNCLAS

1. IN RESPONSE TO THE ARAB-ISRAELI WAR, THE SIXTHFLT HAS BEEN KEPT AT A HIGH STATE OF READINESS FOR THE PAST THREE WEEKS. YOU HAVE BEEN PREPARED TO CARRY OUT ANY MISSION, EITHER HUMANITARIAN OR COMBAT, THAT OUR GOVERNMENT MIGHT ASK US TO PERFORM. YOUR READINESS AND RESPONSE HAS BEEN MOST GRATIFYING.

2. WHEN THE LIBERTY WAS ERRONEOUSLY ATTACKED, YOUR AIRCRAFT WERE LAUNCHED IN A MATTER OF MOMENTS, FULLY ARMED AND PREPARED TO DEFEND HER. YOUR GUN CREWS HAVE STOOD MANY LONG WATCHES AND IT HAS BEEN REASSURING TO KNOW THAT AT ALL TIMES THEY WERE READY TO DEFEND THIS FLEET. DESTROYER COMMANDING OFFICERS HAVE SHOWN COURAGE, SKILL AND GOOD JUDGEMENT IN KEEPING THE RUDE SOVIET INTRUDERS FROM PENETRATING OUR FORMATIONS. MUCH OF OUR TIME HAS BEEN SPENT AT HIGH SPEEDS AND I AM AWARE OF THE EXTRA HOURS THE ENGINEERS HAVE PUT IN KEEPING THEIR PLANTS RUNNING. YOUR COMMUNICATORS, BOTH VISUAL AND RADIO, HAVE BEEN PARTICULARLY ALERT, AND YOUR BRIDGE WATCHES HAVE BEEN SMART IN EXECUTING SIGNALS. IN SHORT, ALL ELEMENTS WERE READY, WILLING AND ABLE.

3. I HAVE GREATEST PRAISE FOR THE SIXTHFLT AND I AM VERY PROUD OF EVERY MAN IN IT FOR THEIR PROFESSIONAL PERFORMANCE DURING THESE PAST TRYING WEEKS. WELL DONE. VADM MARTIN.

Appendix M

On the following several pages are reproduced the full text of the citation that accompanied Captain McGonagle's Medal of Honor, and extracts from several of the citations describing the performances of individual officers and crew members.

> " . . . it is strongly urged that Presidential bestowal of the awards to a representative group be considered and invited. A national tribute is in consonance with the calibre of performance detailed herein."

Vice Admiral W.I. Martin
to the Secretary of the Navy,
August 11, 1967

The President of the United States in the name of The Congress takes pleasure in presenting the MEDAL OF HONOR to

Captain William L. McGonagle
United States Navy

for service as set forth in the following:

CITATION

For conspicuous gallantry and intepidity at the risk of his life above and beyond the call of duty as Commanding Officer, USS LIBERTY (AGTR-5) in the Eastern Mediterranean on 8-9 June 1967. Sailing in international waters, the LIBERTY was attacked without warning by jet fighter aircraft and motor torpedo boats which inflicted many casualties among the crew and caused extreme damage to the ship. Although severely wounded during the first air attack, Captain (then Commander) McGonagle remained at his battle station on the badly damaged bridge and, with full knowledge of the seriousness of his wounds, subordinated his own welfare to the safety and survival of his command. Steadfastly refusing any treatment which would take him away from his post, he calmy continued to exercise firm command of his ship. Despite continuous exposure to fire, he maneuvered his ship, directed its defense, supervised the control of flooding and fire, and saw to the care of the casualties. Captain McGonagle's extraordinary valor under these conditions, inspired the surviving members of the LIBERTY's crew, many of them seriously wounded, to heroic efforts to overcome the battle damage and keep the ship afloat. Subsequent to the attack, although in great pain and weak from the loss of blood, Captain McGonagle remained at his battle station and continued to conn his ship for more than seventeen hours. It was only after rendevous with a United States destroyer that he relinquished personal control of the LIBERTY and permitted himself to be removed from the bridge. Even then, he refused much needed medical attention until convinced that the seriously wounded among his crew had been treated. Captain McGonagle's superb professionalism, courageous fighting spirit, and valiant leadership saved his ship and many lives. His actions sustain and enhance the finest traditions of the United States Naval Service.

Lieutenant Commander Philip McCutcheon Armstrong, Jr., U.S. Navy

"Lieutenant Commander Armstrong was on the bridge when the first strafing attack occurred. A large fire erupted in the vicinity of two 55 gallon gasoline drums stored near the bridge and there was grave danger that the drums might explode and cause a wide-spread uncontrollable conflagration. Without hesitation and with complete disregard for his own personal safety, he fearlessly exposed himself to overwhelmingly accurate rocket and machine gun fire while proceeding to jettison the gasoline drums and organize a party of men to extinguish the blazing lifeboats. At this time he received multiple injuries which proved to be fatal . . ."

Lieutenant Maurice Hogue Bennett, Jr., U.S. Navy

"Though wounded himself . . . without hesitation and with complete disregard for his own personal safety he brought to safety one officer who had been severely injured. . . . in spite of great personal fatigue, he devoted many hours in providing for the comfort, safety and welfare of his shipmates. [Displayed] exceptional inspirational leadership in an hour of awesome peril."

Lieutenant George Houston Golden, U.S. Navy

". . . was in main control during the attack coordinating the operation of machinery for propulsion and power under battle conditions. Three times when told to 'standby for torpedo attack to starboard,' Lieutenant Golden unhesitatingly and with complete disregard for his own personal safety, and although wounded by rocket fire, relieved the phone talker and throttleman on the starboard side of the engineroom at the waterline, assumed their duties and ordered all others away from the area . . ."

Lieutenant (Medical Corps) Richard Francis Kiepfer, U.S. Naval Reserve

". . . with complete disregard for his own personal safety, he exposed himself to overwhelmingly accurate rocket and machine gun fire by going to different stations and compartments to administer first aid after sick bay became untenable and evacuated following a rocket hit. He treated men for pain, shock and took emergency measures to control hemorrhage and later performed a chest operation. After the torpedo hit, he organized personnel for removing the wounded in case of an order to abandon ship. . . . made trips through some of the damaged areas to the medical storeroom for needed supplies. He conducted a major surgical operation, giving the anesthesia (spinal) himself . . ."

Ensign David George Lucas, U.S. Naval Reserve

". . . arrived on the bridge within moments of the initial strafing attack. . . . a large explosion [had] incapacitated the Executive Officer, the Officer of the Deck, the sound powered telephone talkers, and lookouts and caused the instantaneous demise of the Intelligence Officer. . . . though already wounded, he continued to fearlessly expose himself to intense overwhelmingly accurate rocket and machine gun fire to assist the Commanding Officer in maintaining ship control and communications with other vital battle stations throughout the attack. His aggressiveness and coolness under fire was exceptional for a young junior officer with limited afloat experience and inspired his seniors and subordinates alike in an hour of awesome peril..."

Ensign John Deaderick Scott, U.S. Naval Reserve

". . . courageously remained in his fume and smoke filled General Quarters station to direct and coordinate the emergency measures taken by the repair parties to extinguish fires, [and to] minimize and control the flooding of spaces. He personally directed and supervised the emergency plugging and shoring of the ruptured deck in the compartment just aft of his General Quarters station . . ."

Lieutenant Stephen Spencer Toth, U.S. Navy

". . . as Intelligence Officer, was on the starboard wing of the flying bridge, 04 level, when the first strafing attack occurred. It became a vital matter to quickly establish the national identity of the aircraft that had initiated the vicious attack in order to inform higher authority. With complete disregard for his own personal safety he fearlessly exposed himself to overwhelmingly accurate rocket and machine gun fire to obtain this data. While engaged in this task a violent explosion on the starboard side of the bridge inflicted fatal injuries . . ."

Chief Petty Officer Richard John Brooks, U.S. Navy

". . . fearlessly proceeded throughout the main machinery space to check machinery and equipment to try to keep the ship going at the maximum speed possible. Twice he was knocked from one deck to the other by [the impact of] rocket fire and torpedo explosion. Although wounded, he continued restarting equipment and talking to his men to keep up their morale..."

Petty Officer Francis Brown, U.S. Navy

". . . fearlessly exposed himself to overwhelmingly accurate rocket and machine gun fire while [acting as helmsman]. . . . steadfastly maintained the ordered course while many men in the immediate area received serious and fatal injuries. He remained at his post until felled by strafing fire from the torpedo boats at the moment the torpedo struck the ship . . ."

Petty Officer Frank Johnson Brown, U.S. Navy

". . . fearlessly exposed himself to intensely accurate rocket and machine gun fire to fight raging fires above decks. The oxygen breathing apparatus strapped to his chest was completely shot away during the air attack. Having completed his mission above decks, he proceeded to the smoke and steam filled fireroom to relieve and render assistance to personnel overcome by smoke . . ."

Petty Officer Virgil Louie Brownfield, U.S. Navy

". . . fearlessly exposed himself to overwhelmingly accurate rocket and machine gun fire to remain beside the Commanding Officer relaying and receiving crucial orders and information, and continued to do so even after being grievously and painfully wounded . . ."

Petty Officer Jeffery R. Carpenter, U.S. Navy

". . . after the torpedo attack, Petty Officer Carpenter immediately proceeded to the bridge where he rendered first aid to the Commanding Officer and assisted him in relaying crucial orders and directions. Despite painful injuries, his calm, alert actions and initiative assisted the Commanding Officer to remain on the bridge . . ."

Seaman "J" "C" Colston, U.S. Navy

". . . was running forward to his general quarters station at Machine Gun 52 when he stopped to help a wounded shipmate to safety. He continued forward while still exposing himself to extremely heavy rocket and machine gun fire and helped another wounded man to safety. He then answered a call for help to extinguish the burning gasoline cans . . . fearlessly exposed himself to overwhelmingly accurate rocket and machine gun fire while rescuing wounded and fighting fires. He also warned his shipmates when the aircraft started making repeated strafing attacks. He then helped carry several more of his wounded shipmates to safety. His aggressiveness and coolness under fire undoubtedly saved the lives of several . . ."

Seaman Rodney L. Dally, U.S. Navy

". . . was topside fighting numerous fires while the ship was under an intense air attack. With complete disregard for his own personal safety, he fearlessly exposed himself to overwhelmingly accurate rocket and machine gun fire. He was responsible for the control of numerous fires and the evacuation of many wounded . . ."

Petty Officer Russell O'Neal David, Jr., U.S. Navy

". . . in spite of painful back, shoulder and leg wounds, he fearlessly exposed himself to intensely accurate rocket and machine gun fire to aid the wounded and to execute signal hoists . . ."

Petty Officer Duilio Demori, U.S. Navy

". . . fearlessly exposed himself to intense rocket and machine gun fire while assisting in the evacuation of wounded from the exposed forecastle and adjacent weather decks. After insuring that no more wounded were still exposed, he unhesitatingly went below deck to direct maintenance of damage control conditions of compartments below the waterline. He willingly remained below deck during the torpedo attack and immediately afterward directed and assisted the emergency repair teams in minimizing further damage and flooding . . ."

Petty Officer Henry Edward Durzewski, Jr., U.S. Navy

". . . demonstrated exceptional coolness and ability as he unhesitatingly assumed the duties of damage control plotter in addition to his assigned responsibilities. His ability to assimilate, retain and plot reports, as well as pass that information promptly and accurately to Damage Control Central while intense rocket and machine gun fire penetrated decks and bulkheads around him was exemplary. [Later] took charge of the repair party and maintained discipline and organization . . ."

Petty Officer Troy Lawrence Green, U.S. Navy

". . . as an assistant to the corpsmen in the forward battle dressing station, rendered invaluable assistance by alleviating suffering and minimizing casualties. With complete disregard for his own personal safety, he fearlessly exposed himself to overwhelmingly accurate rocket and machine gun fire to rescue wounded and carry them to the battle dressing station for treatment. When the torpedo boats raked the starboard side of the ship with cannon and machine gun fire, he carried the wounded out of the forward battle dressing station to a safer location in the passageway. Throughout the night he not only cared for the wounded, but prepared food, made accurate casualty reports, and in general seized every opportunity to assist or direct work of any nature. Because of his exceptional industry and gentle humor, the spirits of all on board were enhanced during a time of great trial and strain . . ."

Petty Officer Steven Charles Gurchik, U.S. Navy

". . . as a phone talker in Damage Control Central, demonstrated exceptional coolness and ability in relaying promptly and accurately vital information between Damage Control Central and repair parties. His ability to organize and maintain circuit discipline and coordination . . . while intense rocket and machine gun fire penetrated decks and bulkheads around him was exemplary. . . . he continued to perform his vital duties even as fumes and smoke filled his station . . ."

Petty Officer Donald Herold, U.S. Navy

". . . although painfully wounded in the first strafing attack, immediately ran to his Battle Station on machine gun 52. However, the machine gun had been destroyed. Without hesitation and with complete disregard for his own safety, he fearlessly exposed himself to overwhelmingly accurate rocket and machine gun fire to evacuate wounded from the forecastle and other unsheltered areas and continued until wounded again. The wounds were critical . . . His conduct while waiting for treatment was exemplary and enhanced the morale of others . . ."

Seaman Donald A. Hurst, U.S. Navy

". . . as a member of the Forward Repair Party, with complete disregard for his own safety, fearlessly exposed himself to overwhelmingly accurate rocket and machine gun fire while aiding and removing wounded personnel from the forecastle and other unprotected areas. [Later] volunteered to assist a fire party fighting a fire on the bridge at the height of the air attack. When the fire on the 01 level port side was brought under control, he went below to assist in damage control. When the torpedo exploded, he immediately began to plug holes and assist in installing shoring to minimize damage and control flooding . . ."

Chief Petty Officer Carlyle F. Lamkin, U.S. Navy

". . . as assistant repair party officer, personally organized and supervised teams fighting topside fires during the air attack. With complete disregard for his own personal safety, he fearlessly exposed himself to overwhelmingly accurate rocket and machine gun fire . . . [Later] assisted in shoring and plugging operations. He also worked throughout the night assisting in surgical operations, helping save several lives . . ."

Seaman Dale Duane Larkins, U.S. Navy

". . . as loader and telephone talker on machine gun 54, arrived on station shortly after the initial strafing attack. The station was untenable due to intense flames coming from burning gasoline cans on the deck below. With complete disregard for his own personal safety, he fearlessly exposed himself to overwhelmingly accurate rocket and machine gun fire from the attacking aircraft and proceeded to machine gun 53 to assist. Machine gun 53 was soon enveloped in flames from the burning motor whale boat. Seaman Larkins then courageously helped extinguish fires while the aircraft were still attacking. Still with complete disregard for his own safety, he single-handedly manned Mount 51 and fired on the attacking torpedo boats until he received the order to cease fire. He then helped carry several of his wounded shipmates to where they could be given medical aid . . ."

Staff Sergeant Bryce F. Lockwood, U.S. Marine Corps

". . . despite severe burns, the rapid rise of water, heavy smoke and complete darkness, was instrumental in the rescue of personnel from the flooded compartments, thus averting even further loss of life. Without regard for his personal safety or his injuries, he assisted in the rescue until ordered to leave. His calm, rational thinking and actions evidenced a high degree of professional competence and moral fibre."

Petty Officer Charles Monroe Martin, U.S. Navy

". . . in main engine control when the first attack occurred, he immediately started all standby equipment to ensure that the ship was prepared for any speed requested from the bridge. . . . fearlessly exposed himself to machine gun and rocket fire that was entering the machinery space to ensure that all machinery and equipment was in operating condition, and made essential emergency repairs to the fire main pump during the first moments of the attack . . ."

Seaman Frank McInturff III, U.S. Navy

". . . as a stretcher bearer in the Forward Repair Party, exposed himself fearlessly to intense rocket and machine gun fire while assisting in removing the wounded personnel from the weather decks to the forward battle dressing station. Without hesitation and with complete disregard for his own personal safety, he once again exposed himself to overwhelmingly intense and accurate aircraft fire when he courageously joined the fire fighting team on the bridge. After the fires in the vicinity of the bridge were out, he again took up his stretcher and carried two more wounded from the bridge to the battle dressing station . . ."

Petty Officer Garvin L. D. McMakin, U.S. Navy

". . . a repair party phone talker, with complete disregard for his own personal safety, remained at his post even though the intense fumes, smoke and heat twice caused him to lose consciousness. . . . continued to relay information, as well as to help the wounded. When the ship was struck by a torpedo, made certain all the wounded had life jackets and would not leave until all the wounded had been made ready for being placed in life-boats . . ."

Seaman Thomas Robert Moulin, U.S. Navy

". . . as a phone talker in Damage Control Central, demonstrated exceptional skill and coolness in relaying promptly and accurately vital information to and from the bridge, damage control central, and main engine control. His ability to organize and maintain circuit discipline and coordination . . . while overwhelming rocket and machine gun fire penetrated decks and bulkheads around him was exemplary. . . . after the torpedo attack he continued to perform his vital duties as well as give encouragement to a wounded bridge phone talker, even as fumes and smoke filled his station . . ."

Petty Officer Richard Dale Neese, U.S. Navy

". . . as Repair Party 'on the scene leader,' was directly and personally responsible for the control of numerous fires topside during the air attack. With complete disregard for his own safety, he fearlessly exposed himself to overwhelmingly accurate rocket and machine gun fire. After the torpedo hit, he immediately commenced shoring and plugging to control flooding. He assisted with the care of wounded throughout the night . . ."

Seaman Stamatie Pahides, U.S. Navy

". . . as a Messenger in the Forward Repair Party, exposed himself fearlessly to intense rocket and machine gun fire while assisting in carrying wounded personnel from the weather decks to the Forward Battle Dressing Station. [Later] joined the fire fighting team on the bridge. [Still later] returned to his battle station and then, though painfully wounded, assisted in making emergency repairs below deck . . ."

Petty Officer Martin Denny Powledge, U.S. Navy

". . . as bridge telephone talker, fearlessly exposed himself to overwhelmingly accurate rocket and machine gun fire as he aided and comforted the injured and assumed their duties. . . . remained at his station throughout the night, performing his essential functions without relief."

Petty Officer Samuel Leonard Schulman, U.S. Navy

". . . as medical corpsman in charge of the forward battle dressing station, rendered first aid throughout the attack. Abandoned his station after being knocked to the ground and momentarily stunned by several rockets, and then assisted wounded who were in the main deck passageway. . . . performed a tracheotomy to ease the breathing of one man, and saved the life of at least one seaman with artificial respiration. Without his care, several might have perished . . . eventually overcome by fatigue after almost forty hours of continuous work, allowed himself only two hours rest."

Fireman David Skolak, U.S. Navy

". . . Without hesitation and with complete disregard for his own safety, Fireman Skolak fearlessly exposed himself to overwhelmingly accurate rocket and machine-gun fire in an attempt to evacuate the wounded men from the forecastle. While performing these valiant acts, he was fatally wounded. Fireman Skolak's initiative, aggressiveness, courageous actions, and coolness under heavy fire served to inspire all who observed him and were in keeping with the highest traditions of the United States Naval Service."

Petty Officer James Clayton Smith, U.S. Navy

". . . as a member of Repair Party #3, was personally responsible for controlling a large fire on the 01 level port side. With complete disregard for his own safety, fearlessly exposed himself to overwhelmingly accurate rocket and machine gun fire in accomplishing this task. At one point, his fire hose was shot to pieces and the man helping him lost his life. Petty Officer Smith rigged another hose and extinguished the fire, then went on to fight other fires, risking his life to help others. After the torpedo hit, he began shoring and plugging operations to assist in controlling flooding. Then he returned to the mess decks and helped care for the wounded for the rest of the night. His aggressiveness and coolness under fire was inspirational . . ."

Petty Officer Alexander Neil Thompson, U.S. Navy

". . . with complete disregard for his own safety, fearlessly exposed himself to overwhelmingly accurate rocket and machine gun fire from the attacking aircraft . . . Although all of the other men at the station had been killed or seriously wounded during the first pass of aircraft, Petty Officer Thompson courageously and single handedly operated machine gun 51 and continued to fire on the aircraft in the defense of his ship and shipmates until he was fatally wounded by a rocket blast. His aggressiveness and coolness under fire was exceptional inspirational leadership in an hour of awesome peril. Petty Officer Thompson's initiative and courageous actions were in keeping with the highest traditions of the United States Naval Service."

Chief Petty Officer Harold Jesse Thompson, U.S. Navy

". . . as Assistant Repair Officer in the Forward Repair Party, was on the main deck forward when the first strafing attack wounded the Forward Repair Officer. . . . he exposed himself to overwhelmingly accurate rocket and machine gun fire as he assumed the duties of Officer in Charge of the Repair Party, and promptly organized and supervised the evacuation of the exposed wounded personnel and directed the fire fighting teams to the bridge area . . ."

Petty Officer Phillip Francis Tourney, U.S. Navy

". . . as Assistant On-Scene Leader in the Forward Repair Party, assisted in organizing the evacuation of wounded from the exposed weather decks. . . . continued to fearlessly exposed himself to intense rocket and machine gun fire to move a fire fighting team to the bridge. . . . went below to assist damage control efforts. . . . after torpedo explosion, assisted and directed emergency repairs to minimize further flooding . . ."

Petty Officer Lee VanCleave, U.S. Navy

". . . as medical corpsman in charge of the main battle dressing station, administered initial care, stopped major bleeding, splinted fractures, administered medications to relieve pain, cared for burned men, started infusions, and assisted with the major surgical procedures that were done throughout the attack and post-attack recovery phase. When the ship was struck by torpedo, he organized and led a party to the mess deck to take the wounded to safety should it be necessary to abandon ship. . . . continued to work without relief throughout the night, making several dangerous trips to the medical storeroom. . . . His devotion to duty and effectiveness materially contributed to the rapid recovery of the many patients he treated . . ."

Appendix N

EXTRACT FROM
REVIEW OF DEPARTMENT OF DEFENSE,
WORLDWIDE COMMUNICATIONS, PHASE I

REVIEW OF DEPARTMENT OF DEFENSE WORLDWIDE COMMUNICATIONS

PHASE I

REPORT

OF THE

ARMED SERVICES INVESTIGATING SUBCOMMITTEE

OF THE

COMMITTEE ON ARMED SERVICES

HOUSE OF REPRESENTATIVES

NINETY-SECOND CONGRESS

FIRST SESSION

UNDER AUTHORITY OF

H. Res. 201

MAY 10, 1971

U.S. GOVERNMENT PRINTING OFFICE
WASHINGTON : 1971

60-690

COMMUNICATIONS CONCERNING U.S.S. *LIBERTY*
JUNE 7–8, 1967

Hostilities commenced between Israel and the United Arab Republic on June 5, 1967. On that same date at 2015 hours, the Commander, 6th Fleet, ordered all his surface and air units to stand off at least 100 miles from the coasts of the belligerent nations. At the time of that order, U.S.S. *Liberty* was not assigned to 6th Fleet, but was under the operational control of Commander-in-Chief Europe. On June 7th, at 0001 hours, U.S.S. *Liberty* was transferred to the operational control of Commander, 6th Fleet. At the time of her transfer, her operational orders, dated June 1st, directed that the closest permissible approach to the coast of the United Arab Republic would be 12.5 nautical miles, while she could approach no closer than 6.5 nautical miles to the coast of Israel. No action was taken by the Commander, 6th Fleet, on June 7th to cause U.S.S. *Liberty* to conform to his order previously issued to all other 6th Fleet surface and air units.

During the afternoon of June 7th, the Joint Chiefs of Staff decided to reposition U.S.S. *Liberty* to move her farther from the coasts of the belligerent nations. In implementing that decision, a series of five messages from JCS and U.S. commanders in the European Command were directed to U.S.S. *Liberty* and other addressees. None of those messages had reached *Liberty* by 1200Z hours on June 8th, 13½ hours after the first message was released for transmission. The circumstances surrounding the misrouting, loss and delays of those messages constitute one of the most incredible failures of communications in the history of the Department of Defense.

Those five messages will be discussed seriatim. Each is described according to its date-time-group, a six-numeral designation assigned by the originator of the message reflecting the date and hour, month, and year of its release. At the time of the U.S.S. *Liberty* incident, the date-time-group was not an accurate reflection of the time the message had been released by the sender to the communications center, although, in most instances, the difference in the time was an interval of only a few minutes, e.g. JCS 072230Z was released to the communications center at 072241Z. Each date-time-group includes the letter "Z" designating the Greenwich time zone, thus all times are standardized.

JCS 072230Z JUNE 1967 TO CINCEUR

This message contained the first directive from the Joint Chiefs of Staff concerning the relocation of U.S.S. *Liberty*. It was directed to the Commander-in-Chief Europe (CINCEUR), for action. Information copies of the message were addressed to Commander-in-Chief, Naval Forces, Europe (CINCUSNAVEUR); Commander U.S. 6th Fleet; Commander Task Force 64;

U.S.S. *Liberty;* and others. This message modified the operational orders of U.S.S. *Liberty* by directing that her closest permissible approach to the coasts of the United Arab Republic and Israel should be 20 nautical miles and 15 nautical miles, rather than 12.5 and 6.5 nautical miles, respectively.

This message was released from the Joint Chiefs of Staff to the Army Communications Station, at the Pentagon, for transmission at 2241Z hours, June 7th. The action copy of that message to CINCEUR was not transmitted from the Army communications station until 1255Z hours, June 8th, more than 14 hours after its receipt in station. The information copies, addressed to Commander Task Force 67[1] and U.S.S. *Liberty,* were not transmitted until 1315Z hours, June 8th, and then were incorrectly routed to the Naval Communications Station, Philippines. From that station, they were sent to Navy Communications Station, Asmara, where they were placed on Fleet Broadcast at 2135Z hours, June 8th, 23 hours after the date-time-group of the message, and about 9½ hours after the attack on U.S.S. *Liberty.*

This message lost some of its significance, since it was canceled by a subsequent message from the Joint Chiefs of Staff, described in the next section.

JCS 080110Z JUNE 1967 TO CINCEUR

Preliminary telephone call

One hour and nine minutes after releasing the above 072230Z message for transmission, the Joint Chiefs became more concerned over relocating U.S.S. *Liberty* and decided that 20 and 15 nautical miles was too close to the coasts of UAR and Israel for safety. At 072350Z hours, June 7th, a JCS representative made a telephone call to the Command Center duty officer at Commander-in-Chief, U.S. Naval Forces, Europe (CINCUSNAVEUR). In that call, a verbal directive was issued to the CINCUSNAVEUR Command Center duty officer to order U.S.S. *Liberty* to operate no closer than 100 nautical miles to the coasts of the belligerents. The duty officer at CINCUS-NAVEUR was also told that a message formalizing the verbal directive would follow later. However, the JCS might as well have omitted that telephone call since it proved completely ineffective in accelerating action at CINCUS-NAVEUR headquarters. It is true that, as a result of the telephone call, a message incorporating the oral directive was prepared at CINCUSNAVEUR headquarters for dispatch to Commander, 6th Fleet; but despite the urgency indicated by the JCS call, the release of that message for transmission was delayed until the formal notification message from JCS had been received.

Formal message

The promised confirmatory message was not released by the Joint Chiefs

---

1. Department of Defense has informed the subcommittee that the original message was addressed to CTF64, but that an apparent operator error caused it to be addressed to CTF67 when it was prepared for transmission.

of Staff until 080110Z, more than an hour after the telephone call to CINCUSNAVEUR. That delay is not necessarily significant, since JCS could reasonably have expected an immediate and intelligent response to its telephone directive. This message, JCS 080110Z, canceled the earlier JCS 072230Z message and directed that U.S.S. *Liberty* should remain at least 100 nautical miles from the coasts of any of the belligerent nations.

An immediate precedence[2] was assigned to this message, whereas the 072230Z message had been assigned a priority precedence, thus indicating the increased concern of the Joint Chiefs concerning the repositioning of U.S.S. *Liberty.* This message was also released to the Army Communications Station at the Pentagon for transmission. The action copy of this message was again addressed to Commander-in-Chief, Europe, with information copies addressed to CINCUSNAVEUR; Commander, 6th Fleet; Commander, Task Force 64; and U.S.S. *Liberty,* among others. A delay of 44 minutes occurred in the Army Communications Station, Pentagon, before the message was transmitted to CINCEUR, the action addressee at 080211Z. Real [*sic*] Adm. Francis J. Fitzpatrick, Assistant Chief of Naval Operations for Communications, testified before the subcommittee that he thought 44 minutes was an inordinate amount of time for processing such a short message.

The delay in processing the action copy of the message is insignificant, however, when compared with the deplorable handling of the information copies addressed to Commander, Task Force 64, and to U.S.S. *Liberty.* First, there was a delay of 2 hours, 23 minutes before those messages were transmitted from the Army Communications Center, Pentagon, at 080350Z. The only explanation for that delay was that messages of equal or higher precedence were awaiting transmission before this message arrived in station. The Department of Defense, however, was unable to furnish the subcommittee with any documentary evidence which would support that explanation.

The information copies of the message, addressed to U.S.S. *Liberty* and Commander, Task Force 64, were finally transmitted at 0350Z, but, once again, those messages for addressees in the Mediterranean area were misrouted to Naval Communications Station, Philippines. A subcommittee witness testified that the misrouting was due to an erroneous routing indicator which had been assigned to the message by a civilian clerk in the Army Communications Center, Pentagon. Upon its arrival at the Naval Communications Station, Philippines, the error was recognized, the routing indicator was corrected to Naval Communications Station, Morocco, and

2. There are four Department of Defense precedence categories: flash, immediate, priority, and routine, in diminishing order. Those designations indicate the desired speed of delivery. They serve as a guide to operating personnel in processing transmission and delivery of the message.

the message was retransmitted within an hour. That correction should have taken those copies of the message to the Mediterranean area and ultimately to the addressees, except that the message was routed to pass through the Army Communications Station, Pentagon. That station, instead of transmitting the messages to the Navy Communications Station, Morocco, to which they were addressed, sent them to National Security Agency, Fort Meade, Md., where they were filed without further action. The only explanation given for this inexcusable conduct was that clerical personnel had misread the routing indicator. Needless to say, those messages had not reached either U.S.S. *Liberty* or Commander, Task Force 64, by 1200Z hours, June 8, 1967.

USCINCEUR 080625Z JUNE 1967 TO CINCUSNAVEUR

JCS message 080110Z was received at CINCEUR headquarters at 0212Z hours, June 8th. That headquarters, in a telephone conversation with CINCUSNAVEUR headquarters at 0325Z hours, directed CINCUSNAVEUR to take the JCS message for action. That oral order was confirmed by a formal message directed to CINCUSNAVEUR for action, with information copies to Commander, 6th Fleet, and U.S.S. *Liberty,* among others. The formal message, however, was not released until 0625Z hours. No explanation has been offered for the 3-hour delay in preparing that message at CINCEUR headquarters. A further delay of 46 minutes occurred in the message center at CINCEUR before the message was transmitted.

In order to ensure getting this message to its addressees, it was transmitted concurrently over two alternate relay paths. The necessity for the alternate transmission was quickly demonstrated by the loss of the message at the Pirmasens, Germany, Army DCS relay, the first station on one of the transmission paths. As a result of that loss, there was no further transmission of that copy of the message. The explanation offered for the loss of that message was that the [deleted] station was being operated under a combination of adverse conditions caused by the consolidation of commands and relocation of units from France. Heavy traffic volumes resulted from the extensive relocation of units and retermination of teletype circuits. The number of qualified personnel was inadequate to ensure error-free processing of traffic.

The second transmission route succeeded in getting the message to CINCUSNAVEUR and to Commander, 6th Fleet, by 0735Z hours on June [8th]. The information copy directed to U.S.S. *Liberty,* however, had to pass through additional relay stations before it could be placed on fleet broadcast for dissemination to U.S.S. *Liberty.* That meandering route through relay stations consumed another 9 hours. During that time, there were long in-station delays for processing of the message, and there was a delay of more than 2½ hours in passing the message from an Army DCS Communications Station at Asmara to the Navy Communications Station located within a mile of the Army station. Finally, the message was placed on the fleet broadcast at 1646Z hours, June 8th,[3] at which time U.S.S. *Liberty* was limping back to port with her dead and wounded, and so severely damaged that she was subsequently scrapped.

CINCUSNAVEUR 080455Z JUNE 1967 TO COMMANDER, 6TH FLEET

The headquarters, Commander in Chief, U.S. Naval Forces Europe (CIN-CUSNAVEUR) received three separate messages directing the repositioning of U.S.S. *Liberty.* Those messages and the times of their receipt were:

(a) A telephone call from the JCS reconnaissance center at 2350Z, June 7th.

(b) An information copy of JCS 080110Z message which was received at this headquarters at 0312Z hours, June 8th.

(c) A telephone call from CINCEUR at 0325Z hours, June 8th.

Despite the urgency which must have been obvious by that time, no action was taken at that headquarters for more than 3½ hours after the initial telephone call. It was not until after receipt of the telephone call from CINCEUR at 0325Z hours, June 8th that CINCUSNAVEUR headquarters stirred into action. At that time, the duty officer directed that a teletype conference be established with Commander, 6th Fleet. That conference circuit was established, and at 0445Z hours, Commander, 6th Fleet, acknowledged receipt of the order to take action upon the JCS message. The teletype order was confirmed by CINCUSNAVEUR formal message 080455Z which was received by Commander, 6th Fleet, at 0518Z hours, June 8th.

For some unexplained reason, U.S.S. *Liberty* was not informed of either of these messages to Commander, 6th Fleet.

COMMANDER, 6TH FLEET 080917Z JUNE 1967 TO U.S.S. LIBERTY

Upon receipt of the messages from CINCUSNAVEUR, the only action remaining for Commander, 6th Fleet, was issuance of an order to U.S.S. *Liberty* to comply with the minimums directed by the Joint Chiefs of Staff. It was not until 0917Z hours, June 8th, however, more than 4 hours after his receipt of the order, that he released his action message directed to

---

3. A garbled version of this message was placed on fleet broadcast at 1059Z, June 8th, and there was some question whether it had been received by U.S.S. *Liberty.* But as Rear Admiral Fitzpatrick testified, "It is a moot point whether the ship received it or not for two reasons: If it did receive it, it was probably useless to them, and number two, even if they had received it, it wouldn't have made any sense to them because all it said was to take some other JCS message for action, some other commander, and her commander, and they wouldn't have known what that other message was because, as we know, that other message from the Joint Chiefs of Staff, which they had the information copy on, didn't get to them."

U.S.S. *Liberty*. Although his superiors had manifested their concern about repositioning U.S.S. *Liberty* by telephone calls which gave him advance notice of the order, the Commander, 6th Fleet chose not to use the voice circuit when he passed the order to the ship. Rather, he used the normal communications system for transmission of his message.

After its release to the communications center aboard the 6th Fleet flagship, U.S.S. *Little Rock,* that message was delayed for more than 1 hour and a quarter before it was transmitted at 1035Z hours. The explanation for that delay was that there were one flash and seven immediate messages being prepared for transmission at the time the message was received in the message center aboard U.S.S. *Little Rock.* The message arrived at the Army DCS station at Asmara by 1200Z hours, June 8th. That station, however, instead of delivering it to the nearby Navy station for fleet broadcast, missent it to the Navy Communications Station, Greece. It was returned to Army DCS station at Asmara and finally delivered to the Navy Communications Station at 1510Z hours, June 8th, 6 hours, 8 minutes after its release by Commander, 6th Fleet, and more than 10 hours after he had been ordered to act upon the Joint Chiefs of Staff instruction. The message was transmitted on fleet broadcast at 1525Z hours, June 8th, more than 3 hours too late to alert U.S.S. *Liberty* to the danger of her position.

The circumstances surrounding the transmission of those five messages could be considered a comedy of errors were it not for the tragic results of the failure to move U.S.S. *Liberty.* At 1210Z hours, June 8, 1967, U.S.S. *Liberty* was attacked by Israeli aircraft and, at at [sic] 1235Z hours, she was torpedoed by Israeli patrol boats. As a result of those attacks, 34 officers and men were killed, while 75 were wounded, and the ship sustained such severe damages that it was never restored to duty. At the time of those attacks, U.S.S. *Liberty,* through no fault of hers, had not received any of the above-described messages. If the communications system had been responsive, she should have had several hours during which she could have placed some distance between herself and the coast, thereby probably avoiding the attack.

Appendix O

THE SHIP'S OFFICERS

† Lieutenant Commander Philip McCutcheon Armstrong, Jr., USN
* Lieutenant Maurice Hogue Bennett, USN
* Lieutenant James Marquis Ennes, Jr., USNR
* Lieutenant George Houston Golden, USN (plank owner)‡
* Lieutenant Richard Francis Kiepfer, Medical Corps, USNR
* Lieutenant Commander David Edwin Lewis, USN
* Ensign David George Lucas, USNR
* Commander William Loren McGonagle, USN
* Lieutenant James George O'Connor, USNR
Ensign Malcolm Patrick O'Malley, USNR
* Lieutenant (junior grade) Lloyd Clyde Painter, USNR
† Lieutenant James Cecil Pierce, USN
Ensign John Deaderick Scott, USNR
* Ensign Richard Patten Taylor, Jr., USNR
† Lieutenant Stephen Spencer Toth, USN
* Lieutenant (junior grade) Malcolm McEachin Watson, USNR

THE CHIEF PETTY OFFICERS

Chief Petty Officer Joseph A. Benkert
* Chief Petty Officer Richard J. Brooks
* Chief Petty Officer Carlyle F. Lamkin
† Chief Petty Officer Raymond E. Linn
* Chief Petty Officer James A. Matthews
† Chief Petty Officer Melvin D. Smith
Chief Petty Officer Wayne L. Smith
* Chief Petty Officer Harold J. Thompson
Senior Chief Petty Officer Stanley W. White

*Wounded in action.
†Killed in action.
‡ A member of the original crew when the ship was first commissioned is considered a "plank owner"; he is said to "own" a plank in the deck of the ship.

THE PETTY OFFICERS

* Reginald N. Addington
† William B. Allenbaugh
James M. Anderson, Jr.
Alvis L. Armstrong
* Richard K. Baker
* Lowell T. Bingham
* Salvatore Boccella
* Larry L. Bowen
* James Victor Brong
* Frank J. Brown (plank owner)
* Gary Wayne Brummett
Charles E. Byrd
† Ronnie J. Campbell
* David N. Carnahan
Joseph P. Carpenter
* Fred M. Cleveland
† Jerry L. Converse
Juan A. Craig
* James Ray Davidson
* Marvin F. Dodd
* Robert M. Dye (plank owner)
* Dennis M. Eikleberry
Eddie G. Elder
Everrett L. Freese
* Kenneth R. Gauthier
Larry D. Goins
† Curtis A. Graves
* Stephen C. Gurchik
James V. Halman
* David W. Hawkins
* Charles R. Hendricks
† Warren E. Hersey
Wayne L. Hildebrand, Jr.
* John S. Horne, Jr.
* Frederick K. Johns
* James F. Kelly
Kenneth R. Kimble
* Loren W. Kreun
* Calvin L. Landis
* Joseph C. Lentini
* Anthony J. Liefeld
Donald J. Lundin
† Duane R. Marggraf
* John L. Massengale

Americo F. Aimetti
* Timothy P. Ameen
* Joe D. Anderson
Rogelio M. Bagan (plank owner)
Gary L. Barton (plank owner)
* Glenn L. Bloxham
* John E. Booth
Thomas E. Bradley
† Francis Brown (plank owner)
* Virgil L. Brownfield
* Ronald D. Buck
John J. Calligan
* Richard C. Carlson
* Jeffery R. Carpenter
* Calvin L. Chadsey
Charles J. Cocnavitch
James E. Cotten
* Russell O. David, Jr.
Duilio Demori
* Henry E. Durzewski, Jr.
* Lewis D. Eckhart
† Robert B. Eisenberg
John W. Fisher
Ernest A. Gallo
* Ronald D. Gilson (plank owner)
† Jerry L. Goss
Troy L. Green
James T. Halbardier
Charles K. Hauck
* David C. Hazen
* Donald Herold
† Alan Higgins
Jerry G. Hobson
Charles F. Johns
* Melvin P. Johnson
Robert C. Kidd
William M. Kram
* Ronald G. Kukal
* William M. LeMay
Claude L. Lewis, Jr.
* Philip L. Long
† James M. Lupton
Charles M. Martin
Edward H. McClister

* Terry L. McFarland
Garvin L. D. McMakin
James H. Merritt
Thomas R. Moulin
James L. Needham
* John P. Newell
Francis J. O'Classen (plank owner)
* Eugene Owens
* Dennis A. Patten
* Edward G. Perkins (plank owner)
* Carl L. Pleasants
* John G. Popielski
Eugene Prigmore
* John R. Randall
Paddy "E" Rhodes
* Charles L. Rowley
* Robert J. Schnell
* Maurice B. Shafer
* James C. Smith
* Thomas B. Smith
† John C. Spicher (plank owner)
Richard S. Sturman
* Ralph B. Sweet
† Alexander N. Thompson
† Thomas R. Thornton
* Barry R. Timmerman
Ronald E. Trader
* Donaciano Valdez, Jr.
George R. Vanderpool
* Jerry W. Ward
Daniel J. Warwas
Gordon J. Wedig

* David L. McFeggan
† Anthony P. Mendle
* Stephen E. Meyer
David V. Myers
* Richard D. Neese
Richard L. Newton
Glenn R. Oliphant
* David W. Page
* Garland W. Payne
David T. Plasterer
* Floyd H. Pollard
Martin D. Powledge
* Albert E. Rammelsburg
Richard J. Reger
* Douglas C. Ritenburg
* Kenneth M. Schaley
* Samuel L. Schulman
* Harold E. Six
† John C. Smith, Jr.
* Dennis C. Snader
* Joseph D. Stoudt
John R. Sutter
* Charles J. Thome
* Larry B. Thorn
† Phillipe C. Tiedtke
* Phillip F. Tourney
*Sammy M. Uber
* Thomas Lee VanCleave
† Frederick J. Walton
Joseph P. Ward
Clyde W. Way
* Gregory L. Welch

THE SEAMEN

Gary L. Aftoora
* Richard E. Anderson
* Joseph W. Ashworth
John W. Beattie
* Nathan D. Benedict, Jr.
* Gerald R. Bisher
* Calvin Bostic II
David W. Bundy

Benjamin G. Aishe
Theodore L. Arfsten
Thomas G. Bacskay
* Edward H. Bechtel
* Lee R. Bennett
† Gary R. Blanchard
* Don R. Botcher
* Danny R. Byrd

* William E. Casper
* Rodney C. Concepcion
* George R. Cornish
* Dale E. Daniels
James P. DiGeronimo
Alan W. Easton
* Donald F. Follin, Jr.
Edward D. Handy
* Warren D. Heaney
Glen J. Holden
Donald A. Hurst
Duane D. Johnson
* James P. Kavanaugh
* Glenn D. Kelly
* Eugene H. Kirk
* Stephen J. Krasnasky
* John D. LaMar
* Steven J. Latorre
* Terry W. Lehman
† James L. Lenau
Benjamin L. Lomasang
* Gerald F. Losasso
* James A. Maraio
† David W. Marlborough
* Robert L. McAllister
* Frank McInturff III
Remegio N. Mercado
Richard G. Mumford
* Donald W. Pageler
* Herbert J. Parker
* Herbert C. Peetoom
* Harvey L. Purcell
* Thomas A. Quintero
* Robert B. Reilly
Stephen J. Richard
William R. Russell
* Robert A. Scarborough
* David A. Shaw
† David Skolak
Jerry D. Smith
Michael J. Tobin
* Jeffery L. Triplett
* Robert B. Vandeventer

* "J" "C" Colston, Jr.
* Eddie Lamar Cook
* Rodney Lee Dally
Rodolfo A. Diana
* Kenneth B. Eakins
* Kenneth P. Ecker
* Ronald F. Grantski
† Lawrence P. Hayden
† Carl L. Hoar
* John M. Hrankowski
* Thomas F. Jackson
Perry W. Johnson
† Richard W. Keene
Frederick W. Kerner
* David J. Kisiel
* Alan F. Kriner
Dale D. Larkins
* Joel W. Lehman
* Thomas W. Lemond
Ronald L. Lipply
Robert W. Long
Randy W. Lucas
* Sofronio P. Marfil (plank owner)
* Jimmie L. Mathews
* Patrick H. McAndrews
* Joseph L. Meadors
* David B. Miller
† Carl C. Nygren
* Stamatie Pahides
* Salvador Payan
* Gerald H. Pierson
Anthony A. Quintero
David Ramey
* Thomas J. Reilly
* Victor J. Rossi, Jr.
Reynald S. Sarno
* Ronald W. Schneider
* Michael R. Simpson
* Larry J. Slavens
* Larry L. Soper
Stephen B. Tracy
* Thomas E. Vanderschuur
* Carl J. Vickers

Richard W. Wainwright
Pedro P. Watan
Tommy W. Wheeler
* Daniel B. Wood

* Robert M. Waltz
* Richard L. Weaver
* George W. Wilson, Jr.
* Robert R. Zagar

THE MARINES

* Staff Sergeant Bryce F. Lockwood
† Sergeant Jack L. Raper
† Corporal Edward E. Rehmeyer

CIVILIANS

* Donald L. Blalock
† Allen M. Blue
Robert L. Wilson

Appendix P

EXTRACT FROM COMBAT INFORMATION CENTER WATCH OFFICER'S LOG

Entries were made in this log as events occurred throughout the afternoon. Bridge logs, on the other hand, were reconstructed later.

1310	GENERAL QUARTERS DRILL
1317	CHEMICAL ATTACK PROBABLE (SIMULATED)
1324	CHEMICAL ATTACK (SIMULATED)
1348	SECURE FROM GENERAL QUARTERS
1358	ATTACKED BY TWO JETS—MACHINE GUN FIRE—REPEATED BOMB-INGS
1406	FIRE ON BRIDGE
1410	CONTINUED ATTACKS
1424	THREE GUNBOATS SIGHTED
1430	BRIDGE ORDERS HOLD FIRE
1431	STAND BY FOR TORPEDO ATTACK
1433	DEMOLITION BILL IN EFFECT
1435	TORPEDO STARBOARD SIDE
1515	SIGHTED TWO ISRAELI HELICOPTERS MAKING REPEATED PASSES OVERHEAD
1516	TORPEDO BOATS HAVE NOW LEFT MAIN AREA
1517	HELICOPTERS FRIENDLY
1519	POWER AVAILABLE NOW (RUDDER DOES NOT ANSWER)
1520	AFTER STEERING HAS CONTROL
1524	CONDITION ZEBRA RESET
1536	TORPEDO BOATS NOW REAPPROACHING
1538	APPEARS TO BE UNIDENTIFIED DESTROYER BEHIND TORPEDO BOAT
1539	HOISTING CODE LIMA INDIA
1542	TORPEDO BOATS REVERSED COURSE—ONE SEEMS TO BE SMOKING
1607	BOAT APPROACHING STARBOARD SIDE AT HIGH SPEED (APPROX 12 MILES)
1611	HOISTED INTERNATIONAL SIGNAL FLAG
1615	TWO UNIDENTIFIED JETS APPROACHING SHIP, STARBOARD SIDE
1621	ALL ENGINES STOP—NO STEERING
1623	LEFT STANDARD RUDDER—ALL ENGINES AHEAD ONE-THIRD
1628	SHIFT RUDDER

1630   HIGH SPEED PATROL BOAT NUMBER 204-17 CIRCLED SHIP

1631   MAINTAIN EIGHT KNOTS

1632   BOATS FLYING ISRAELI ENSIGN

1632   "TORPEDO BOATS SEEM TO BE ISRAELI"—CAPTAIN'S STATEMENT

1632   GUNBOATS RETREATING

1630   SHIP IS UNDERWAY COURSE 340° MAGNETIC, SPEED EIGHT KNOTS

1642   CHANGE SPEED TO ALL AHEAD ONE-THIRD, AFTER STEERING HAVING TROUBLE MAINTAINING COURSE

1648   THREE GUN BOATS HAVE TURNED AWAY

1653   CHANGE COURSE TO 000° MAGNETIC

1655   WORD PASSED TO COMSIXTHFLT THAT PHOTOS WERE TAKEN OF ATTACKING AIRCRAFT

1702   POWER TO ANCHOR WINDLASS

Appendix Q

RESOLUTION OF THE AMERICAN LEGION CONVENTION

THE 49TH ANNUAL NATIONAL CONVENTION OF THE AMERICAN LEGION
AUGUST 29, 30, 31, 1967
RESOLUTION NO. 508

Committee: Foreign Relations
Subject: U.S.S. *LIBERTY* Incident

Whereas, on June 8, 1967, the U.S.S. Liberty—while operating in international waters in the Eastern Mediterranean—was the target of an apparent deliberate attack by Israel's war planes and torpedo boats; and

Whereas, this unwarranted and unprovoked attack killed 34 members of the Liberty's crew and wounded 75 other U.S. Navy personnel on board, in addition to causing extensive damage to the ship; and

Whereas, the U.S. Government's official inquiry covered the circumstances surrounding the incident, including the fact that the ship was "properly marked as to her identity and nationality, and in calm, clear weather" when attacked, but the published report fails to provide the American public with a satisfactory answer as to the reason for the attack; now, therefore, be it

Resolved, by the American Legion in National Convention assembled in Boston, Massachusetts, August 29, 30, 31, 1967, That The American Legion denounces and condemns Israel's irresponsible attack on the U.S.S. Liberty, a United States ship and its crew; and be it

Further Resolved, That The American Legion insists that the United States Government conduct a complete and thorough investigation of this incident, with the results to be made public insofar as security permits; and be it

Further resolved, That The United States Government demand full payment from the Israeli Government for:
   (1) compensation to the next of kin for the deceased;
   (2) compensation to the wounded for injuries and residual disabilities; and
   (3) damages to the property of the United States.

Appendix R

ISRAEL'S APOLOGY FOR THE ATTACK

Embassy of Israel
Washington, D.C.

The Ambassador of Israel presents his compliments to the Honorable the Secretary of State and has the honor to inform him that he has been requested by the Government of Israel to renew its sincere expression of deep regret for the tragic accident in which, at the height of hostilities in the area, the USS Liberty was hit by Israeli fire. The Government of Israel deeply regrets this tragic accident.

The Ambassador of Israel has been instructed to inform the Honorable the Secretary of State that the Government of Israel is prepared to make amends for the tragic loss of life and material damage.

The Ambassador of Israel expresses once again in the name of the Government of Israel its deep condolences to the Government of the United States and its sympathy to all the bereaved families.

The Ambassador of Israel avails himself of this opportunity to renew to the Honorable the Secretary of State the expression of his highest consideration.

Washington, D.C.
June 10, 1967

Appendix S

AMERICAN REPLY TO THE ISRAELI APOLOGY

The Secretary of State presents his compliments to His Excellency the Ambassador of Israel and has the honor to refer to the Ambassador's note of June 10, 1967, concerning the attack by Israeli aircraft and torpedo boats on the United States naval vessel U.S.S. Liberty, which was carried out at 1605 and 1625 hours local time [*sic*], respectively, on June 8, 1967, while the U.S.S. Liberty was engaged in peaceful activities in international waters.

At the time of the attack, the U.S.S. Liberty was flying the American flag and its identification was clearly indicated in large white letters and numerals on its hull. It was broad daylight and the weather conditions were excellent. Experience demonstrates that both the flag and the identification number of the vessel were readily visible from the air. At 1450 hours local time [*sic*] on June 8, 1967, two Israeli aircraft circled the U.S.S. Liberty three times, with the evident purpose of identifying the vessel. Accordingly there is every reason to believe that the U.S.S. Liberty was identified, or at least her nationality determined, by Israeli aircraft approximately one hour before the attack. In these circumstances, the later military attack by Israeli aircraft on the U.S.S. Liberty is quite literally incomprehensible. [At] a minimum, the attack must be condemned as an act of military recklessness reflecting wanton disregard for human life.

The subsequent attack by Israeli torpedo boats, substantially after the vessel was or should have been identified by Israeli military forces, manifests the same reckless disregard for human life. The silhouette and conduct of U.S.S. Liberty readily distinguished it from any vessel that could have been considered hostile. The U.S.S. Liberty was peacefully engaged, posed no threat whatsoever to the torpedo boats, [and] obviously carried no armament affording it a combat capability. It could and should have been scrutinized visually at close range before torpedoes were fired.

While the Ambassador of Israel has informed the Secretary of State that "the Government of Israel is prepared to make amends for the tragic loss of life and material damage," the Secretary of State wishes to make clear that the United States Government expects the Government of Israel also to take disciplinary measures which international law requires in the event of wrongful conduct by the military personnel of a State. He wishes also to make clear that the United States Government expects the Government of Israel to issue instructions necessary to ensure that United States personnel and property will not again be endangered by the wrongful actions of Israeli military personnel.

The United States Government expects that the Government of Israel will provide compensation in accordance with international law to the extent that it is possible to compensate for the losses sustained in this tragic event. The Department of State will, in the near future, present to the Government of Israel a full monetary statement of its claim.

Washington, D.C.
June 10, 1967

Appendix T

ISRAELI REBUTTAL TO THE AMERICAN RESPONSE

Embassy of Israel
Washington, D.C.

The Ambassador of Israel presents his compliments to the Honorable the Secretary of State and has the honor to refer to the Secretary's note of June 10, 1967, concerning the attack by Israeli aircraft and torpedo boats on the United States naval vessel U.S.S. Liberty.

The Government of Israel feels that the statement that "there is every reason to believe that the U.S.S. Liberty was identified, or at least her nationality determined, by Israeli aircraft approximately one hour before the attack" is unfounded.

Nor can the Government of Israel accept the statement that "the attack must be condemned as an act of military recklessness reflecting wanton disregard for human life."

The Government of Israel is of the view that the drawing of such conclusions before a full investigation has been made is unwarranted.

The Government of Israel has already announced the establishment by the Chief-of-Staff of the Israel Defense Forces of a Commission of Enquiry to make a full investigation of all the facts and circumstances. The Government of Israel will make available to the Government of the United States the findings of this investigation, and, for its part, would hope that the Government of the United States will make available to the Government of Israel the findings of its own investigation.

The Government of Israel recalls that as soon as this tragic error occurred it immediately informed the Government of the United States what had taken place. The Government of Israel immediately assumed responsibility for this error and conveyed its apologies and deep regret for what had occurred and for the grievous loss of life.

Subsequently, as mentioned in the Secretary of State's note of June 10, 1967, the Government of Israel took the initiative to offer to make amends for the tragic loss of life and material damage. Further, all assistance was offered by the personnel of the Israel Defense Forces to the U.S.S. Liberty, but these personnel were informed by the U.S.S. Liberty that such help was not needed. The area around the U.S.S. Liberty was immediately searched by Israel Defense Forces personnel, by plane and boat, and subsequently search efforts were renewed.

The Government of Israel has standard instructions of the most stringent nature to all its military personnel that the personnel and property of the United States, as of all countries not involved in hostilities, shall not be endangered. These instructions have been renewed.

The Government of Israel regrets that it was not given prior information by the Government of the United States of the presence of a United States vessel in an area which the United Arab Republic had warned neutral vessels to avoid, as it was an area of hostilities. The area was in fact being used by the United Arab Republic for purposes of hostilities against Israel. It would be appreciated if the Government of Israel could be given timely information of the approach of United States vessels to shores where the Israel Defense Forces are in authority.

The Government of Israel renews its offer to make amends and has instructed the Ambassador of Israel to reiterate its profound regret for the consequences of what was admittedly a tragic error.

The Ambassador of Israel avails himself of this opportunity to renew to the Honorable the Secretary of State the assurances of his highest regard.

Washington, D.C.
June 12, 1967

INDEX

A

abandon ship, order to, 88, 91, 94, 97, 149, 181
Abernethy, Congressman Thomas, 4
Abidjan, Ivory Coast, 9–12, 45
air attack, 39–81, 146–148, 244, 281
air support
  promised, 38–39
  bungled, 74, 76–78, 91–93, 98–99, 237, 281
Aishe, Benjamin G., 83, 111
Algeria, 42
America, USS, 76, 91, 116, 126, 237–241
American embassy
  Tel Aviv, Israel, 155, 242; *see also* Castle, Ernest C.
  Malta, 167–168
American Legion, resolution of, 283
Anderson, columnist Jack, 4
Andrew Jackson, USS, 218
Armstrong, Philip McC., 10, 16, 21, 25, 31, 36, 41–42, 51, 60, 147
  profile, 30–33
  during attack, 43, 63, 78–80, 105, 107, 108, 108n
  honored, 176, 260
  buried, 181
Ashdod, Israeli naval base at, 96
Atkinson, Captain Bert M., Jr., 145
authentication, 75, 75n
awards for heroism, 258

B

Banner, USS, 191n
Barbour, Ambassador (to Israel) Walworth, *see* American embassy: Tel Aviv, Israel
Barry, USS, 131
Battle Efficiency Award, 33, 251
Beattie, John W., 89
Beecher, William, 191
Belmont, USS, 8
Benkert, Joseph A., 23–24, 42, 107, 115, 169–170, 181, 201
Bennett, Maurice H., 42, 57, 111, 113, 189, 206, 215, 260
Big Ear, 218
Blanchard, Gary R., 113
Bloch, Israeli Lieutenant Colonel Michael, 153, 160
Blue, Allen M., 19, 85
Boston, Captain Ward M., Jr., 145
Boston *Globe,* 170
boxcar, *see* reconnaissance
brawling, *see Liberty*: crew
Breelove, Major, 46
Brewer, Jane, 13, 132
Brooks, Richard J., 66, 83, 97, 261
Brown, Francis, 71, 80–81, 176, 262
Brown, Frank J., 262
Brownfield, Virgil L., 204, 262
Bundy, Presential Adviser McGeorge, 98, 100
Bunting, Captain, 251

C

D

M

N

ABOUT THE AUTHOR

JAMES M. ENNES, JR., was born in Newark, New Jersey, in 1933 and spent his early years in Alameda, California. During the Korean War, at age seventeen, he enlisted in the Navy.

Most of Mr. Ennes's adult life has been spent in the Navy. He left the service briefly to earn a B.A. degree in business administration at San Francisco State College in 1961. He was commissioned an ensign in 1962, and from 1965 until he retired from the Navy in 1978 he was assigned to cryptologic duties.

The author now lives and writes in the Pacific Northwest. He and his wife, Terry, have three children, Mark, Julie and Carolyn.